LATE-BREAKING DEVELOPMENTS: SEC ISSUES NEW RULES ON INDEPENDENCE

At the time this *Guide* was being printed, the SEC, on November 15, 2000, announced adoption of new rules on auditor independence. The authors suggest that instead of reading the proposed rules as presented in Appendix C, go to www.sec.gov and read the final rules titled, *Revision of the Commission's Auditor Independence Requirements*. The purpose of this insert is to summarize the significant changes in the new rules and to reference the chapters in the *Guide* that will be affected by the changes. Additional updates and new developments will be posted on the Wiley website at www.wiley.com/ethics.

Definition of Member for Purposes of Investing (Chapter 8)

The SEC redefines "member" as the CPA firm and covered persons. **Covered persons** include partners, principals, shareholders, and employees of the CPA firm who

1. Are on the audit engagement team (including concurring partners and all persons who consult with others on the audit, review, or attest engagement).
2. Are in the chain of command who (a) supervise or have direct responsibility for the engagement (including all levels through the CPA firm's chief executive), (b) evaluate the performance or recommend the compensation of the engagement partner, (c) provide quality control or oversight of the engagement.
3. Provide ten or more hours of nonaudit services during the fiscal year (beginning on the date the individual performs the tenth hour of service) through the audit report date or who expect to provide ten or more hours of nonaudit services on a recurring basis (excluding nonmanagerial employees).
4. Are partners, principals, or shareholders in the office of the CPA firm in which the lead engagement partner practices.
5. Are members of the **immediate family** (spouse, spousal equivalent, and dependents) of any of the above (their investments are attributed to covered persons).

NOTE: The current AICPA definition of "member" excludes 3. above (less restrictive than the SEC) and includes all owners without regard to office location (more restrictive than the SEC).

Investments in Audit Clients Held by Close Family Members (Chapters 8 and 9)

Current AICPA/SEC requirements attribute certain investments held by close relatives to the "member." The amended SEC rules indicate that only investments made by the covered person and his or her immediate family are attributed to the covered person. However, if any partner, principal, shareholder, or professional employee (i.e., those who are not covered persons) or their immediate family members, or any **close family member** (parent, nondependent child, and sibling) of a covered person has a beneficial ownership of more than 5% or controls an audit client, the CPA firm's independence is impaired. In addition, if a close family member of any partner, principal, or shareholder controls an audit client, the CPA firm is not independent.

Employment by Audit Client of Immediate Family Members and Close Family Members (Chapter 17)

The new SEC amendment limits employment relationships to a covered person's immediate family members and close family members when employed by an audit client in an accounting or financial reporting oversight role. When an audit client employs such individuals, independence is impaired.

NOTE: The amendment is less restrictive than existing AICPA requirements in terms of persons covered and employment positions.

Other Financial Interests (Chapters 9 and 15)

1. **Insurance Products**--Independence is impaired if any covered person/immediate family member has an insurance policy issued by an insurer audit client unless: (a) the policy was obtained prior to becoming a covered person, and (b) the likelihood of the client becoming insolvent is remote.
2. **Futures Commission Merchants**--Independence is impaired if any covered person/immediate family member has a futures or commodity account with a futures commission merchant audit client.
3. **Credit Cards**--The amendment sets an aggregate outstanding balance that must be reduced to $10,000 at payment due date.

   NOTE: The current AICPA limit is $5,000.

Performance of Nonaudit Services (Chapters 6, 13, and 21)

1. **Bookkeeping**--Continues prohibition of any service to an audit client involving (a) maintaining or preparing client accounting records, (b) preparing financial statements (filed or supporting filed financial statements), or (c) preparing source documents. There are two exceptions: (1) a rare emergency situation, and (2) certain bookkeeping services (as discussed in Chapter 13) for foreign divisions and subsidiaries.

2. **Financial Information Systems Design and Implementation**--Similar to existing AICPA rules, but includes requirements that involve the client's acknowledgment in writing to the CPA firm and the client's audit committee (or board) of the client's responsibility for internal accounting controls and the adequacy of the financial reporting system.

3. **Appraisal or Valuation Services or Fairness Opinions**--Generally follows existing AICPA/SECPS requirements presented in Chapter 13. The CPA firm is not independent if it provides any of these services when the results would be material to the financial statements. There are four exceptions that would not impair independence: (a) the client or specialist employed by the client provides primary support for the recorded balances, (b) for pension and related liabilities, the client takes responsibility for all significant assumptions and data, (c) the valuation is performed in the context of a tax engagement, (d) the valuation does not affect the financial statements.

4. **Actuarial Services**--Follows AICPA/SECPS requirements. The rule is explicit in stating that actuarial services involving determination of an insurance company's policy reserves and related accounts would render the CPA firm not independent. There are three exceptions: (a) the audit client has its own or third party actuaries to perform the primary work, (b) management accepts responsibility for significant methods and assumptions, and (c) the CPA firm's involvement is not continuous.

5. **Internal Audit Services** (Chapter 21)--Same as AICPA requirements except that (a) services are limited to 40% of total hours expended on internal audit work related to accounting systems, controls over such systems, and financial statements (not applicable to audit clients with less than $200 M in assets), and (b) client has to acknowledge in writing to the CPA firm and the audit committee (or board) its responsibility for internal accounting control.

6. **Management Functions**--Same as AICPA requirements.

7. **Human Resources**--Same as SECPS and AICPA requirements.

8. **Broker-Dealer Services** (Chapters 6 and 13)--Same as AICPA requirements.

9. **Legal Services** (Chapter 6)--Follows long-standing SEC policy of prohibiting the performance of legal services for audit clients.

NOTE: The proposed rule would have prohibited the provision of expert services to audit clients. The final rules do not adopt a restriction on expert services, but integrity and objectivity must be maintained.

Quality Control Provision Covering all Employees and Associated Entities of the CPA Firm Participating in the Engagement (Chapter 26)

Inadvertent violations of independence requirements will not cause the CPA firm to lose independence if

1. The covered person did not know of the circumstances causing the lack of independence.
2. The CPA firm corrects the problem as promptly as possible after discovery.
3. The CPA firm (with more than 500 SEC registrants as audit, review, attest clients) has certain defined elements of quality control.

Effective Dates

The SEC's final rule is effective sixty days from publication in the Federal Register. There are two exceptions: (1) for nonaudit services relating to appraisal or valuation services or fairness opinions and internal audit services, the effective date is eighteen months from the above date, and (2) for financial interests and employment relationships, the effective date is three months from the above date. Until the effective dates, preexisting requirements of the SEC, Independence Standards Board, or the accounting profession in the US (the AICPA, state boards, and state societies) should be followed. After the effective dates, if conflicts exist among the above organizations, the most stringent requirement should be followed.

WILEY

The CPA's Guide to
Professional
Ethics

Dan M. Guy, CPA, PhD
D. R. Carmichael, CPA, CFE, PhD
Linda A. Lach, CPA

JOHN WILEY & SONS, INC.
New York • Chichester • Weinheim • Brisbane • Singapore • Toronto

This publication is designed to provide accurate and authoritative information in regard to the subject matter covered. It is sold with the understanding that the publisher is not engaged in rendering legal, accounting, or other professional service. If legal advice or other expert assistance is required, the service of a competent professional person should be sought.

To order books, or for customer service call, (800)-CALLWILEY (225-5945)

ISBN 0-471-38037-7

Printed in the United States of America

10 9 8 7 6 5 4 3 2 1

CONTENTS

PREFACE

The CPA's Guide to Professional Ethics will help CPAs, both in public practice and not in public practice, to understand and apply the guidance on ethics. It is designed to be a comprehensive and integrated analysis of ethics requirements that is easy to read and easy to use.

The book integrates the various requirements of the AICPA's *Code of Professional Conduct*, the SEC, the Independence Standards Board, the Department of Labor, the GAO's Yellow Book, and state societies and state boards. The book also contains information on ethical standards for consulting and tax services, and provides a clear and concise analysis of international ethics requirements.

The book provides invaluable guidance on how a CPA should respond to an ethics investigation. An overview of the Joint Ethics Enforcement Process is presented, along with steps to take if selected for a disciplinary action.

The book is presented using the Information Mapping format. This format separates information into small units based on purpose or function for the reader, rather than by topic. It allows a reader to either go through the book in detail or scan quickly for relevant points to resolve an ethics question or issue. The format has been successfully used in hundreds of training, procedural, and reference manuals, in both paper and online modes.

The book includes numerous examples and graphics designed to illustrate complex ethics issues that CPAs and their firms face. Each chapter contains a section that provides guidance on the authoritative sources for the topics discussed in the chapter. The book also provides information on where CPAs can go to get more information on ethics issues. Finally, a glossary provides a quick reference for key definitions.

Low-cost self-study continuing education for eight hours of CPE is included within the book.

The authors bring to this book over seventy years of experience of accounting and auditing, and the ethical issues involved in these disciplines. Mr. Guy and Mr. Carmichael, both former vice presidents at the AICPA, have served as consultants to the SEC on ethical issues, represented CPAs in state board of accountancy ethics investigations, and testified as experts on ethical matters. Ms. Lach adds her expertise as the former director of professional development at the AICPA, responsible for all of the AICPA's continuing education programs.

This edition of the book is current through all pronouncements issued as of October 31, 2000. Updates will be provided on the John Wiley & Sons, Inc. at website www.wiley.com/ethics within thirty days of the issuance of a new pronouncement.

We welcome comments, suggestions, and questions about this book. Please direct all correspondence to

Dan M. Guy, PhD, CPA
314 Paseo de Peralta
Santa Fe, MN 87501
Dmguy@worldnet.att.net

Douglas R. Carmichael, PhD, CPA, CFE
Baruch College, CUNY
Department of Accountancy
17 Lexington Avenue
New York, NY 10010
Douglas.carmichael@worldnet.att.net

Linda A. Lach, MS, CPA
21 Papurah Road
Fairfield, CT 06432
LindaLach@aol.com

Dan M. Guy
Santa Fe, New Mexico

Douglas R. Carmichael
New York, New York

Linda A. Lach
Fairfield, Connecticut

October 2000

ABOUT THE AUTHORS

Dan M. Guy, PhD, CPA, lives in Santa Fe, New Mexico, where he is a writer and consultant in litigation services. He completed an 18-year career with the AICPA in New York City in January 1998, where he had overall responsibility for, among other things, the Auditing Standards Board and the Accounting and Review Services Committee. Dr. Guy was Vice President, Auditing, at the AICPA from 1983 until 1996, when he became Vice President, Professional Standards and Services. Dr. Guy has written numerous books on auditing, sampling, and compilation and review. He has represented the profession on numerous occasions before Congress, various regulatory agencies, and at the international level. Prior to joining the AICPA, Dr. Guy was a professor of accounting at Texas Tech University and a visiting professor at the University of Texas at Austin. He was in public practice with KPMG Peat Marwick and Arthur Andersen. In 1998, he received the John J. McCloy Award for outstanding contributions to audit quality in the US. The award was presented by the Public Oversight Board that monitors the SEC Practice Section of the AICPA's Division for CPA Firms.

D. R. Carmichael, PhD, CPA, CFE, is the Wollman Distinguished Professor of Accountancy in the Stan Ross Department of Accountancy of the Zicklin School of Business at Bernard M. Baruch College, City University of New York. Until 1983, he was the Vice President, Auditing, at the AICPA, where he directly participated in the development of accounting and auditing standards. Dr. Carmichael has written numerous books and articles on accounting and auditing. He acts as a consultant on accounting, auditing, and control matters to CPA firms, public corporations, attorneys, government agencies, and financial institutions. Dr. Carmichael has served as a consultant to the AICPA, the Securities and Exchange Commission (SEC), the General Accounting Office (GAO), the Federal Deposit Insurance Corporation (FDIC), and other federal and state government agencies. He has also investigated numerous cases involving allegations of fraudulent financial reporting and provided expert witness testimony on those matters.

Linda A. Lach, CPA, writes and edits books and continuing education materials for accountants, auditors, and financial executives. She is the former Director of Professional Development for the American Institute of Certified Public Accountants. In that position, she was responsible for conferences, seminars, and self-study courses developed for the accounting profession. She has made numerous presentations and written articles on continuing education issues. Before joining the AICPA, she held various financial management positions and worked as an auditor for Touche Ross (currently Deloitte & Touche).

ACKNOWLEDGMENTS

We are grateful to the individuals who contributed to *The CPA's Guide to Professional Ethics*. In particular, we express our appreciation to the Independence Education Project (IEP), (especially Bob Sack, Mike Sutton, Joe Godwin, Jim Detrick, and an anonymous practitioner). The IEP was sponsored by one of the large CPA firms as a public service for CPAs and others wanting to know more about independence. We are also especially thankful to our spouses Terri Guy, Carol Schaller, CPA, and Richard Nichols, for their technical skills as well as their patience and encouragement. Finally, we wish to thank everyone at John Wiley & Sons, Inc. including John DeRemigis, Judy Howarth, and Pam Miller, for helping to make this book possible.

PART A

INTRODUCTION TO ETHICS

1 INTRODUCTION

Purpose of This Book

This book is designed to help practitioners understand and apply the ethics requirements of the AICPA's *Code of Professional Conduct*, along with ethics requirements of

- The SEC
- The Independence Standards Board
- The DOL
- The GAO's Yellow Book
- State societies and state boards

Applicability of Code of Professional Conduct

The AICPA's *Code of Professional Conduct* was adopted by the membership of the AICPA to provide guidance to all members in carrying out professional responsibilities.

Therefore, the Code applies to

- Members in public practice
- Members in industry
- Members in government
- Members in education

Applicability of Chapters

Each chapter indicates whether the chapter applies only to members in public practice, only to members **not** in public practice, or to all members. The following chart guides members in determining whether the guidance in a chapter applies.

Format of Book

This book is presented in an information mapping format. The format separates information into small units based on the purpose or function for the reader, rather than the topic. It allows a reader to either go through the book in detail or scan quickly for relevant points.

This method has been in use in industry since 1972 and is used extensively in hundreds of training, procedural, and reference manuals, in both paper and electronic modes.

Organization of This Book

This book is divided into the following parts:

- **Part A** introduces the organizations involved in setting and enforcing ethics requirements. It also summarized the ethics enforcement process.
- **Part B** provides an overview of the key concepts of independence, integrity, and objectivity.
- **Part C** provides detailed guidance on understanding and applying the complex independence requirements of the AICPA and other organizations.
- **Part D** covers other ethics rules in the AICPA's *Code of Professional Conduct.*
- **Part E** provides additional guidance for tax and consulting services and covers international ethics requirements. It also gives the practitioner guidance on where to go for more information.

How to Use This Book

This book is designed to be easy to use. To find a topic or subject in this book, use the Table of Contents or the Topical Index on page I-1. The information mapping format makes it easy to scan each chapter and find information easily and quickly.

To find the meaning of a technical term, refer to Appendix A, Glossary.

---

2 ORGANIZATIONS INVOLVED IN THE DEVELOPMENT, REGULATION, AND ENFORCEMENT OF ETHICS REQUIREMENTS

In This Chapter

For information on	See section
AICPA	A
SEC	B
Independence Standards Board	C
State societies of CPAs	D
State boards of accountancy	E
Other organizations	F

Overview

The AICPA establishes ethics requirements that apply to AICPA members.

State societies of CPAs and state boards of accountancy establish their own ethics codes, but the independence requirements are generally the same as those of the AICPA.

The AICPA and most state societies cooperate in the Joint Ethics Enforcement Program (JEEP) in bringing enforcement actions against their members. Each state board of accountancy independently enforces its requirements against the CPAs it licenses to practice.

The Independence Standards Board (ISB) establishes independence requirements for auditors of public companies. The SEC enforces those requirements. The SEC also provides guidance on insider trading and advertising.

NOTE: The securities laws require that public companies file statements with the SEC that have been audited by an independent accountant. Because the SEC is charged with the responsibility to administer the securities laws, the Commission and the Staff have established and interpreted independence rules for CPAs who audit public companies. Following the formation of the ISB in 1997 and its recognition by the SEC in 1998, the SEC has indicated that it would look to the ISB for leadership in establishing and improving auditor independence regulations. The SEC continues its oversight and enforcement role. In addition, on June 27, 2000, the SEC proposed new rule changes that would affect independence requirements. See Appendix C.

Section A: AICPA

Introduction	The American Institute of Certified Public Accountants (AICPA) is the national professional organization for all certified public accountants (CPAs).
	Its purpose is to provide the necessary support to ensure that CPAs serve the public interest in performing the highest quality of professional services.
Ethics Requirements	The *Code of Professional Conduct* ("the Code") was adopted by the membership of the AICPA to provide guidance and rules to all members.
	Membership in the AICPA is voluntary, but by accepting membership, a CPA assumes an obligation of self-discipline and agrees to adhere to the Code.
Composition of the Code	The Code contains principles, rules, interpretations, and rulings. The *principles* are positive statements of responsibility that provide the framework for the rules, which govern performance.
	Rules are broad but specific descriptions of conduct that would violate the responsibilities stated in the principles.
	Interpretations provide guidelines on the scope and application of the rules, but do not limit their scope or application.
	Ethics Rulings summarize the application of rules and interpretations to a particular set of factual circumstances.

Principles

The six *principles* in the Code are described as follows:

Article I	Responsibilities	Members should use sensitive professional and moral judgments in all their professional activities.
Article II	The Public Interest	Members should act in a way that will • Serve the public interest • Honor the public trust • Demonstrate commitment to professionalism
Article III	Integrity	Members should perform all professional responsibilities with the highest sense of integrity.
Article IV	Objectivity and Independence	A member should • Maintain objectivity • Be free of conflicts of interest in discharging professional responsibilities A member in public practice should be independent in fact and appearance when providing auditing and other attestation services.
Article V	Due Care	A member should • Observe the profession's technical and ethical standards • Strive continually to improve competence and the quality of services • Discharge professional responsibilities to the best of the member's ability
Article VI	Scope and Nature of Services	A member in public practice should observe these principles in determining the scope and nature of services to be provided.

Professional Ethics Executive Committee (PEEC)

The PEEC is the AICPA's senior technical committee that promulgates professional ethics requirements.

Rules and changes in rules must be approved by the AICPA membership.

Interpretations and rulings are issued on PEEC's own authority after due process procedures that include exposure to interested parties.

Coverage of Rules, Interpretations, and Rulings on Ethics

The rules on independence, integrity, and objectivity are described generally in Chapters 4, 5, and 6. Related interpretations and rulings on independence are explained throughout Chapters 7 through 26.

The remaining rules and their related interpretations and rulings are explained in Chapters 27 through 33.

Section B: The SEC

Introduction

The Securities and Exchange Commission (SEC) is a federal government regulatory agency with responsibility for administering the federal securities laws.

These federal securities laws are intended to protect investors and to ensure that the securities markets operate fairly and that investors have access to disclosure of all material information concerning publicly traded securities.

Relation to Independent Auditors

The federal securities laws require that independent public accountants audit financial statements filed with the SEC to protect public investors.

SEC regulations (Rule 2-01 of Regulation S-X) provide that the SEC "will not recognize any certified public accountant or public accountant as independent who is not in fact independent."

Prohibitions Against Relationships and Interests That Impair Independence

SEC regulations [Rule 2-01(b)] specifically identify the following situations that will be considered to impair independence:

- Connection to the client (or any of its parents, its subsidiaries, or other affiliates) as a promoter, underwriter, voting trustee, director, officer, or employee.

  *NOTE: The term **affiliates** is construed broadly and includes persons associated with the client in a decision-making capacity such as officers, directors, and substantial stockholders, as well as entities that, directly or indirectly, control, are controlled by, or are under common control with the client.*

  *Whenever the term **client** is used in this book in reference to an SEC requirement, the term also includes its parents, subsidiaries, or affiliates.*

- Holding or being committed to acquire any direct financial interest or material indirect financial interest in the client or any of its parents, its subsidiaries, or other affiliates.

  NOTE: These specific prohibitions are similar to those specified in AICPA Interpretation 101-1 and are described in more detail throughout this book, including particularly Chapters 9, 10, 15, and 16.

SEC Interpretations of Independence Requirements

The SEC has authority and responsibility under the federal securities laws for determining whether auditors who audit financial statements filed with it are independent.

From 1934 on, the SEC exercised its authority by having its staff issue interpretations of the independence requirements and by bringing enforcement actions for violations.

The SEC also refers auditors to independence requirements adopted by the AICPA to the extent they did not conflict with the SEC's own requirements.

*NOTE: SEC interpretations are codified in **Codification of Financial Reporting Policies: Section 602, "Requirements and Interpretations Relating to Independence."***

These interpretations are integrated and referred to at appropriate points throughout the book.

Recognition of the Independence Standards Board

Without abdicating its statutory responsibilities, the SEC has stated that it intends to look to the Independence Standards Board (ISB) to establish and maintain the independence requirements applicable to auditors of public companies. (The ISB is discussed in Section C.)

The SEC will consider an auditor to be *not independent* unless the auditor has substantial authoritative support for the position that an interest or relationship does not impair independence.

The SEC will consider principles, standards, interpretations, and practices established or issued by the ISB as having substantial authoritative support for the resolution of auditor independence issues.

Retention of Enforcement Authority

The SEC retains its existing authority to institute enforcement actions as it deems appropriate under Rule 102(e) against auditors who appear or practice before it.

The SEC may deny, temporarily or permanently, the privilege of appearing or practicing before it to a person found to have engaged in unethical or improper professional conduct.

NOTE: "Improper professional conduct" means

    1. Intentional or knowing conduct, including reckless conduct, that results in a violation of applicable professional standards; or
    2. Either of the following two types of negligent conduct:

> a. *A single instance of highly unreasonable conduct that results in a violation of applicable professional standards in circumstances in which an accountant knows, or should know, that heightened scrutiny is warranted.*
> b. *Repeated instances of unreasonable conduct each resulting in a violation of applicable professional standards, that indicate a lack of competence before the Commission.*

This means the SEC may deny the ability of an individual auditor or a CPA firm to perform audits of public companies.

Retention of Oversight Authority

The SEC retains its ultimate authority to not accept, or to modify or supplement, the ISB independence standards and interpretations.

Proposed SEC Rule Changes

On June 27, 2000, the SEC issued proposed rule changes that are designed to

1. Reduce the number of investments made by auditors and their family members that would impair independence
2. Reduce the number of people within CPA firms whose families would be affected by employment restrictions necessary to maintain independence
3. Expand the types of nonaudit services that would impair independence

The proposal also articulates four principles on which independence restrictions are based. An accountant is not independent when he or she

1. Has a mutual or conflicting interest with the audit client
2. Audits their own work
3. Functions as a member of management or an employee of the audit client
4. Acts as an advocate for the audit client

The proposal had a 75-day comment period, including public hearings. The proposed rule changes are provided in Appendix C. Additional background information about these changes is available at the SEC's website, www.sec.gov.

Additional Guidance on Ethics

The SEC also provides guidance on

- Insider trading (Chapter 28)
- Advertising by investment advisors (Chapter 31)

Section C: Independence Standards Board

Introduction	The Independence Standards Board (ISB) is a standard-setting body designated by the AICPA to **establish independence requirements for auditors of public companies**.
Relationship to the AICPA	The ISB operates as an independent body, but is funded by the AICPA's SEC Practice Section of its Division for CPA Firms (SECPS).
	The ISB, as well as all other SECPS activities, operate under the general oversight of the Public Oversight Board (POB).
	NOTE: The POB's Panel on Audit Effectiveness has recommended that the ISB operate under the direct oversight of the Public Oversight Board (POB).
ISB Structure	The ISB has eight members serving on a part-time basis.
	Four, including the chair, are public members.
	Three are senior partners of SECPS member firms and one is the president of the AICPA.
	NOTE: The POB's Panel on Audit Effectiveness has recommended a change in the composition of the ISB to seven members. Four, including the chair, would be public members.
Applicability of ISB Independence Requirements	The independence requirements established by the ISB apply only to auditors of public companies.
	The independence requirements of the AICPA's *Code of Professional Conduct* (the Code) apply to members providing audit, other attestation, or compilation services whether those services are provided to public or private clients.
	The auditor of a public company would be required to follow the Code to the extent its requirements did not conflict with those of the ISB or SEC.
	The requirements of the ISB and SEC are usually more restrictive than those of the AICPA code.

Relationship to the SEC	The ISB adopted as its standards the existing independence guidance of the SEC.
	The SEC has recognized the independence guidance issued by the ISB as having substantial authoritative support for resolving auditor independence issues.

Independence Issues Committee	The Independence Issues Committee (IIC) is drawn from SECPS member firms.
	The IIC is charged with assisting the ISB in establishing standards by identifying and discussing emerging independence issues within the framework of existing authoritative literature.
	Consensus positions of the IIC are available. (Information on accessing the ISB publications and documents can be found in Chapter 37.)

ISB Staff	The full-time staff of the ISB fields telephone inquiries on independence issues in addition to assisting the ISB and IIC.
	ISB staff interpretations apply only to the particular parties directly affected unless ratified by the ISB, but the SEC considers them as having substantial authoritative support.
	ISB staff interpretations are generally publicly available. (See Chapter 37.)

Standards Issued by the ISB	The ISB has issued

- Standard No. 1--*Independence Discussions With Audit Committees* (discussed in the next section)
- Standard No. 2--*Certain Independence Implications of Audits of Mutual Funds and Related Entities.* (ISB Standard No. 2 is discussed in Chapter 9, Subsections I and J.)
- Standard No. 3--*Employment With Audit Clients* (ISB Standard No. 3 is discussed in Chapter 16.)

The ISB has also issued the following interpretations:

- Interpretation 99-1, *Impact on Auditor Independence of Assisting Clients in the Implementation of FAS 133 (Derivatives)*

- Interpretation 00-1, *The Applicability of ISB Standard No. 1 when "Secondary Auditors" Are Involved in the Audit of a Registrant*
- Interpretation 00-2, *An Amendment of Interpretation 00-1*

Required Independence Communications with Audit Committee (ISB No. 1)

ISB Standard No. 1 requires that an auditor disclose to the audit committee, in writing, (1) all relationships between the auditor and the public company that may reasonably be thought to bear on independence, and (2) confirm the existence of independence.

The auditor must also discuss independence with the audit committee.

These written and oral communications are required at least annually.

*NOTE: When secondary auditors are involved in the audit of consolidated financial statements, the secondary auditors must comply with ISB No. 1 **when a subsidiary or investee is itself a registrant**. Otherwise the responsibility to comply with ISB No. 1 rests solely with the primary auditor. In that situation, the primary auditor's report to the audit committee should include independence issues involving secondary auditors, if any.*

Section D: State Societies of CPAs

Introduction

State societies are voluntary organizations of CPAs within each individual state.

They are self-regulatory organizations.

Code of Professional Conduct

Generally, each state society has its own code of professional conduct.

Generally, these codes are modeled after the AICPA code but sometimes have important differences. For example, state requirements may differ from AICPA rules in the area of commissions and contingent fees.

In the area of independence requirements, however, there are not significant differences.

Enforcement of State Society Codes

Most state societies cooperate with the AICPA in the Joint Ethics Enforcement Program (JEEP). See Chapter 3.

Contacting State Societies

Appendix B provides information on how to contact state societies.

Section E: State Boards of Accountancy

Introduction

State boards are state government regulatory organizations.
Each state government issues a license to practice within the particular state under that state's accountancy statute.

State accountancy statutes are enacted into law as part of the normal legislative process in each state.

A state board in a particular state may be a component of a larger organization that regulates several professions or vocations within the state.

NOTE: The designated agency may be a part of a state department of regulation or board of regents.

Code of Conduct

The code of conduct of the state board may be a part of the state accountancy statute. Generally, independence requirements are the same as those of the AICPA.

National Association of State Boards of Accountancy (NASBA)

NASBA is a voluntary organization composed of the state boards of accountancy.

It promotes communication, coordination, and uniformity among state boards.

In conjunction with the AICPA, NASBA has developed a Uniform Accountancy Act (UAA).

The UAA is for the information of state legislators, and adoption of all or part of its provisions is up to the legislators in the individual states.

Enforcement of State Board Codes

The enforcement mechanism within each state depends on the laws and regulations of the state.

A state board has authority to suspend or remove a CPA's license to practice in that state.

Contacting State Boards

Appendix B provides information on how to contact state boards.

Section F: Other Organizations

Introduction	A variety of regulatory or self-regulatory organizations may be involved in the establishment of independence requirements.

Department of Labor (DOL)	The Employee Retirement Income Security Act of 1974 (ERISA) requires that the audit of an employee benefit plan's financial statements be performed by an "independent qualified public accountant."

DOL regulations impose independence requirements that are stricter, in some ways, than those of the AICPA.

Generally, those areas in which DOL requirements are more stringent tend to be the same as those of the SEC. (See Chapter 23.) |

General Accounting Office (GAO)	The GAO establishes standards for audits of governmental organizations, programs, activities, and functions.

Generally, CPAs in public accounting practice will be considered independent if they are independent under AICPA requirements.

However, difficult situations can arise because of the complexity of organizational relationships that may be encountered. (See Chapter 22.) |

SECPS	Within the SECPS structure is the Joint Task Force on Independence and Quality Controls.

The task force establishes SECPS membership requirements related to independence quality controls.

Example

Specific requirements have been developed related to maintaining a database of SEC registrant attest clients. |

FDIC

The Federal Deposit Insurance Corporation (FDIC) requires that each depository institution engage an independent public accountant to audit and report on its financial statements. The FDIC states that the independent public accountant should comply with the AICPA's *Code of Professional Conduct* and meet the independence requirements and interpretations of the SEC and its staff. See Chapter 37 for the FDIC's website.

Auditing Standards Board (ASB)

The ASB issues Statements on Quality Control Standards (SQCS) that establish requirements for quality controls, including policies and procedures related to independence, integrity, and objectivity. (See Chapter 26.)

The ASB issues pronouncements on auditing and other attestation services that require independence in the performance of those services. (See Chapters 4 and 7.)

Accounting and Review Services Committee (ARSC)

The ARSC issues Statements on Standards for Accounting and Review Services that require independence in the performance of reviews. An accountant may perform a compilation when he or she is not independent, but must disclose the lack of independence in the compilation report (or in the engagement letter if a compilation report will not be issued for a management-use-only compilation).

Authoritative Sources

1. SEC *Codification of Financial Reporting Policies*, Section 601, Role of Independence in the Auditing Process.
2. Independence Standards Board Operating Policies.
3. Bylaws of the AICPA.
4. AICPA *Code of Professional Conduct.*
5. ISB Standard No. 1, *Independence Discussions With Audit Committees.*
6. ISB Interpretation 00-1, *The Applicability of ISB Standard No. 1 When "Secondary Auditors" Are Involved in the Audit of a Registrant.*

3 ETHICS ENFORCEMENT–WHAT A MEMBER NEEDS TO KNOW

In This Chapter

For information on	*See section*
Overview of the Joint Ethics Enforcement Program (JEEP)	A
Conduct of an investigation and trial board hearing	B
Authors' advice to a member involved in a disciplinary action	C

Overview

The AICPA and virtually all of the state societies of CPAs have joined together in the Joint Ethics Enforcement Program (JEEP). This chapter describes JEEP and the major phases and possible outcomes of ethics investigations and hearings, and provides guidance on what a member should do if notified of a potential disciplinary action under JEEP.

Section A: Overview of the Joint Ethics Enforcement Program (JEEP)

What Is JEEP?

The AICPA and virtually all of the state societies of CPAs have joined together in a program to permit joint enforcement of their Codes of Professional Conduct.

What Is the Purpose of JEEP?

The purpose of JEEP is to eliminate duplicate investigation of a potential matter by both the AICPA Professional Ethics Division and the ethics committee of one or more participating state societies.

Who Performs an Ethics Investigation Under JEEP?

The ethics committee of a participating state society investigates a potential disciplinary matter unless it requests the AICPA to conduct the investigation or the AICPA, under established policy, has the right to conduct the investigation.

An investigation by the executive committee of the AICPA's Professional Ethics Division may be performed by a committee member and staff member, or an ad hoc investigator appointed specifically for a particular matter.

What Are the Possible Outcomes of an Investigation?

The possible findings of an ethics committee under JEEP are as follows:

- No violation.
- Letter of required corrective action with directives.
- Offer of a settlement agreement.
- Trial board referral.

If a matter is referred to the trial board, ethics committee representatives present the action as the Ethics Charging Authority (ECA).

What Is the Role of the Joint Trial Board?

A hearing panel of five members of the Joint Trial Board hears cases referred by the ethics committee and recommends appropriate disciplinary, remedial, or corrective action.

The Joint Trial Board consists of at least 36 members elected for a three-year term by AICPA Council.

NOTE: In a trial board hearing, the ECA (ethics committee representatives) act as the plaintiff's attorney, the hearing panel chairman acts as the judge, and the hearing panel is the jury.

What Is Automatic Discipline?

Members of the AICPA can be automatically suspended from membership without a hearing if they are convicted for

- A crime punishable by imprisonment for more the one year.
- Willful failure to file any income tax return that the member, as an individual taxpayer, is required to file by law.
- Filing a false or fraudulent income tax return on a client's behalf or for the member's own benefit.
- Willfully aiding in the preparation and presentation of a false and fraudulent income tax return of a client.

Automatic suspension can also result from suspension of the member's certificate as a CPA or license or permit to practice public accountancy as a disciplinary measure by any governmental agency.

What Is Failure to Cooperate?

A member who refuses to honor his or her obligation to make a substantive response to an ethics committee's written interrogatories or requests for documents is said to have failed to cooperate with the committee in its investigation.

Failure to cooperate subjects a member to an automatic charge before a hearing panel of violation of

- Rule 501, *Acts Discreditable* (see Chapter 30).
- Rule 102, *Integrity and Objectivity* (see Chapter 6).
- Bylaws of the AICPA or participating state society.

Section B: Conduct of an Investigation and Trial Board Hearing

Major Phases of Investigation and Hearing

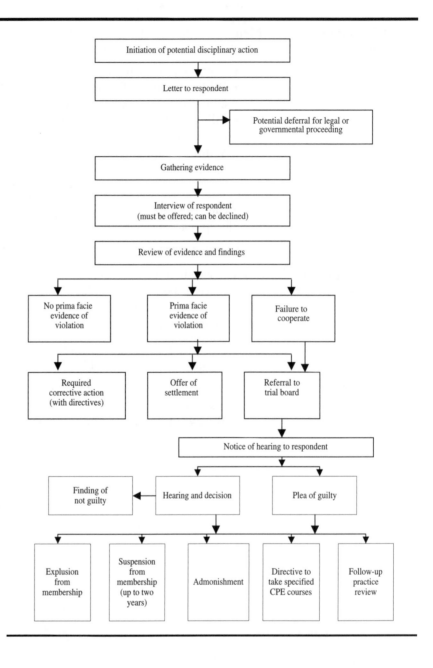

What Can Cause the Initiation of a Disciplinary Action?

A potential disciplinary matter may come to the attention of an ethics committee as a result of

- A complaint.
- Other information.

Other information can be any information from any source whatsoever, including

- AICPA programs and activities, such as the Division for Firms.
- Participating state societies.
- Federal, state, or local governmental agencies.
- Newspaper articles or other media reports.
- Announced decisions of judicial or regulatory authorities.
- Anonymous tips.

When Can a Disciplinary Action Be Deferred?

If a member makes a written request and provides evidence of the following, a disciplinary action will be deferred.

- A legal proceeding before a state or federal civil or criminal court.
- A proceeding or investigation by a state or federal regulatory agency, such as the SEC or a state board of accountancy.
- An appeal actively undertaken from a decision of a state or federal civil or criminal court or regulatory agency.

How Will a Member Know a Disciplinary Action Has Started?

The ethics committee investigating the matter will send an opening letter to each member identified as a respondent.

The letter might request responses to written interrogatories and documents such as working papers and financial reports.

What Are the Member's Obligations in an Investigation?

A member has a duty to cooperate in an investigation by providing a written response to interrogatories and furnishing requested documents.

If a substantive response is not received to a letter of inquiry within 30 days, a follow-up letter will be sent.

If a substantive response is not received within 30 days of the follow-up request, the matter will be referred to the full committee for action due to failure to cooperate.

What are the Member's Rights in an Investigation?

A member has several rights, including the right to

- Be represented by legal counsel, firm representatives, and an expert witness at any meetings or discussions during the investigation, and, if there is a referral, at a hearing panel.
- Have the opportunity to meet or have a telephone interview with members of the committee, and offer evidence that should be considered in making a finding.
- Have the opportunity to read and correct and comment on the written summary of the interview.
- Have the investigation conducted in a **confidential** manner and have his or her name and the findings published only in specified circumstances.

When Will the Name of a Member and the Findings of an Investigation Be Published?

The results of the investigation and the name of the member will not be published in *The CPA Letter* unless

- The matter is presented to a hearing panel and the panel finds the member guilty, or
- As part of a settlement agreement, the member agrees to publication.

When Will the Ethics Committee Refer a Matter to the Trial Board?

If the ethics committee concludes that a violation is of sufficient gravity to warrant formal disciplinary action, the matter will be referred to the trial board.

One or more of the following conditions could result in referral:

- Harm to the public or the profession.
- Disregard for standards.
- Disregard for facts.
- Subordination of professional judgment.
- Failure to act on findings of a prior quality control or peer review.
- Repeated violations.
- Reflections on the respondent's honesty.

Can a Guilty Decision of the Trial Board Be Appealed?

A respondent found guilty by a hearing panel may request a review by filing a letter within 30 days of the decision.

A review of the request is performed by an ad hoc committee of at least five members of the trial board who did not participate in the prior proceedings.

A decision by the ad hoc committee denying a request is final.
If the request is granted, a new review panel conducts a hearing that may affirm, modify, or reverse an initial panel decision.

Section C: Authors' Advice to a Member Involved in a Disciplinary Action

Introduction	A member who receives notice of a potential disciplinary action under the JEEP has to treat the matter very seriously because

- Even though the most severe penalty is loss of AICPA or state society membership, a guilty finding can significantly damage a member's public reputation and personal self-esteem.
- A companion action by a state board can cause the loss of the member's CPA license.

NOTE: Many state boards do not have the resources to perform their own investigations and rely on the JEEP investigation.

Respond on a Timely Basis to Requests of the Ethics Committee	By not responding within the established time limits, the member will be found to have failed to cooperate with an ethics investigation. The matter will automatically be referred to the trial board as a violation of ethics rules or membership bylaws.

Engage Professionals as Representatives	A member should promptly hire competent legal counsel and an experienced expert witness before responding. This is a right of the member that should be exercised. The ethics committee will have the legal and technical resources of the AICPA and state society available. A member needs comparable or better support.

Go to the Interview and Be Thoroughly Prepared	The interview by the investigators is an opportunity the investigators must offer that should be accepted. It is the best chance a member has to persuade investigators that no disciplinary action is necessary. The member and his or her representatives should be thoroughly prepared to explain why relevant professional standards were not violated or to present meaningful mitigating circumstances.

In Written and Oral Responses, Limit the Response to the Request	Requests for information should be responded to honestly and with diligence, but the responses should not provide any information beyond what is requested.
	An ethics investigation is not limited in scope to the allegations or implications included in the complaint or other information that gave rise to the investigation.
	Any responses should avoid raising other issues by being limited to what was explicitly requested.
Carefully Consider Acceptance of a Letter of Required Corrective Action	If the ethics committee finds there is prima facie evidence of a violation after the interview, the mildest penalty is an agreement for corrective action.
	Even when the member disagrees with the finding, professional pride should not stand in the way of accepting the penalty because
	• There will be no publication of the finding and the member's name in *The CPA Letter.*
	• The corrective action is usually taking specified CPE courses and the member will have to take courses anyway to comply with mandatory CPE requirements.
In a Hearing, Try to Persuade a Sufficient Number of Decision Makers	An affirmative vote of two-thirds of those present and voting is required to expel a member.
	An affirmative vote of a majority of those present and voting is required for other sanctions.
	NOTE: The goal should be to persuade three members of the five-member panel that no sanction is necessary because there was no violation of relevant professional standards or that mitigating circumstances indicate sanctions are not warranted.
Persuasive Mitigating Circumstances or Arguments	If the facts of the case support them, the member and the member's representatives should try to make the following points:
	• There was no intentional disregard of the standards or the facts.
	• The member has acted promptly and diligently whenever a peer review or internal inspection has found the need for improvement.
	• The member has cooperated fully and responded honestly to all inquiries.

- Any violations of standards that might have occurred were isolated events and inadvertent.
- The member has consistently endeavored to remain competent and current by taking CPE courses and other means.
- For all these reasons, no sanction is necessary to prevent harm to the public or the profession.

Authoritative Sources

1. *Joint Ethics Enforcement Program (JEEP) Manual of Procedures.*
2. *Rules of Procedure and Practice of the Joint Trial Board.*

PART B

OVERVIEW OF INDEPENDENCE, INTEGRITY, AND OBJECTIVITY

4 IMPORTANCE OF INDEPENDENCE

Overview

Independence is essential when a CPA in the practice of public accounting issues a report that provides assurance on the reliability of a written assertion that is the responsibility of another party. This type of engagement is referred to broadly as an *attestation service.*

An opinion based on an audit of financial statements is a widely known form of attestation service.

This chapter explains the importance of independence when providing auditing (section A) and other attestation services (section B).

Section A: Importance of Independence in Providing Audit Services

Introduction	Independence is an essential auditing standard because the auditor's opinion is provided to enhance confidence in the reliability of financial statements that are the representations of management.
	If the auditor were not independent of management, the auditor's opinion would add nothing to the financial statements.
Basic Principle	A member in public practice should be independent in fact and appearance when providing auditing and other attestation services.
Rationale	No matter what technical proficiency the auditor possesses, the auditor's impartiality is the indispensable quality that inspires confidence in the dependability of the auditor's opinion, and therefore the reliability of the audited financial statements.
The Auditing Standard	The second general standard of generally accepted auditing standards (GAAS) is
	In all matters relating to the assignment, an independence in mental attitude is to be maintained by the auditor or auditors.
Significance of Independence to the Profession	It is of utmost importance to the profession that the general public maintain confidence in the independence of independent auditors.
	The prestige and trust of auditors as a professional group depend on the continued achievement of public confidence in the independence of auditors.
Consequences of Not Being Independent	If an auditor is not independent, any procedures the auditor might perform would not be in accordance with GAAS, and the auditor would be precluded from expressing an opinion on the financial statements.

No matter how extensive the procedures performed by the auditor, if the auditor is not independent, the financial statements are, for all practical purposes, unaudited.

Example

In several instances in which the SEC has determined that a CPA firm was not independent, the SEC has notified the client that its annual financial statements filed with the SEC would have to be reaudited by another firm. The filed financial statements were not considered to meet the SEC's requirement for audited financial statements because of the original firm's lack of independence.

Other Possible Consequences of Not Being Independent

A lack of independence may subject an auditor or a CPA firm to disciplinary action by regulators and professional organizations as well as to litigation by clients, investors, and others who relied on the financial statements.

Penalties can include payment of monetary damages to plaintiffs and loss of the license to practice and membership in professional organizations.

Consequences to the Profession of Lack of Independence

Publicly reported instances of violations of the independence rules could damage the faith of the public in the reliability of audited financial statements.

The result could be a significant loss in the value of the audit function and a deterioration in the public trust of all members of the profession.

The Current Status of Auditor Independence

Auditors as a group, and the accounting profession generally, enjoy a high level of public trust and confidence because of an established reputation for professional independence, objectivity, and integrity.

Maintaining public trust and confidence will require every auditor to continue to take seriously the requirements for independence, integrity, and objectivity, and to adhere to the letter and spirit of those requirements in daily practice.

Section B: Importance of Independence in Providing Other Attestation Services

Introduction

In addition to an audit of financial statements, there are several other types of engagements that require independence.

These types of engagements are described in detail in Chapter 7, Engagements That Require Independence.

This section describes the importance of independence to the broad category of engagements generally referred to as *attestation services.*

The Attestation Standard

The fourth general standard of the attestation standards is

> In all matters relating to the engagement, an independence in mental attitude shall be maintained by the practitioner or practitioners.

Significance of the Independence Standard to Attestation Services

Independence is a cornerstone of the attest function.

It presumes an undeviating concern for an unbiased conclusion about the reliability of an assertion no matter what the assertion may be.

Rationale for Independence

Because a practitioner providing an attestation service is giving assurance on the reliability of assertions that are the responsibility of another party, the practitioner must be free of influence by that other party.

Authoritative Sources

1. *AICPA Codification of Statements on Auditing Standards.*
   a. AU Section 220, Independence.
   b. AU Section 504, Association With Financial Statements.
2. *United States v. Arthur Young & Co.*, 465 U.S. 805, 1984.
3. *Statements on Standards for Attestation Engagements*, AT Section 100, Attestation Standards.

5 BASIC CONCEPTS OF
RULE 101–*INDEPENDENCE,* AND
RULE 102–*INTEGRITY AND OBJECTIVITY*

In This Chapter	*For information on*	*See section*
	Basic concepts of independence	A
	Related requirements on integrity, objectivity, and freedom from conflict of interest	B

Overview

CPAs need to perform all professional responsibilities with the highest sense of integrity.

CPAs also need to maintain objectivity and be free of conflicts of interest in discharging all professional responsibilities.

CPAs in public practice have additional responsibilities related to being independent when providing auditing and other attestation services. Section A explains the basic concepts related to these additional responsibilities. Section B explains the key features and relationships among ethics requirements on independence, integrity, and objectivity.

Section A: Basic Concepts of Independence

Introduction

The public relies on the independence, objectivity, and integrity of independent auditors to maintain the orderly functioning of commerce.

This reliance imposes a public interest responsibility on auditors.

Basic Principle

A member in public practice should be independent in fact and appearance when providing auditing and other attestation services.

Rationale

The purpose of an audit of financial statements is to enhance confidence in their reliability.

Public confidence in the auditor's report on financial statements could be impaired by

- Evidence that independence was actually lacking (*independence in fact*), and
- Circumstances that reasonable people might believe likely to impair independence (*independence in appearance*).

Requirements for Independence in Fact

To be *independent in fact,* the auditor must have

- **Integrity**--a fundamental character of intellectual honesty and candor, and
- **Objectivity**--a state of mind of judicial impartiality that recognizes an obligation for fairness to
  - Management and owners of a client,
  - Creditors,
  - Prospective owners or creditors, and
  - Others who might rely (including governments and the business and financial community).

Requirements for Independence in Appearance

To be **recognized** as independent, the auditor must be free from any obligation to or interest in the client, its management, or its owners.

Such interests or obligations could cause those who rely on audited financial statements to believe the auditor is biased with respect to the client, its management, or its owners.

Example

An independent auditor auditing the financial statements of a corporation of which the auditor is a director might be intellectually honest. However, it is unlikely that the public would accept the auditor as independent. The auditor would, in effect, be auditing decisions that he or she had a part in making.

Precepts Against Presumed Loss of Independence

The accounting profession and regulators--for example, the SEC--have adopted requirements to guard against the **presumption** of loss of independence.

These requirements are stated in the form of rules and their interpretations that provide objective tests.

These requirements have the force of professional law for independent auditors.

Example

A member with a direct financial interest in a client is **presumed** under these requirements to not be independent. The presumption relates to conformity with an objective test and not the personal qualities of the auditor. An auditor with a financial interest in a corporation might still be unbiased in expressing an opinion on its financial statements. However, the rule has been adopted to avoid situations that are likely to lead outsiders to doubt the independence of auditors.

Section B: Related Requirements on Integrity, Objectivity, and Freedom From Conflicts of Interest,

Introduction

A CPA in public practice, providing auditing and other attestation services, should be independent in fact and appearance.

In providing all services, a CPA should maintain the objectivity, freedom from conflicts of interest, and integrity required to be independent in fact. However, independence in appearance is not always required or possible.

Reasons for Separate Requirements on Integrity and Objectivity

Not all professional services require independence in appearance, and CPAs not in public practice cannot maintain the appearance of independence, because they are employed by others.

Examples

A CPA representing a client in tax court must be intellectually honest and objective, but is acting as the client's advocate and cannot exercise the judicial impartiality of an auditor.

A CPA preparing financial statements as a corporate controller cannot be free of any conflict of interest in making accounting judgments, but must be intellectually honest in applying accounting principles.

Responsibilities of CPAs Employed by Others

CPAs employed by others to prepare financial statements or to perform internal auditing, tax, or consulting services are charged with the same responsibility for objectivity as those in public practice.

They must be scrupulous in the application of generally accepted accounting principles and candid in all their dealings with CPAs in public practice.

Structure of the Rules on Independence, Integrity, and Objectivity

There are two related rules that are concerned with independence, integrity, and objectivity as follows:

Rule 101--Independence. A member in public practice shall be independent in the performance of professional services as required by standards promulgated by bodies designated by Council.

Rule 102--Integrity and Objectivity. In the performance of any professional service, a member shall maintain objectivity and integrity, shall be free of conflicts of interest, and shall not knowingly misrepresent facts or subordinate his or her judgment to others.

Applicability of the Rule on Independence

Rule 101 applies to CPAs in public practice who provide professional services that must be performed in accordance with standards that specify an independence requirement.

Examples

Generally accepted auditing standards that apply to audit services include a standard that requires independence.

Attestation standards that apply to examination, review, and agreed-upon procedure services include a standard that requires independence.

Other services that require independence are explained in Chapter 7, Engagements That Require Independence.

Applicability of the Rule on Integrity and Objectivity

Rule 102 applies to all CPAs, no matter where they are employed, who are engaged in performing professional services.

Example

CPAs in public practice who render attest, tax, and consulting services, CPAs employed by others who prepare financial statements, who perform internal auditing services, or who serve in financial and management capacities in industry, education, and government are all subject to Rule 102.

Enforcement of the Rules on Independence, Integrity and Objectivity

A variety of self-regulatory and regulatory organizations enforce the requirements on independence, integrity, and objectivity.

- The AICPA and state societies of CPAs enforce the requirements against all members in a cooperative program called the Joint Ethics Enforcement Program (JEEP). See Chapter 3.
- State boards of accountancy enforce the requirements against CPAs licensed in their particular states.
- The SEC enforces the requirements against auditors who audit financial statements and against CPAs who are involved in the preparation of financial information filed with it.
- Other government agencies, such as the Department of Labor (DOL), enforce the requirements against CPAs subject to their jurisdiction.

NOTE: See Chapter 2, Organizations Involved in the Development, Regulation and Enforcement of Ethics Requirements, for a more extensive discussion of these organizations.

Authoritative Sources

1. *AICPA Codification of Statements on Auditing Standards,* AU Section 220, Independence.
2. *AICPA Code of Professional Conduct*

    a. Article II--The Public Interest (ET Section 53).
    b. Article III--Integrity (ET Section 54).
    c. Article IV--Objectivity and Independence (ET Section 55).

3. *FASB* Statement of Financial Accounting Concepts 1, *Objectives of Financial Reporting by Business Enterprises.*
4. AICPA *Code of Professional Conduct*

    a. Rule 101, *Independence* (ET Section 101.01).
    b. Rule 102, *Integrity and Objectivity* (ET Section 102.01).

6 REQUIREMENTS FOR INTEGRITY AND OBJECTIVITY (INCLUDING FREEDOM FROM CONFLICTS OF INTEREST)

In This Chapter	*For information on*	*See section*
	Basic rule, definitions, and rationale	A
	Guidelines for members in public practice	B
	Guidelines for members not in public practice	C

Overview

Rule 102: Integrity and Objectivity states:

> In the performance of any professional service, a member shall maintain objectivity and integrity, shall be free of conflicts of interests and shall not knowingly misrepresent facts or subordinate his or her judgment to others.

In addition to discussing integrity and objectivity, this chapter discusses the meaning of "conflicts of interest" and how such conflicts may impair independence in an engagement requiring independence.

Additional prohibitions relating to conflicts of interest are set forth in SEC rules. These are referred to as "occupational conflicting interests." These prohibitions are also discussed in this chapter.

Section A: Basic Rule, Definitions and Rationale on Integrity and Objectivity

Rule 102	In the performance of any professional service, a member shall • Maintain objectivity and integrity. • Be free of conflicts of interest. • Not knowingly misrepresent facts or subordinate his or her judgment to others.
Definition of Integrity	Integrity is an element of character fundamental to professional recognition. It is the quality from which public trust derives and the benchmark against which a member must ultimately test all decisions. Integrity is measured in terms of what is right and just.
Definition of Objectivity	Objectivity is a state of mind, a quality that lends value to a member's services. The principle of objectivity imposes the obligation to be • Impartial. • Intellectually honest. • Free of conflicts of interest.
Definition of Professional Services	Professional services include **all services** performed by a member while **holding out** as a CPA. Holding out as a CPA includes any action initiated by a member, whether or not in public practice, that informs others of his or her status as a CPA. For example • Any oral or written representation to another regarding CPA status. • Use of the CPA designation on business cards or letterhead. • Display of a certificate evidencing a member's CPA designation. • Listing as a CPA in local telephone directories.

NOTE: This definition of "holding out" is different from that used in state laws and regulations where it is used to define the practice of public accounting.

Definition of Member

In the context of Rule 102, as opposed to Rule 101 on independence (see Chapter 5), the term "member" is used in the limited sense of a member, associate member, or international associate of the AICPA.

Definition of Conflict of Interest

A conflict of interest may occur if a member performs a professional service for a client or employer, and the member or his or her firm has

- A relationship with another person, entity, product, or service that could, in the member's professional judgment, be viewed by the client, employer, or other appropriate parties as impairing the member's objectivity.

NOTE: The member's professional judgment is subject to the test of reasonableness and appropriateness in the circumstances.

Rationale

To maintain and broaden public confidence, members should perform all professional responsibilities with the highest sense of integrity.

Service and the public trust should not be subordinated to personal gain and advantage.

Regardless of service or capacity, members should protect the integrity of their work, maintain objectivity, and avoid any subordination of their judgment.

Section B: Guidelines for Members in Public Practice

Relationship to Independence	A member should maintain objectivity and be free of conflicts of interest in discharging **all** professional responsibilities.

A member in public practice has an **additional obligation** to be independent in fact and appearance when providing auditing and other attestation services.

Independence in fact presumes the ability and willingness to act with integrity and objectivity and be free of conflicts of interest.

Implications for a Firm's Quality Control

An actual conflict of interest under Rule 102 would also impair independence under Rule 101.

Thus, a firm's quality control system should provide for

- Checking for conflicts of interest in the acceptance or continuance of auditing or other attestation engagements.
- Obtaining written representations from all professional personnel, on hiring and annually thereafter, stating they are familiar with, and are in compliance with, professional standards and the firm's policies and procedures regarding independence, integrity, and objectivity (including freedom from conflicts of interest).

Examples of Conflicts of Interest

In addition to being free from conflicts of interest in auditing and other attestation engagements, a member and the member's firm should be free of conflicts of interest in providing other professional services.

The following situations should cause a member to consider whether others would view the relationship as impairing objectivity:

- Providing litigation services to a plaintiff suing the firm's client.
- Providing tax services to both parties involved in a divorce proceeding who were previously a married couple client.
- Suggesting to a personal financial planning client an investment in a business in which the CPA has a financial interest.
- Providing personal financial planning services to several members of a family who may have opposing interests.

- Providing consulting services to a company that is a major competitor of a company in which the CPA has a position of influence.
- Serving on a city's board of tax appeals which considers matters involving several of the member's clients.
- Providing consulting services related to the acquisition by one client of real estate owned by another client.
- Referring clients to an insurance broker that refers clients to the member under an exclusive arrangement.
- Referring a client to a service bureau in which the member or partners in the member's firm hold material financial interests.

These examples are not all-inclusive and only illustrate situations that could be viewed as impairments.

Consent Permits Performance of Other Services with a Conflict

If a significant relationship that creates a conflict of interest is disclosed to, and consent is obtained from, the client, employer, or other appropriate parties, performance of professional services, other than auditing or other attestation engagements, is permitted.

*NOTE: In audit and other attest engagements, it may be impractical or impossible to obtain consent or disclose consent of parties. Auditors' or accountants' reports ordinarily are not restricted as to use. If the report is restricted, it may be practical to make disclosure and obtain consent of all other parties. See AU 532, **Restricting the Use of an Auditor's Report**. When making the disclosure, the member should be mindful of Rule 301 on not disclosing confidential information. This means it may be necessary to obtain specific consent to make the disclosure as well as consent for the conflict of interest.*

Example

A member is approached by a company, for which he or she may or may not perform other professional services, to provide personal financial planning or tax services for its executives. The executives are aware of the company's relationship with the member and have agreed to the arrangement. The member may accept the engagement if the member can perform these investment advisory services with objectivity, since the member may find, in performing these services, that the member may recommend actions to the executives that are unfavorable to the company.

As mentioned above, the member should also consider Rule 301, (Chapter 28) and not disclose confidential information. In this case, the clients are both the company and the executives.

The member should consider informing the company and the executives of possible results of the engagement.

Individual Considers or Accepts Employment with Client

A member may find that an individual participated in an engagement while considering, or after accepting, employment with the client. The member should evaluate whether all work had been performed with objectivity and integrity as required under Rule 102. If the client is a public company, the member should also follow the guidance in ISB Standard 3, *Employment with Audit Clients* (see Chapter 16).

Professional Services Involving Client Advocacy

Some requested professional services involving client advocacy may pose an unacceptable risk of impairing the reputation of a member and his or her firm with respect to independence, integrity, and objectivity because they may

- Stretch the bounds of performance standards.
- Go beyond sound and reasonable professional practice.
- Compromise credibility.

Example

A CPA is asked to advocate, in a meeting with regulators, a client's position on a financial reporting issue that clearly conflicts with an authoritative pronouncement. The CPA should refuse to perform this service.

Service as Director of a Nonclient Bank

The AICPA discourages a member from serving as a director of a non-client bank, if the member has clients (requiring independence or otherwise) that are customers of the bank.

The AICPA discourages bank directorships, to avoid situations in which the member would have

- A conflict of interest under Interpretation 102-2, or
- A problem with confidential client information under Rule 301 (Chapter 28).

NOTE: A more appropriate way for the member to serve the nonclient bank would be as a consultant to the board of directors.

Service as Director of a Consumer Credit Company

A member in public practice may serve as a director or officer of a consumer credit company that purchases installment sales contracts from retailers and receives payments from consumers, as long as he or she does not

- Audit the company.
- Participate in matters that might involve a conflict of interest.

Occupational Conflicting Interests

The SEC prohibits auditors from being involved in certain services or occupations. According to the SEC, these services or occupations are either not compatible with the auditor's appearance of complete objectivity, or are fundamentally different from the practice of accountancy.

The SEC prohibits the auditor from

1. Acting as or providing legal counsel to a client.

   Rationale: Serving as legal counsel is concerned with personal rights and interests, a role which is inconsistent with the appearance of independence.

2. Engaging in a commercial business that is directly competitive with the business of a client.

   Rationale: This would appear to a third party as influencing the auditor's objectivity, because the auditor would have access to records, policies, and practices of a business competitor.

   NOTE: There are situations that appear to breach this rule but are acceptable to the SEC. The acceptability by the SEC of a competitive situation is highly dependent on the particular facts. The authors believe that a competitive impairment can be mitigated, but how it can be mitigated depends on the facts and circumstances.

3. Being a broker-dealer.

   Rationale: This activity involves recommending securities, soliciting customers, and the execution of orders that could involve issuer or investor clients. Such activities would cause third parties to question the auditor's ability to be impartial and objective.

Example of conflicts of interest

A consultant to CPA Firm was also a director and member of the audit committee of a client audited by CPA Firm. The consultant's compensation from each of these two relationships was significant in relation to the consultant's total earnings. The SEC concluded that because of the consultant's dual role, CPA Firm's independence was impaired.

Section C: Guidelines for Members Not in Public Practice

Basic Principle

Integrity requires a member to observe both the form and spirit of technical and ethical standards

Circumvention of those standards constitutes subordination of judgment.

In This Section

This section contains the following topics:

Duty Not to Make Knowing Misrepresentations in the Preparation of Financial Statements

A member shall have knowingly misrepresented facts in violation of Rule 102 when a member

- Knowingly makes, or permits or directs another to make, materially false and misleading entries in an entity's financial statements or records.
- Knowingly fails to correct an entity's financial statements or records that are false or misleading when the member has authority to record an entry.
- Knowingly signs, or permits or directs another to sign, a document containing materially false and misleading information.

NOTE: A member who has the authority but fails to correct financial statements or records that are known to be false or misleading violates Rule 102 to the same extent as a member who knowingly makes false or misleading entries.

Duty to Be Candid with Employer's External Accountant	In dealing with his or her employer's external accountant, a member must be candid and not knowingly fail to disclose material facts.
	For example, this duty would include being honest and disclosing all relevant facts in responding to oral or written requests for representations made by the employer's external accountant.

Steps to Follow for Disagreement with Supervisor on Proper Accounting	The following table leads you through the process for dealing with a disagreement with a supervisor related to the preparation of financial statements or the recording of transactions.

Step	*Description*	*Refer to page*
1	Consider whether there is a material misrepresentation	6-9
2	Make concerns about potential material misrepresentation known within the entity	6-10
3	Consider the responsibility for further communication outside the entity.	6-11

Step 1: Consider Whether There Is a Material Misrepresentation

Is the Supervisor's Proposal an Acceptable Alternative?	Consider whether (1) the entry or failure to record a transaction in the records, or (2) the financial statement presentation or the nature or omission of disclosure in the financial statements, as proposed by the supervisor, represents the use of an acceptable alternative and does not materially misrepresent the facts.
	NOTE: The member should do appropriate research and consult authoritative literature or an independent authoritative source and make a personal judgment. It is a subordination of judgment to simply accept the supervisor's judgment that the matter is not material or has authoritative support. It is appropriate to consult an outside source such as the AICPA's technical information service.

If the Answer Is Clearly Yes	If, after appropriate research or consultation, the member concludes that the matter has authoritative support or does not result in a material misrepresentation, the member need do nothing further.

If the Answer Is No or Is Unclear	If, after appropriate research or consultation, the member concludes there is a material misrepresentation or concludes the answer is unclear, the member should take Step 2.

Step 2: Make Concerns About Potential Material Misrepresentation Known Within the Entity

If the Member Concludes Financial Statements or Records Could Be Materially Misstated

Make concerns known to the appropriate higher levels of management within the entity.

For example, communicate with the supervisor's immediate superior, senior management, the audit committee or equivalent, the board of directors, or the company's owner.

NOTE: The proper level of communication depends on the nature of the misstatements and the apparent involvement of higher levels in the misstatement. Generally, the communication should be to the next higher level above those who appear to be involved. The authors recommend that when a member of senior management appears to be involved, the communication should be to the audit committee or board of directors or owners.

Consider Documenting Concerns

Consider documenting the following matters:

- Understanding of facts.
- Accounting principles involved.
- Application of principles to facts.
- Parties with whom matters were discussed.

NOTE: The authors recommend that the member make a comprehensive contemporaneous record of these matters.

If Appropriate Action Is Not Taken

If, after discussing his or her concerns with appropriate persons in the entity, the member concludes that appropriate action was not taken, go to Step 3.

Step 3: Consider The Responsibility for Further Communication Outside the Entity

Consider Need for Legal Counsel	The member may wish to consult with his or her own legal counsel. *NOTE: The authors recommend engaging personal legal counsel before proceeding any further. Legal counsel can help the member understand the member's legal duties in the circumstances as well as provide advice on how to protect against retribution by the entity or potential violation of the law by the member.*
Consider Whether to Continue Relationship with Employer	The member should consider whether the relationship with the employer should continue.
Consider Responsibility to Communicate to Third Parties	The member should consider any responsibility that may exist to communicate to third parties, such as regulatory authorities or the employer's (former employer's) external accountant.

Members Performing Educational Services	Educational services are professional services and Rule 102 applies to those services. Educational services include • Teaching full- or part-time at a university. • Teaching a continuing professional education course. • Engaging in research or scholarship.
Use of the CPA Designation by Member Not in Public Practice	A member not in public practice may use his or her designation on business cards or letterhead, or in connection with financial statements or correspondence. To avoid violating Rule 102, the member should use his or her employment title to indicate that he or she is an employee and not independent of the employer. If the member states in a transmittal that a financial statement is presented in conformity with GAAP, the member must comply with Rule 203, *Accounting Principles* (Chapter 27).

Authoritative Sources

1. Rule 102, *Integrity and Objectivity* (ET 102.01).
2. Interpretation 102-1, *Knowing Misrepresentations in the Preparations of Financial Statements or Records* (ET 102.02).
3. Interpretation 102-2, *Conflicts of Interest* (ET 102.03).
4. Interpretation 102-3, *Obligations of a Member to His or Her Employer's External Accountant* (ET 102.04).
5. Interpretation 102-4, *Subordination of Judgment by a Member* (ET 102.05).
6. Interpretation 102-5, *Applicability of Rule 102 to Members Performing Educational Services* (ET 102.06).
7. Interpretation 102-6, *Professional Services Involving Client Advocacy* (ET 102.07).
8. SEC *Codification of Financial Reporting Policies,* Occupational Conflicting Interests (sec 602.02.e).
9. Ethics Ruling No. 65, *Use of CPA Designation by Member Not in Public Practice* (ET 191.130-.131).
10. Ethics Ruling No. 77, *Individual Considering or Accepting Employment With the Client* (ET 191.154-.155).
11. Ethics Ruling No. 85, *Bank Director,* (ET 191.170-.171).
12. Ethics Ruling No. 99, *Members Providing Services for Company Executives* (ET 191.198-.199).
13. Ethics Ruling No. 117, *Consumer Credit Company Director* (ET 591.233-.234).

PART C

INDEPENDENCE REQUIREMENTS FOR MEMBERS IN PUBLIC PRACTICE

7 ENGAGEMENTS THAT REQUIIRE INDEPENDENCE[*]

Introduction

Rule 101, *Independence* (ET 101.01), requires a "member" (as defined in Chapter 8) to be independent **in the performance of professional services as required by standards**. This chapter identifies those engagements that require independence. The Statements on Auditing Standards (SASs), Statements on Standards for Accounting and Review Services (SSARSs), and the Statements on Standards for Attestation Engagements (SSAEs) are the authoritative standards that require independence.

Some engagements require a member and a member's firm as defined in Chapter 8 to be independent; but, agreed-upon procedures engagements (Chapter 24) require only that the engagement team be independent--a more narrow requirement. In this section, you will learn what types of engagements require firm (as opposed to engagement team) independence.

Basic Principle

Firm independence applies to all audit, examination, and review engagements. Engagement team independence applies to agreed-upon procedures engagements.

---

[*]*On April 15, 2000, the Professional Ethics Division of the AICPA issued an Exposure Draft which would revise Ruling 100, **Actions Permitted When Independence Is Impaired**. The revision to this ruling would introduce an engagement-team independence approach and would permit a member's firm to perform "postaudit work," as described in the ethics ruling, when the firm is no longer independent of the client, provided that any such procedures are performed by individuals who are currently independent of the client. Please check the John Wiley & Sons, Inc. website at www.wiley.com/ethics for more information.*

Audits

The concept of members as defined in Chapter 8 is applied in all audit engagements.

The term "audit" includes engagements to audit

- Financial statements based on GAAP or an other comprehensive basis of accounting.
- Specified elements, accounts, or items of a financial statement.

Examinations

The concept of members as defined in Chapter 8 is applied in all examination engagements. Examination is a type of attest engagement that provides the highest level of assurance--reasonable assurance--on the subject matter.

The term "examination" includes engagements to examine

- Prospective financial statements--forecasts and projections.
- Design and operating effectiveness of internal control over financial reporting, or a segment thereof.
- Suitability of design of internal control over financial reporting.
- Specific requirements of an entity's compliance with laws and regulations.
- Management's discussion and analysis.
- Pro forma financial information.
- An entity's written assertion about a defined subject matter.

Reviews

The concept of members as defined in Chapter 8 is applied in all review engagements.

A review engagement may include an engagement to review

- Interim financial information of a public entity.
- Annual or interim financial statements of a private entity.
- Annual financial statements of a public entity when that entity does not have its annual financial statements audited.
- Pro forma financial information.
- An entity's written assertion about a defined subject matter.

Comfort Letters Require Independence

Engagements to issue comfort letters for underwriters and certain other requesting parties require the member and the member's firm to be independent. If the comfort letter relates to a filing under the Securities Act of 1933, the SEC's additional independence requirements apply.

NOTE: For other requesting parties, such as municipalities, the AICPA rules apply.

Compilations

A member or member's firm does not have to be independent to perform a compilation, but the report (or the engagement letter for a management-use-only compilation) has to be modified to recognize the lack of independence. To know when this special report or report language has to be used, you have to apply the definition of member and member's firm to determine independence.

The term "compilation" includes engagements to compile

- Financial statements of a private company.
- Prospective financial statements (forecasts and projections).

Compilation Reports When Not Independent

If a member or member's firm as defined in Chapter 8 is not independent, the compilation report on both private company financial statements and prospective financial statements must be modified to indicate

> We are not independent with respect to XYZ Company.

NOTE: The reason the accountant is not independent should not be described in the report.

Reporting When Not Independent on a Public Company's Financial Statements

A compilation report **cannot** be issued on the financial statements of a public company. Therefore, in this situation, the accountant is required to disclaim an opinion and state that the firm is not independent.

SAS No. 26, *Association with Financial Statements*, requires the following report to be issued:

> We are not independent with respect to XYZ Company, and the accompanying balance sheet as of December 31, 20X1, and the related statements of income and retained earnings and cash flows for the year then ended were not audited by us and accordingly, we do not express an opinion on them.

NOTE: The reason the accountant is not independent should not be described in the report.

Use of Nonindependent CPA Firm on an Engagement

CPA Firm A is independent with respect to XYZ audit client. CPA Firm A is using CPA Firm B's partners, shareholders, or professional employees on the XYZ audit engagement. CPA Firm B is not independent. In this circumstance, CPA Firm A is also not independent. However, Firm A may use the work of individuals from Firm B in a manner similar to internal auditors. Thus, Firm A would remain independent.

Independence Is Impaired After Member's Report Is Issued

A member was independent when the audit report was initially issued. Afterwards, the member's independence was impaired. The member may reissue the report or consent to its use after independence is impaired.

Authoritative Sources

1. Rule 101, *Independence* (ET 101.01).
2. *Codification of Statements on Auditing Standards*, which includes the Statements on Standards for Attestation Engagements (1999 edition).
   a. AU 623, *Special Reports*.
   b. AU 634, *Letters for Underwriters and Certain Other Requesting Parties*.
   c. AU 722, *Interim Financial Information*.
   d. AT 100, *Attestation Standards*.
   e. AT 200, *Financial Forecasts and Projections*.
   f. AT 300, *Reporting on Pro Forma Financial Information*.
   g. AT 400, *Reporting on an Entity's Internal Control Over Financial Reporting*.
   h. AT 500, *Compliance Attestation*.
   i. AT 700, *Management's Discussion and Analysis*.
3. *Codification of Statements on Standards for Accounting and Review Services* (1999), AR 100, *Compilation and Review of Financial Statements*.
4. Ethics Ruling No. 71, *Use of Nonindependent CPA Firm on an Engagement* (ET 191.142-.143).
5. Ethics Ruling No. 74, *Audits, Reviews, or Compilations and a Lack of Independence* (ET 191.148-.149).
6. Ethics Ruling No. 100, *Actions Permitted When Independence Is Impaired* (ET 191.200-.201).

8 DEFINITION OF MEMBER FOR PURPOSE OF INDEPENDENCE REQUIREMENTS

In This Chapter	*For information on*	*See section*
	Who is a member?	A
	Who else is a member?	B

Overview

A member in public practice must be independent when performing certain services such as audits of financial statements or examinations of prospective financial statements.

Section A defines the meaning of individuals within the CPA firm who are considered members.

Section B identifies individuals external to the CPA firm that are deemed to be members because of their relationship with a member.

NOTE: Refer to Chapter 24 for the definition of member when engaged to perform an agreed-upon procedures engagement.

Section A: Who Is a Member?

Introduction	To apply the independence rules and the guidance on integrity and objectivity, you must be able to define and apply the concept of a member and a member's firm.
Member's Firm	A member's firm is the form of organization permitted by state law or regulation whose characteristics conform to the resolution of AICPA Council on form of organization and name (ET Appendix B). A member's firm includes the individual owners.
Who Is a Member?	Members fall into five categories.

Category 1--Owners
Category 2--Professional employees who participate in the
        engagement
Category 3--Managerial individuals in participating office
Category 4--Any entity controlled by Categories 1, 2 and 3
Category 5--Other members

NOTE: The definition of member for purposes of applying the independence requirements is unrelated to membership in the AICPA or any other organization.

Category 1--Owners

A member includes all

- Proprietors
- Partners
- Shareholders

Without regard to

- Line of service (e.g., audit, tax, consulting client).
- Participation in a given client engagement.

**Category 2--
Professional
Employees Who
Participate in the
Engagement**

Members also include all individuals (i.e., professional employees) and independent contractors retained by the member (except those deemed to be specialists under SAS No. 73, *Using the Work of a Specialist*) who participate in the audit engagement. However, individuals who simply provide clerical assistance such as word processing or photocopying are excluded.

NOTE: SAS No. 73 permits an auditor to retain a specialist that is related to the client (i.e., not independent) provided the auditor

1. *Evaluates the relationship and whether it might impair the specialist's objectivity, and*
2. *If objectivity might be impaired, applies additional procedures to the specialist's assumptions, methods, or findings.*

The SEC expands the AICPA definition to include any professional employee

1. Providing any professional service to the client.
2. In any line of service (e.g., audit, tax, consulting).

Example

A staff accountant in a CPA firm's consulting services department may work on developing a new customer complaint system for XYZ Company, an audit client. Under the AICPA's definition of member, the staff accountant would not be a member, but under the SEC's definition, the staff accountant would be a member.

**Category 3--
Managerial
Individuals in
Participating Office**

All individuals, including consultants (except for the SAS No. 73 exclusion), having a *managerial/administrative position* located in the engagement office or any other office participating in a *significant portion of the engagement.*

**Category 4--Any
Entity Controlled
by Categories 1, 2
and 3**

Any entity (e.g., partnership, corporation, trust, joint venture, pool) whose operating, financial or accounting policies can be controlled by anyone or any combination of individuals in categories 1, 2, or 3 above.

*NOTE: The AICPA Code refers to control as defined by GAAP for consolidation purposes. Currently, FASB Statement No. 94, **Consolidation of All Majority-Owned Subsidiaries**, defines control for purposes of consolidation (over 50% signals control). However, that definition of control does not apply to many of the entities listed above because those entities do not have voting shares. The authors believe, in that situation, that the guidance on control in FASB Statement No. 57, **Related Party Disclosures**, should be followed. That is, one party controls another when the controlling* *party can significantly influence the management or operating policies of an entity to the extent that the entity may be prevented from fully pursuing its own intent.*

Example

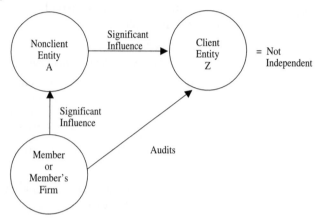

NOTE: For additional guidance concerning a member who controls a separate business that performs any services for which standards are promulgated by bodies designated by Council, see Section C, Chapter 33, Rule 505--Form of Organization and Name.

Category 5--Other Members

Any individual (who is not in category 1, 2, or 3 above) in an office having significant participation in an engagement who provides services to clients and is associated with a client as a

1. Promoter, underwriter, or voting trustee, director, officer, or employee, or in any capacity equivalent to a member of management.
2. Trustee for a pension or profit-sharing trust of the client.

Example

A new staff accountant joins the tax department of a CPA firm's Dallas office. The staff accountant is a director of his father's private company, an audit client of the CPA firm's Dallas office. The staff accountant will not provide any services to the private company. He also does not fall within categories 1, 2, or 3 above. Since the Dallas office staff accountant is a director of the private company, a member according to Category 5 above, the firm would not be independent. However, if the audit client were located in San Antonio and was an audit client of that office, the new staff accountant would not be a member. The firm would be independent.

Meaning of "Managerial Position"

To apply category 3 above, you should know the meaning of "managerial/administrative position." Whether an individual has a managerial/administrative position depends on

- His or her responsibilities, and
- How the position is held out to clients and third parties.

Examples of managerial/administrative duties include responsibilities for

- Overall planning and supervision of engagements for specified clients.
- Determining if an engagement is complete, subject to final partner/principal approval.
- Collecting fees.
- Marketing services of the firm.
- Establishing firm policies on technical matters.
- Managing the firm.
- Implementing or overseeing compliance with the elements of quality control (as set forth in Statement on Quality Control Standards No. 2, *System of Quality Control for a CPA Firm's Accounting and Auditing Practice*).

In addition, if any individual obtains a significant amount of his or her compensation from profit sharing, he or she is deemed to be "in a managerial/administrative position."

Meaning of "Office Participating in a Significant Portion of the Engagement"

To apply Category 3 above, you also have to know the meaning of "office participating in a significant portion of the engagement."

Offices participating in a significant portion of the engagement

1. Include the office having primary client responsibility (i.e., the engagement office) for a multi-office engagement.
2. Depends on the significance of work performed relative to the overall engagement effort. To assess this, you should use professional judgment and consider the materiality of the

   a. Engagement hours or fees of a given office as compared to the total engagement hours or fees.
   b. The percentage of assets or income (loss) before income taxes a given office has responsibility for in relation to client totals of those items.

What CPA Firm Employees Are Typically Excluded From the Definition of Members?

Professional employees below the managerial/administrative level who are not assigned to any engagement involving the client are not members (the only exception is Category 5 above). Likewise, those administrative employees that meet all of the following criteria are not members.

1. Have no client responsibilities,
2. Are not involved in marketing services,
3. Are not involved in establishing firm policies on technical matters, and
4. Have no responsibility related to the implementation of, or compliance with, the elements of quality control.

For example, an employee assigned to supervise the secretarial pool or the mailroom employees is not a member.

Section B: Who Else Is A Member?

Introduction

Now that you can define and apply the meaning of members based on their role within the CPA firm, you need to recognize others who are deemed to be members as a result of a relationship with a CPA firm individual who is a member.

Spouses or Dependents

The term member also includes

- Spouses, whether or not dependent.
- Dependents, whether or not related.
- Cohabitants, whether or not dependent, considering all facts and circumstances from a third-party perspective.

NOTE: A former spouse would not be included in the member category provided the member and the former spouse are legally divorced. A cohabitant is always deemed to be a member when the relationship is equivalent to that of a spouse or partner. Also, other cohabitants may be considered members. In considering other cohabitants, evaluate the relationship from the perspective of a third party--the appearance of independence--having knowledge of the strength and personal bond between the individuals. Would the third party conclude that there is a threat to independence?

Close Relatives

The term member does not include "close relatives" (e.g., parents, brothers and sisters, nondependent children). However, a close relative of a member having an investment in a client (Chapter 9) or employed by a client (Chapter 17) may impair independence.

The Main Consideration

It is impossible to enumerate all the circumstances where the appearance of a member's independence may be impaired by the relationship with a relative.

Therefore, members must consider

- The strength of the personal and business association.
- Whether a reasonable person who is aware of all the facts, and considering normal character and behavior, would conclude that there is a threat to the member's independence.

In assessing independence, members must consider the particular facts and circumstances from the perspective of a third party. Independence rules, interpretations, and ethics rulings should never be applied in a mechanical fashion.

Authoritative Sources

1. Interpretation 101-9, *The Meaning of Certain Independence Terminology and the Effect of Family Relationships on Independence* (ET 101.11, as revised May 2000).
2. SEC Regulation S-X, Article 2, *Qualifications and Reports of Accountants*, Reg. 210.2-.01.(a).
3. Ethics Ruling No. 106, *Member Has Significant Influence Over an Entity That Has Significant Influence Over a Client* (ET 191.212-213).

9 DIRECT AND INDIRECT FINANCIAL INTERESTS IN CLIENTS

Introduction

Independence is impaired if during (1) the period of engagement[1] or (2) at the time of expressing an opinion, a member or member's firm

- Had or was committed to acquire any direct or material indirect financial interest in a client.
- Was a trustee of any trust, or executor or administrator of any estate, that had or was committed to acquire any direct or material indirect financial interest in a client.

NOTE: A commitment to acquire a financial interest (e.g., agreeing to purchase stock upon issuance) impairs independence at the time of signing the stock subscription contract.

Basic Principle

A member's direct financial interest in a client impairs independence **without regard to materiality**.

If material, a member's indirect financial interest in a client impairs independence. Materiality is determined primarily by reference to the net worth of the member, the member's firm, and the client.

A member may dispose of a disqualifying direct or material indirect financial interest prior to acceptance of the engagement requiring independence and cure the independence problem.

Example

A CPA firm received a five percent, ten-year debenture of the client in a settlement of accounting fees pursuant to a plan of reorganization approved by the US District Court. If the financial interest is disposed of promptly, the CPA firm's independence is not impaired.

---

[1] *See Appendix A for the definition of "period of professional engagement."*

*NOTE: The SEC has a less restrictive independence requirement for a foreign accountant who audits a financial statement of a **nonmaterial** division, subsidiary or investee of an international business. The foreign accountant is considered independent if securities of the parent company, subsidiary, or investee are **not** owned by **any member** of the foreign accounting firm who is located in the firm's office that audits the division, subsidiary, or investee entity.*

Definitions of Direct and Indirect

Simply stated, a **direct financial interest** is created when a member invests in a client entity; whereas, an **indirect financial interest** is created when a member invests in a nonclient entity that has a financial interest in a client.

*NOTE: These terms are not defined in the AICPA **Code of Professional Conduct** or in the SEC **Codification of Financial Reporting Policies**. Their application is somewhat situational and the resulting identification of a financial interest as direct or indirect is determined by whether it is acceptable to apply materiality to the interest.*

Exception for Direct Financial Interest in Company That Acquires Audit Client

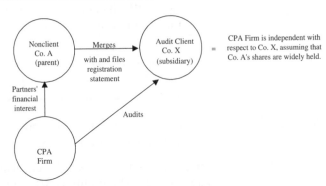

NOTE: If Partners in CPA Firm were in a position to influence the actions of Co. A, independence is impaired. In addition, if Co. X were to continue as a subsidiary of Co. A, CPA Firm would not be independent for subsequent audits unless Partners promptly dispose of their financial interest in Co. A.

Examples of Direct Financial Interests

Direct financial interests are investments made by a member

- In bonds, preferred stock, or common stock of a client.
- As trustee, executor, or administrator in bonds, preferred stock, or common stock of a client.
- As a general partner in a partnership that invests in client securities.
- In an investment club that acquires securities of a client.

- In insurance contracts or retirement plans that invest in a client if the member has the ability to direct the investments.
- In a client mutual fund or the fund's investment advisor.

Examples of Indirect Financial Interest

Indirect financial interests include

- A member's investment as a limited partner in a partnership that invests in a client.
- A member's investment in the product of a nonclient financial services company that invests in a client (when the member can not direct the investments).
- A financial interest in the client held by a close relative of an individual participating in the engagement.
- Under SEC requirements, a financial interest in the client held by a close relative of a proprietor, partner, or shareholder, whether or not such person participates in the engagement.
- A member's investments in a nonclient regulated mutual fund that invests in client securities.

Materiality

Whether an indirect financial interest impairs independence depends on materiality. In determining materiality, the member should consider the net worth of the

1. Member (including the net worth of spouse, cohabitant, and dependents).
2. Member's firm.
3. Client.

The member should select the smallest measure of the above three items.

NOTE: Unless otherwise specified in regulations, a frequently used rule-of-thumb for calculating materiality is five percent. Generally, an indirect financial interest would be considered material when it amounts to five percent or more and would be considered not material if less than five percent of items 1, 2, or 3 above.

Setting up Blind and Irrevocable Trusts

A member's lack of independence concerning a direct or indirect financial interest **cannot** be remedied by placing securities

1. In a blind trust, or
2. In an irrevocable trust that is controlled by an unassociated trustee for the benefit of a member's spouse, cohabitant, or dependents.

To maintain independence, a member must also ensure that such trusts do not acquire a direct or material indirect financial interest in clients.

Trustee of a Trust or Executor/ Administrator of an Estate

If a member or the member's firm is a trustee of any trust or executor or administrator of any estate that has or is committed to acquire any direct or material indirect financial interest in a client, the member is not independent.

NOTE: Mere designation of a member to become a trustee, executor, or administrator does not impair independence, but actual service does. The SEC sometimes makes exceptions to the above requirement for foreign accountants serving as trustees of trusts holding immaterial direct financial interests in clients.

Financial Interest Held by a Close Relative

If an individual participating in the engagement or (under SEC requirements) a proprietor, partner, or shareholder has a close relative that has a financial interest in the client that is material to that relative, and the individual has knowledge of the relative's financial interest, independence is impaired.

NOTE: Close relatives are the individual's

- *Nondependent children (including grandchildren and stepchildren).*
- *Brothers and sisters.*
- *Grandparents, parents, and parents-in-law.*
- *Spouses of any of the above.*
- *A spouse's brothers and sisters and their spouses (only for SEC registrants).*

Specific Investments That Would and Would Not Impair Independence

Type of investment	See subsection
Partnerships	A
Investment clubs	B
Deposits in a client financial institution	C
Accounts with client broker-dealer	D
Financial products of a nonclient financial service company	E
Retirement plan managed by a client insurance company	F
Employee benefit, health and welfare, retirement, savings, or similar plan of clients and nonclients	G
Securities in social clubs	H
Nonclient mutual funds	I
Client mutual funds	J

Subsection A: Partnerships

General Partner	If a member has a **direct** financial interest in a partnership that invests in a client, and the member is a general partner or functions in a similar manner, independence is impaired.
Limited Partner	If a member has a **direct** financial interest in a partnership that invests in a client, and the member is a limited partner having a material interest (to the member's net worth), independence is impaired.
Direct vs. Indirect Financial Interest	A general partner/member's investment in a partnership that invests in a client is a direct financial interest. A limited partner/member's investment in a partnership that invests in a client is an indirect financial interest.

Subsection B: Investment Clubs

Definition of Investment Club	An investment club is a group of individuals who pool their money, select investments, and invest the pooled funds in the selected investment.
Direct Financial Interest	Any investment made by a member in an investment club is a direct financial interest. Therefore, if club investments are made in clients, independence is impaired without regard to materiality.

Subsection C: Deposits in a Client Financial Institution

Account Balances Insured	If a member has checking accounts, savings accounts, certificates of deposit, or money market accounts in a client financial institution, independence is **not** impaired if all such accounts' balances are equal to or less than the state or federal government insurance limits.

Uninsured Account Balances	If a member has the above accounts in a client financial institution, independence **is** impaired if the aggregate uninsured balances are material to the member's net worth.

Subsection D: Accounts With Client Broker-Dealer

Self-Directed IRA	A member may maintain a self-directed IRA account with a client broker-dealer without impairing independence.

Items That Impair Independence

Independence is impaired

1. If the broker-dealer has discretionary authority to execute transactions for the member.
2. If the member leaves cash or securities with the broker-dealer beyond a normal settlement period.
3. If the broker-dealer extends credit to the member (Chapter 15, Loans to and from Clients).

Subsection E: Financial Products of a Nonclient Financial Services Company

Ability to Direct Investment

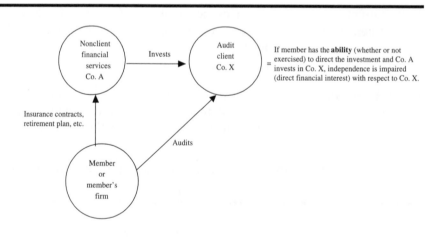

Does Not Have Ability to Direct Investment	If the above member does not have the ability to direct the investments and Co. A invests in a client (but not exclusively in clients), the interest is an indirect financial interest and independence is impaired only if material.
Portfolio is Invested in Clients Only	If Co. A above invests only in clients of the member, the interest is a direct financial interest and independence is impaired.

Subsection F: Retirement Plan Managed by a Client Insurance Company

Retirement Funds Maintained in a Pooled Separate Account	A member may contribute to a retirement plan that is invested/managed by a client insurance company and be independent with respect to the insurance company.
	To maintain independence, the retirement funds must be maintained in a pooled separate account, not part of the general assets of the insurance company.

Subsection G: Employee Benefit, Health and Welfare, Retirement, Savings, or Similar Plan of Clients and Nonclients

Member Participates in Client or Nonclient Plan	If a member participates in an employee benefit, health and welfare, retirement, savings, or similar plan **of a client**, independence is impaired with respect to the client and such plans.
	If a member participates in any of the above plans **of clients or nonclients that invest in the client or in other clients**, independence is impaired with respect to the client or those other clients (investees).
Health and Welfare Plan Exception	If the member's participation in a health and welfare plan arises as a result of a spouse's or cohabitant's employment, participation does not impair independence if **all** of the following conditions are met: 1. The spouse's or cohabitant's position with the client does not impair independence (Chapter 17, Employment of a Spouse, Dependent or Close Relative by a Client). 2. The plan is normally offered to all employees in equivalent positions.

NOTE: Although the AICPA has not officially changed Ruling 107 (the health and welfare plan exception) to apply to spouses and dependents rather than spouses and cohabitants, as it has done for Ruling 108 (the retirement and savings plan exception), the authors believe that the AICPA may incorporate such changes into Ruling 107 and other rulings in the future.

Retirement and Savings Plan Exception

If the member's participation in a retirement, savings, or similar plan arises as a result of a spouse's or dependent's employment, participation is permitted if **all** the following conditions are met:

1. The spouse/dependent's position with the client does not impair independence (Chapter 17).
2. The plan is normally offered to all employees in equivalent positions.
3. The member does not participate in the engagement.
4. The member is not in a position to influence the engagement, meaning that the member does not have direct management responsibility for, or does not provide direct technical consultation, quality control, or oversight, of the engagement or engagement team.

    NOTE: A member's relationship with a cohabitant may be the same as that of a spouse.

5. If the right of possession does not exist, the investment should not be material to the member's net worth. (If an investment is material, a sufficient amount may be forfeited so that the remaining holdings are not material.)
6. The member does not participate in the client/sponsor engagement if the investment is in that client. If the investment is in another client, the member does not participate in that engagement.

Additional Restriction

Electing to invest in a client through a spouse's, cohabitant's, or dependent's benefit plan when there are nonclient investment options available in the plan constitutes a direct investment in the client and impairs independence even if the right of possession does not exist.

Subsection H: Securities in Social Clubs

Required to Acquire Securities

A member who is required by a condition of membership of a social club (e.g., country club or tennis club) to acquire a pro rata share of the club's securities is independent with respect to such club, provided

1. Membership in the club is essentially social.
2. The member does not serve on the club's governing board or otherwise participate in management of the club.

Subsection I: Nonclient Mutual Funds

Indirect Financial Interest

Investments in a nonclient regulated mutual fund are indirect financial interests. For the average diversified mutual fund, a member's indirect financial interest in any one of the fund's securities is unlikely to be material.

Specialized Fund

If the mutual fund has a limited number of securities in its portfolio, a member's indirect financial interest may be material, causing independence to be impaired.

Audits of Investment Adviser, Sister Funds, or Related Nonfund Entities

ISB Standard No. 2, *Certain Independence Implications of Audits of Mutual Funds and Related Entities*, must be considered if the member's investment in a nonclient fund is part of a mutual fund complex that has other funds or nonfund entities that are audited by the member's firm (see Subsection J).

Subsection J: Client Mutual Funds, Including Open-End and Closed-End Funds, and Unit Investment Trusts

Audit of Any Fund or Nonfund Entity in the Fund Complex

To maintain independence, (1) the audit firm and the firm's retirement plans (except for self-directed defined contribution plans), (2) the engagement team, and (3) those in a position to influence the audit must be independent of **all**

• Sister funds (having a common investment adviser).

- Related nonfund entities (e.g., investment adviser, broker-dealer, bank, or insurance company in the mutual fund complex).

In addition, the partners in the firm, either individually or collectively, do not have significant influence over any audited fund, sister fund or nonfund entity.

NOTE: In auditing a nonfund entity, the same independence requirements apply to all funds in the mutual fund complex.

Permitted Investments

Partners and employees (other than those on the engagement team or in a position to influence the audit) **would be** permitted under ISB No. 2, *Certain Independence Implications of Audits of Mutual Funds and Related Entities*, to make direct investments in nonclient sister funds.

Spouses, cohabitants, and dependents of partners (other than those on the engagement team or in a position to influence the audit) would be permitted to invest in an employer-sponsored benefit plan in mutual funds that are audit clients.

NOTE: The SEC's definition of members and the AICPA requirements pertaining to spousal employee benefit plans are more restrictive than the above. Therefore, members must follow the more restrictive rules until those organizations amend their existing requirements.

Authoritative Sources

1. Interpretation 101-1, *Interpretation of Rule 101* (ET 101.02.A.1 and 2).
2. Interpretation 101-9, *The Meaning of Certain Independence Terminology and the Effect of Family Relationships on Independence* (ET 101.11, as revised May 2000).
3. SEC *Codification of Financial Reporting Policies,* Financial Interest in Client Company (sec. 602.02.b.ii.).
4. SEC *Codification of Financial Reporting Policies,* Financial Interests in Client Company or Its Affiliates by a Foreign Accountant (sec. 602.02.b.iv.).
5. ISB Standard No. 2, *Certain Independence Implications of Audits of Mutual Funds and Related Entities*.
6. Ethics Ruling No. 11, *Member as Executor or Trustee* (ET 191.021-.022).
7. Ethics Ruling No. 17, *Member of Social Club* (ET 191.033-.04).

8. Ethics Ruling No. 35, *Stockholder in Mutual Funds* (ET 191.069-.070).
9. Ethics Ruling No. 36, *Participant in Investment Club* (ET 191.071-.072).
10. Ethics Ruling No. 41, *Member as Auditor of Insurance Co*mpany (ET 191.081-.082).
11. Ethics Ruling No. 66, *Member's Retirement or Savings Plan Has Financial Interest In Client* (Revised)(ET 191.132-.133).
12. Ethics Ruling No. 68, *Blind Trust* (ET 191.136-.137).
13. Ethics Ruling No. 70, *Member's Depository Relationship With Client Financial Institution* (ET 191.140-.141).
14. Ethics Ruling No. 79, *Member's Investment in a Partnership That Invests in Member's Clients* (ET 191.158-.159).
15. Ethics Ruling No. 81, *Member's Investment in a Limited Partnership* (ET 191.162-.163).
16. Ethics Ruling No. 107, *Participation in Health and Welfare Plan of Client* (ET 191.214-.215).
17. Ethics Ruling No. 108, *Participation of Member or Spouse in Retirement, Savings, or Similar Plan Sponsored by, or That Invests in, Client* (Revised) (ET 191.216-.217).
18. Ethics Ruling No. 109, *Member's Investment in Financial Services Products That Invest in Clients* (ET 191.218-.219).

10 FINANCIAL INTERESTS IN NONCLIENTS THAT ARE RELATED TO CLIENTS

Introduction

A financial interest in a nonclient that is related in some way to a client may impair independence. This chapter explains and graphically illustrates those investments in nonclients that may impair independence.

Basic Principle

Independence may be impaired because of a member's financial interest in a nonclient who is related in various ways to a client. A financial interest in a nonclient may result in a financial interest in a client or place the member in a capacity equivalent to a member of management.

Important Definitions

To apply the guidance in this chapter, you need to understand the following definitions:

1. Significant influence--According to Accounting Principles Board Opinion No. 18, *The Equity Method of Accounting for Investments in Common Stock*, significant influence exists when the investor owns from 20 to 50 percent of the investee's voting shares, although circumstances exist where such influence is present with under 20 percent ownership, or conversely is absent with holdings of 20 percent or greater.
2. Investor--A partner, general partner, or a natural person or corporation that has the ability to exercise significant influence.
3. Investee--A subsidiary or an entity over which an investor has the ability to exercise significant influence.

**Client has Material
Investment in
Nonclient**

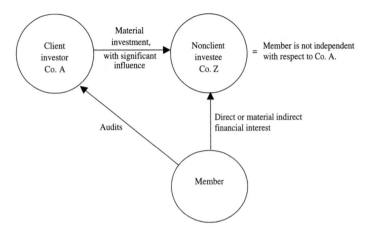

Rationale: Member's direct or material indirect financial interest in
Co. Z is tantamount to member having a financial interest in Co. A.

**Client has
Immaterial
Investment in
Nonclient**

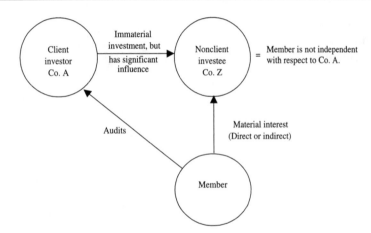

Rationale: Client Co. A's ability to influence Co. Z could enhance or
diminish the value of the member's financial interest in Co. Z by an
amount material to the member's net worth without a material effect
on its own financial statements. As a result, the member would not
appear to be independent.

*NOTE: If the member had an immaterial (direct or indirect) financial
interest in Co. Z, the member would be independent with respect to Co. A.
The SEC quantifies materiality as not exceeding five percent of Co. A's
consolidated total assets. In addition, Co. A's equity in Co. Z's income from
continuing operations before income taxes cannot exceed five percent of Co.
A's consolidated income from continuing operations before income taxes.*

Nonclient Has Material Investment in Client

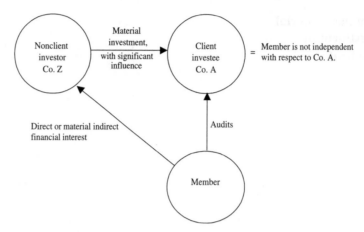

Rationale: Member's direct or material indirect interest in Co. Z is tantamount to member having a financial interest in Co. A.

Nonclient Has Immaterial Investment in Client

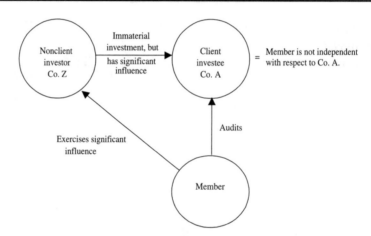

Rationale: A financial interest sufficient to allow the member to significantly influence the actions of Co. Z could permit the member to exercise a degree of control over Co. A that would place the member in a capacity equivalent to a member of management.

Member's Investment in Limited Partnership (LP) Having Client General Investor

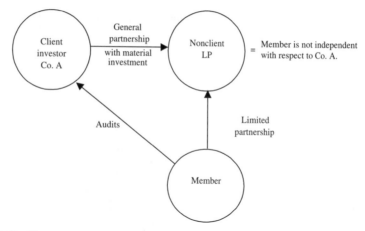

NOTE: *However, if (1) Co. A's financial interest in LP is not material and (2) member's financial interest in LP is immaterial, member's independence with respect to Co. A is not impaired.*

Other Relationships

Other relationships, for example, brother-sister entities (under common control) and client-nonclient joint ventures may affect independence.

To determine if they do

1. Make inquiry(ies) to your client to determine if such relationships exist. (If you can **not** reasonably obtain information about the relationships, independence is **not** impaired.)
2. If relationships exist, would a reasonable observer conclude that independence is threatened?

Example: Brother/Sister Entities

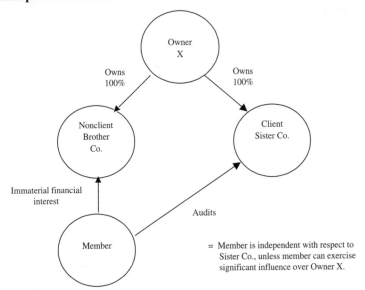

NOTE: *If member's financial interest in Brother Company is material, member is not independent with respect to Sister Company.*

Example: Joint Ventures

The same logic applied to Brother/Sister above applies to joint ventures. An immaterial financial interest in a nonclient investor would not impair independence, provided the member could not exercise significant influence over the nonclient investor. For example

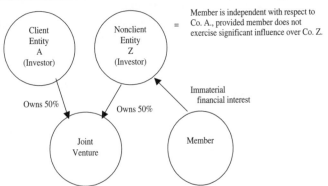

Authoritative Sources

1. Interpretation 101-8, *Effect on Independence of Financial Interests In Nonclients Having Investor or Investee Relationships with a Member's Client* (ET 101.10).
2. SEC *Codification of Financial Reporting Polices,* Interests in Nonclient Affiliates and Investee Companies (sec. 602.02.b.iii).
3. Ethics Ruling No. 81, *Member's Investment in a Limited Partnership* (ET 191.162-.163).
4. See also Ethics Ruling No. 69, *Invest with a General Partner* (ET-138-.139), which is discussed in Chapter 14, *Business Relationships; Joint, Closely Held Business Investments; Cooperative Arrangements; and Lease Arrangements.*
5. See also Ethics Ruling No. 79, *Member's Investment in a Partnership That Invests in Member's Client* (ET .158-.159), which is discussed in Chapter 9, *Direct and Indirect Financial Interests in Client.*

11 FORMER PRACTITIONERS

Introduction	The independence of a CPA firm might be affected by a former practitioner's financial interest in, or official association with, a client.
Definition of Former Practitioner	A proprietor, partner, shareholder or equivalent of a firm, who leaves by resignation, termination, retirement, or sale of all or part of the practice.
Basic Principle (AICPA Rule)	Independence of the firm may be impaired if the former practitioner is considered a member as a result of the actual, or appearance of, influence or participation in the firm.
	If a former practitioner who is considered a "member" has a financial interest in or official association with a firm's client, independence is impaired.
Criteria for Determining Firm's Independence	In determining a firm's compliance with independence requirements, the key is deciding whether a former practitioner is included in the term "a member or a member's firm."
	The criteria for making this determination relate to
	<ul><li>Payments to the former practitioner.</li><li>Participation in the firm's business or professional activities.</li><li>Appearance of participation or association with the firm.</li></ul>
Restrictions on Payments	Payments of amounts due the former practitioner for his or her capital interest in the firm and for unfunded vested retirement benefits must be

- Subject to a written agreement.
- Not material to the CPA firm.
- Calculated based on an underlying formula that remains fixed during the payout period. (Retirement benefits may be adjusted for inflation.)

NOTE: The SEC imposes additional restrictions on payments as discussed later in this chapter. ISB 3 also creates restrictions that are discussed later in this chapter.

Restrictions on Actual Participation

The former practitioner cannot participate in the firm's business or professional activities (whether or not compensated).

NOTE: The AICPA provides an exception to this restriction for a reasonable period of time during the transition period upon leaving the firm for consultations on an advisory basis.

Restrictions on Appearance of Participation or Association

An unacceptable appearance of participation or association would result from actions such as inclusion of the former practitioner's name

- Under the firm's name in an office building directory.
- As a member of the firm in membership lists of business, professional, or civic organizations.
- In the firm's internal directory without being designated as retired.

An unacceptable appearance of participation or association would not be created by the firm providing office amenities such as office space and secretarial and telephone services, except as noted below concerning a position of significant influence with the client and additional restrictions of the SEC.

Restrictions Related to a Position of Significant Influence with a Client

If a former practitioner assumes a position of significant influence with a client, office amenities can no longer be provided.

Additional Restrictions of the SEC

The SEC requires that all active connections with the firm must be severed and imposes the following additional restrictions on the influence or participation of former practitioners

- Payments cannot be related to current firm revenues. (Payments must be in predetermined annual amounts from a fixed settlement amount.)
- Appearance of continuing influence may exist if the practitioner was closely associated with professional services provided the client before leaving the firm and very shortly after leaving acquires an interest in or becomes associated with the client.
- Appearance of continuing influence may also exist if the firm provides office amenities or if the former practitioner's name continues to be listed in the firm letterhead or firm directories, whether or not the practitioner is identified as retired.

ISB Rule When Former Practitioner is Employed by Client

According to ISB 3, *Employment with Audit Clients*, a CPA firm may not be independent if a firm professional (FP) is employed by an audit client. If FP has knowledge of, and relationships with the firm that could adversely influence the audit, independence is impaired unless the firm implements the following safeguards.

Accepting Employment-- Safeguards

1. The audit engagement team considers whether the audit plan needs to be modified to reduce the risk of circumvention.
2. If FP will have significant interaction with the audit team, the firm takes steps to ensure that the existing audit team has the stature and objectivity to deal with FP.
3. If FP joins the client (a) within one year of leaving the firm and (b) has significant interaction with the audit team, the next annual audit is separately reviewed by a professional uninvolved in the audit. The purpose of the review is to determine if the audit team exercises appropriate skepticism in evaluating representations and work of FP. The extent of the review depends in part on the position that FP has at the audit client.
4. The firm requires (a) prompt liquidation of all capital balances, (b) settlement of all retirement balances (unless they are immaterial to the firm and fixed as to amount/payment), and (c) settlement of immaterial retirement balances if within five years of leaving the firm, FP's name as an officer or employee of the audit client is required to be disclosed by the SEC in a proxy statement or an annual report.

NOTE: The definition of retirement balances used above excludes a defined contribution plan (e.g., a 401(K)) if the firm has no funding obligation after CPA leaves the firm. The above ISB requirements are effective for employment with audit client situations arising after December 31, 2000.

Authoritative Sources

1. Interpretation 101-2, *Former Practitioners and Firm Independence* (ET 101.04).
2. SEC Codification of Financial Reporting Policies, *Retired Partners* (sec. 602.02.f).
3. ISB Standard No. 3, *Employment with Audit Clients.*

12 UNPAID FEES[*]

Introduction	Unpaid fees may impair independence. Both the AICPA and the SEC have rules that govern unpaid fees, and those rules are substantially different. This chapter explains the AICPA and SEC rules and highlights their differences.
Basic Principle	Unpaid fees may impair independence because they are tantamount to having a financial interest in, or making a loan to, a client.
Definitions of Unpaid Fees	Unpaid fees are fees for (1) audit and (2) other professional services that relate to certain prior periods that are delinquent as of the • Date the current year's audit engagement begins, if the client is an SEC registrant, or • Date the audit report is issued for non SEC clients (i.e., AICPA rule).
AICPA Rule	Independence is impaired, if when the audit report is issued for the current year, professional fees for (1) billed services, (2) unbilled services, or (3) uncollected notes receivable (arising from professional fees) are delinquent for more than one year prior to the current audit report date. *NOTE: Materiality of the delinquent fees is not considered, and the above rule does not apply to professional fees from a client in bankruptcy.*

[*]*Contingent fees and commissions are prohibited for any service performed for a client when the member also performs an audit, certain attestation services, or a compilation for that client. These matters are discussed in Chapter 29, Rule 302--Contingent Fees, and Chapter 32, Rule 503--Commissions and Referral Fees.*

Example:

	Period 1	*Period 2*
Current audit report issued on 2/15/02	Fees for services performed from 2/15/01 to 2/15/02 do not impair independence	Fees for services performed before 2/15/01 do impair independence

SEC Rule

Independence is impaired, if unpaid fees for any professional service are material in relation to the fee expected for the current audit at the date the current audit begins.

NOTE: Unpaid fees personally owed by a principal shareholder of a client can also impair independence.

There are two exceptions to the SEC's general rule that apply only to audits of financial statements in filed annual reports. Independence is not impaired, if at the time the current audit begins

1. A definite commitment is made by the client to pay delinquent fees before the current year audit report is issued, or
2. An arrangement is agreed to for periodic payments to pay the delinquent fees, and there is reasonable assurance that such fees will be paid before beginning the audit for the next year.

NOTE: The exceptions above do not apply to a registration of securities under the Securities Act of 1933. Generally, prior year audit and other professional fees should be paid before the current audit begins in order to avoid independence problems.

Authoritative Sources

1. SEC *Codification of Financial Reporting Policies*, Unpaid Prior Professional Fees (sec 602.02.b.v).
2. Ethics Ruling No. 52, *Unpaid Fees* (ET 191.103-.104).

13 PERFORMANCE OF OTHER SERVICES FOR CLIENTS

Introduction

A member or member's firm may perform services for a client that require independence (attest services) and also perform other nonattest services for the same client.

The member must evaluate the effect of the nonattest services on independence.

> **Example:**
>
> A member's firm might perform audit services for a client and also be asked to design an inventory control system for that client. The member must evaluate the nature of the services related to the design of the inventory control system to determine whether the services impair audit independence.

Basic Principle

To avoid an impairment of independence, the member should take care not to perform **management functions** or make **management decisions** for the attest client.

The SEC, in addition, believes that judgments about appropriate accounting principles and methods of recording, classifying, and presenting financial data cannot subsequently be evaluated on an impartial and objective basis, and generally views involvement in recordkeeping as an impairment of independence.

Essential Understanding with Client

The member should establish an understanding with the client regarding

- Objectives of the engagement.
- Services to be performed.
- Management's responsibilities.
- Member's responsibilities.

It should be clear that the member will not make management decisions or perform management functions.

NOTE: It is preferable that the understanding be documented in an engagement letter.

Other Client Responsibilities

The member should be satisfied that the client

- Is in a position to have an **informed judgment** on the results of the nonattest services.
- Understands its responsibility to

    1. Designate a management level individual (or individuals) to be responsible for overseeing the nonattest services provided.
    2. Evaluate the adequacy of the nonattest services and the findings.
    3. Make management decisions, including accepting responsibility for the results of nonattest services.
    4. Establish and maintain internal controls, including monitoring ongoing activities.

General Examples of Activities That Would Impair Independence

- Authorizing, executing, or consummating a transaction.
- Otherwise having or executing authority on behalf of a client.
- Having custody of client assets.
- Reporting to the board of directors on behalf of management.
- Supervising client employees in the performance of normal recurring activities.
- Determining which of the member's recommendations should be implemented.
- Serving as the client's registrar, stock transfer or escrow agent, or general counsel.
- Preparing source documents or originating data in electronic or other form evidencing the occurrence of a transaction.

    Example:

    Source documents include purchase orders, payroll time cards, and customer orders. They are the documents on which the evidence of an accounting transaction is initially recorded.

NOTE: The SEC regards bookkeeping services of all types as impairing independence.

SEC Position on Bookkeeping Services

If an auditor has participated closely, either manually or through computer services, in maintenance of the basic accounting records and preparation of financial statements, the auditor is not independent.

If an auditor performs other accounting services involving participating with management in operational decisions, the auditor is not independent.

Exceptions to the SEC's Position on Bookkeeping Services

The SEC will not deem independence to have been impaired in the following circumstances:

- The auditor's work is limited to processing and production of summaries and listings, and reports that do not become part of the basic accounting records.
- No accounting services have been provided in the latest full year; services in earlier years were limited in extent or mechanical in nature; **and** strict application of the normal prohibition would cause an unreasonable hardship on a company going public for the first time.
- Accounting services for a foreign component of a domestic client, provided **all** of the following eight conditions are met:

  1. The services are provided by a foreign office or a foreign firm associated with a domestic accounting firm.
  2. The services are limited, routine, or ministerial bookkeeping services.
  3. The services are provided to a foreign division, subsidiary or investee of a domestic registrant which is a client of the domestic firm.
  4. It is impractical to make other arrangements.
  5. The foreign entity is not material to the consolidated financial statements.
  6. The foreign entity does not have employees capable or competent to perform the services.
  7. Total fees for the bookkeeping services for all foreign entities do not exceed one percent of the total audit fee for the registrant.
  8. The services are consistent with the professional ethics rules in the foreign location.

SEC Versus AICPA on Services to Nonclients Related to the Client

The SEC regards all persons and entities related to the client, such as officers, directors, principal stockholders, affiliates, or an employee benefit plan sponsored by the client, to be the same as the client for purposes of evaluating independence.

The SEC position is that *services that would impair independence if provided to the client would also impair independence if provided to related persons or entities.*

Example:

A partner in a firm is also a lawyer and is engaged to represent the CEO of an audit client in personal litigation. Independence is impaired because legal representation requires advocacy.

The AICPA generally regards these related entities and persons as separate clients, but imposes restrictions on services to employee benefit plans sponsored by the client. (See Subsection L.)

SECPS Restrictions on Consulting Services

SEC Practice Section members should not perform services for clients that are inconsistent with the firm's responsibilities to the public. The SECPS prohibits the following services for audit clients:

- Psychological testing
- Public opinion polls
- Merger and acquisition assistance for a finder's fee.
- Executive recruitment (see discussion below and Subsection G).
- Actuarial services to insurance companies (see discussion on next page and Subsection F).

NOTE: These are restrictions on the scope of service. They may not necessarily indicate impairment of independence.

Executive Recruitment Services That Would and Would Not Be Prohibited by the SECPS

An SECPS member firm should not

- Accept an engagement to search for candidates for managerial, executive, or director positions with audit clients.
- Engage in psychological testing, other formal testing or evaluation programs, or undertake reference checks for executive or director positions.
- Act as a negotiator on the client's behalf.
- Recommend a specific candidate for a specific job.

An SECPS member firm may

- Interview candidates or advise the client, at the client's request, on a candidate's competence for accounting-related positions.

Actuarial Services That Would and Would Not Be Prohibited by the SECPS

When auditing publicly held insurance companies, an SECPS member firm should not render actuarially-oriented advisory services unless it is satisfied that it is acting in an advisory capacity and that the client accepts the responsibility for any significant actuarial methods and assumptions. The firm should not render services

- Involving the determination of policy reserves and related accounts to clients unless such clients use their own or third-party actuaries to provide management with the primary actuarial capabilities. The CPA firm may use their own actuaries to audit such reserves.
- When the CPA firm's involvement is continuous and may be perceived as serving as management.

Specific Examples of Activities That Would and Would Not Impair Independence by Type of Service

Type of service	*See subsection*
Bookeeping	A
Payroll and other disbursement	B
Benefit plan administration	C
Investment advisory or investment management	D
Corporate finance--consulting or advisory	E
Appraisal, valuation, or actuarial	F
Executive or employee search	G
Business risk consulting	H
Information systems design, installation, or integration	I
Management advisory	J
Representative of creditor's committee	K
Employee benefit plan sponsored by client	L
Assisting clients in implementing SFAS 133 (Derivatives)	M

Subsection A: Bookkeeping

Example Activities That Would *Not* Impair Independence

- Record transactions for which management has determined or approved the appropriate account classification, or post coded transactions to a client's general ledger.
- Prepare financial statements based on information in the trial balance.
- Post client-approved entries to a client's trial balance.

- Propose standard, adjusting, or correcting journal entries or other changes affecting the financial statements to the client.
- Provide data-processing services.

NOTE: The SEC takes a much more restrictive position on bookkeeping services than the AICPA. See the earlier discussion in this chapter for a description of the limited exceptions to the SEC's position.

Example Activities That Would Impair Independence

- Determine or change journal entries, account codings or classification for transactions, or other accounting records without obtaining client approval.
- Authorize or approve transactions.
- Prepare source documents or originate data.
- Make changes to source documents or entries without client approval.

Subsection B: Payroll and Other Disbursement

Example Activities That Would *Not* Impair Independence

- Using payroll time records provided and approved by the client, generate unsigned checks, or process client's payroll.
- Transmit client-approved payroll or other disbursement information to a financial institution provided the client has authorized the member to make the transmission and has made arrangements for the financial institution to limit the corresponding individual payments as to amount and payee. In addition, once transmitted, the client must authorize the financial institution to process the information.
- Make electronic payroll tax payments in accordance with US Treasury Department or comparable guidelines provided the client has made arrangements for its financial institution to limit such payments to a named payee.

Example Activities That Would Impair Independence

- Accept responsibility to authorize payment of client funds, electronically or otherwise, except as specifically provided for with respect to electronic payroll tax payments.
- Accept responsibility to sign or cosign client checks, even if only in emergency situations.
- Maintain a client's bank account or otherwise have custody of a client's funds or make credit or banking decisions for the client.

- Sign the payroll tax return on behalf of client management.
- Approve vendor invoices for payment.

NOTE: The SEC takes a much more restrictive position on bookkeeping services than the AICPA. See the earlier discussion in this chapter for a description of the limited exceptions to the SEC's position.

Subsection C: Benefit Plan Administration

Example Activities That Would *Not* Impair Independence	• Communicate summary plan data to plan trustee. • Advise client management regarding the application or impact of provisions of the plan document. • Process transactions (e.g., investment/benefit elections or increase/decrease contributions to the plan; data entry; participant confirmations; and processing of distributions and loans) initiated by plan participants through the member's electronic medium, such as an interactive voice response system or Internet connection or other media. • Prepare account valuations for plan participants using data collected through the member's electronic or other medium.
Example Activities That Would Impair Independence	• Make policy decisions on behalf of client management. • When dealing with plan participants, interpret the plan document on behalf of management without first obtaining management's concurrence. • Make disbursements on behalf of the plan. • Have custody of assets of a plan. • Serve a plan as a fiduciary as defined by ERISA.

NOTE: See Subsection L for a discussion of the effect of providing services to a benefit plan on independence with respect to the sponsor.

Subsection D: Investment Advisory or Investment Management

Example Activities That Would *Not* Impair Independence	• Recommend the allocation of funds that a client should invest in various asset classes, depending upon the client's desired rate of return, risk tolerance, etc. • Perform recordkeeping and reporting of client's portfolio balances including providing a comparative analysis of the client's investments to third-party benchmarks. • Review the manner in which a client's portfolio is being managed by investment account managers, including determining whether the managers are (1) following the guidelines of the client's investment policy statement; (2) meeting the client's investment objectives; and (3) conforming to the client's stated investment styles. • Transmit a client's investment selection to a broker-dealer or equivalent provided the client has authorized the broker-dealer or equivalent to execute the transaction.
Example Activities That Would Impair Independence	• Make investment decisions on behalf of client management or otherwise have discretionary authority over a client's investments. • Execute a transaction to buy or sell a client's investment. • Have custody of client assets, such as taking temporary possession of securities purchased by a client.

Subsection E: Corporate Finance--Consulting or Advisory

Example Activities That Would *Not* Impair Independence	• Assist in developing corporate strategies. • Assist in identifying or introducing the client to possible sources of capital that meet the client's specifications or criteria. • Assist in analyzing the effects of proposed transactions including providing advice to a client during negotiations with potential buyers, sellers, or capital sources. • Assist in drafting an offering document or memorandum. • Participate in transaction negotiations in an advisory capacity. • Be named as a financial advisor in a client's private placement memoranda or offering document.

Example Activities That Would Impair Independence	• Commit the client to the terms of a transaction or consummate a transaction on behalf of the client.
	• Act as a promoter, underwriter, broker dealer, or guarantor of client securities, or distributor of private placement memoranda or offering documents.
	• Maintain custody of client securities.

Subsection F: Appraisal, Valuation, or Actuarial

Example Activities That Would *Not* Impair Independence	• Test the reasonableness of the value placed on an asset or liability included in a client's financial statements by preparing a separate valuation of that asset or liability.
	• Perform a valuation of a client's business when all significant matters of judgment are approved by the client and the client is in a position to have an informed judgement on the results of the valuation.

Example Activities That Would Impair Independence	• Prepare a valuation of an employer's securities contained in an employee stock ownership plan (ESOP) to support transactions with participants, and allocations within the ESOP, when the client is not in a position to have an informed judgment on the results of this valuation.
	• Prepare an appraisal, valuation, or actuarial report using assumptions determined by the member and not approved by the client.

NOTE: If the appraisal, valuation, or actuarial services result in the original determination of amounts to be included in the financial statements, the SEC would regard the auditors as being involved in the preparation of the financial statements, and independence would be impaired.

Subsection G: Executive or Employee Search

Example Activities That Would *Not* Impair Independence	• Recommend a position description or candidate specifications. • Solicit and perform screening of candidates and recommend qualified candidates to a client based on the client-approved criteria (e.g., required skills and experience). • Participate in employee hiring or compensation discussions in an advisory capacity.
Example Activities That Would Impair Independence	• Commit the client to employee compensation or benefits arrangements. • Hire or terminate client employees. *NOTE: Firms that are members of the SECPS should also refer to the membership requirements that restrict the performance of certain executive recruiting services (see page 13-4).*

Subsection H: Business Risk Consulting

Example Activities That Would *Not* Impair Independence	• Provide assistance in assessing the client's business risks and control processes. • Recommend a plan for making improvements to a client's control processes and assist in implementing these improvements.
Example Activities That Would Impair Independence	• Make or approve business risk decisions. • Present business risk considerations to the board or others on behalf of management.

Subsection I: Information Systems--Design, Installation, or Integration

---

Example Activities That Would *Not* Impair Independence	• Design, install or integrate a client's information system, provided the client makes all management decisions. • Customize a prepackaged accounting or information system, provided the client makes all management decisions. • Provide the initial training and instruction to client employees on a newly implemented information and control system.

Example Activities That Would Impair Independence	• Supervise client personnel in the daily operation of a client's information system. • Operate a client's local area network (LAN) system when the client has not designated a competent individual, preferably within senior management, to be responsible for the LAN.

Subsection J: Management Advisory

Example Activities That Would *Not* Impair Independence	As long as the member's role is advisory in nature, independence would not be considered to be impaired even if the services are very extensive. **Example:** A member has attended board meetings; interpreted financial statements, forecasts and other analyses; counseled on expansion plans; and counseled on banking relationships. Even though the member's involvement has been extensive, independence is not impaired because the services have been limited to providing advice in all these areas.

Subsection K: Representative of Creditor's Committee

Examples of Activities That Would Impair Independence with Respect to the Debtor Corporation

- Sign or cosign checks issued by the debtor corporation.
- Sign or cosign purchase orders in excess of established amounts.
- Exercise general supervision to insure compliance with budgetary controls and pricing formulas established by management, with the consent of creditors, as part of an overall program aimed at the liquidation of deferred indebtedness.

NOTE: All of the activities are management functions and would impair independence with respect to the debtor.

Subsection L: Employee Benefit Plan Sponsored by Client

Nature of Services Provided to Employee Benefit Plan

Asset management or investment services that may include having custody of assets, performing management functions, or making management decisions are provided to an employee benefit plan sponsored by an audit client or other attest service client.

NOTE: Independence would be impaired for the plan--The issue is independence with respect to the sponsor. (See Chapter 23, Independence Requirements for Audits of Employee Benefit Plans, for a discussion of plan-related independence issues.)

AICPA Position on Defined Benefit Plan

If the assets under management or in the custody of the member are material to the plan or the client sponsor, independence is impaired with respect to the sponsor.

AICPA Position on Defined Contribution Plan

Impairment of independence with respect to the sponsor would occur if the member makes management decisions or performs management functions on behalf of the sponsor or has custody of the sponsor's assets.

NOTE: The AICPA views the plan and its participants as separate clients from the sponsor.

Position of Regulatory Agencies	Government regulatory agencies such as the SEC and DOL do not accept the AICPA position that the plan and its participants are separate clients. Services that would impair independence for the plan would generally have the same effect with respect to the sponsor.

Subsection M: Assisting Clients in Implementing SFAS 133 (Derivatives)

Introduction	Statement of Financial Accounting Standards (SFAS) 133, *Accounting for Derivative Instruments and Hedging Activities*, is complex and clients may need assistance in implementation.
	ISB Interpretation 99-1 provides guidance on the effect of assistance on (1) accounting application and (2) valuation consulting on the auditor's independence.
Basic Principle	Independence is impaired by acting in a capacity equivalent to that of management or auditing the results of the auditor's own work or the work of someone else in the auditor's firm.
Rationale	The auditor cannot be placed in the position of making professional judgments about the results of the auditor's own work (or that of others in the firm) because a "self-review" cannot be sufficiently objective.
	The auditor also cannot be in the position of accepting responsibility for the choices and judgments inherent in the preparation of financial statements to the extent that the auditor is acting as a member of management.
Examples of Accounting Application Assistance That Would *Not* Impair Independence	• Discuss the requirements of SFAS 133 and the related concepts, terminology and implementation issues. • Provide sample journal entries used to apply SFAS 133. • Provide guidance on compiling an inventory of derivatives. • Provide guidance in determining whether specific derivatives meet the criteria as hedges. • Provide examples and discuss factors to be considered in formally documenting hedging relationships and the client's risk management objective and hedging strategies.

- Discuss factors to be considered in making critical judgments such as separation of the intrinsic value of instruments from their time value.
- Provide guidance in determining the accounting for hedged items.
- Provide guidance or assist management in developing and adapting systems to account for derivatives and hedged items.

Examples of Accounting Application Assistance That Would Impair Independence	Perform services that would be subject to audit procedures such as the following: • Compiling the inventory of derivatives. • Creating the initial journal entries to be recorded. • Initially determining whether specific derivatives meet the relevant criteria as hedges. • Making management decisions concerning the implementation of SFAS 133.
Examples of Valuation Consulting Assistance That Would *Not* Impair Independence	• Provide guidance or assist in developing the client's own valuation model. • Provide guidance on the nature or relevant model inputs (volatility, yield curves, etc.). • Validate client or third-party models used. • Validate reasonableness of inputs to models (client assumptions). • Provide a generic or standardized model (similar to a Black-Scholes or binomial software model).
Examples of Valuation Consulting Assistance That Would Impair Independence	• Compute derivative values (using either auditor- or client-approved assumptions and an auditor-developed or third-party model approved by the client). • Develop or be responsible for key assumptions or inputs (for use in any valuation model or product). • Provide an auditor-developed nonstandardized model for the client's use to value derivatives.

Authoritative Sources

1. Interpretation 101-3, *Performance of Other Services* (ET 101.05).
2. SEC's *Codification of Financial Reporting Policies,* Bookkeeping and Related Professional Services (sec 602.02.c).
3. Ethics Ruling No. 8, *Member Providing Advisor Services* (ET 191.015-.016).
4. Ethics Ruling No. 9, *Member as Representative of Creditor's Committee* (ET 191.017-.018).
5. Ethics Ruling 111, *Employee Benefit Plan Sponsored by a Client* (ET 191.222-.223).
6. ISB Interpretation 99-1, *Impact on Auditor Independence of Assisting Clients in the Implementation of SFAS 133 (Derivatives).*

14 BUSINESS RELATIONSHIPS; JOINT CLOSELY HELD BUSINESS INVESTMENTS; COOPERATIVE ARRANGEMENTS; AND LEASE ARRANGEMENTS

In This Chapter

For information on	*See section*
SEC Position on Business Relationships	A
Joint Closely Held Business Investments	B
Cooperative Arrangements	C
Lease Arrangements	D

Overview

The SEC considers all direct and material indirect business relationships with clients as impairing independence. Section A discusses the SEC's position on business relationships.

The AICPA prohibits members from having a joint, closely held business investment with the client. The AICPA provides some relief to the prohibition, if the investment is not material. Section B discusses joint closely held business investments, including the SEC's position on such investments.

The AICPA prohibits members from having cooperative arrangements with the client. Again, the AICPA provides some relief for arrangements that are not material. Section C discusses cooperative arrangements, including the SEC position on such arrangements.

Section D explains the AICPA and SEC requirements on lease arrangements with clients.

Section A: SEC Position on Business Relationships

Introduction

The SEC prohibits business relationships with clients and does not specifically address or recognize AICPA concepts involving joint closely held business investments and cooperative arrangements. This prohibition applies (1) during the period of the professional engagement,* and (2) at the time of expressing an opinion.

Basic Principle

Direct and material indirect business relationships, **other than a consumer in the normal course of business**, with a client or officers, directors, or substantial stockholders, impair independence.

Specifically Prohibited Relationships

The SEC prohibits

- Joint business ventures.
- Limited partnership agreements.
- Investments in supplier or customer companies.
- Sales by the member of items other than professional services.

   NOTE: See section D for SEC restrictions on leasing interests.

Decision Criteria

When making decisions on independence matters involving business relationships, the member should consider

- Whether a mutuality or identity of interest with the client exists, that
- Would cause the member to lose the appearance of objectivity and impartiality.

*See Appendix A for the definition of "period of professional engagement."

Section B: Joint, Closely Held Business Investments

Introduction	If (1) during the period of the professional engagement,* or (2) at the time of expressing an opinion, a member or the member's firm had a material joint, closely held business investment with any client or officer, director, or principal stockholder(s) of such client, independence is impaired.
Basic Principle	If a member or member's firm has a **material** joint, closely held business investment with a client, the mutuality of interest with that client causes independence to be impaired. *NOTE: The SEC prohibits business relationships, such as joint, closely held investments, without regard to materiality.*
What Is a Joint Closely Held Business Investment?	A joint closely held business investment is an investment that is subject to control by the • Member, or the member's firm, • Client, or its officers, directors, or principal stockholders, or • Any combination of the above. *NOTE: Ethics Ruling No. 80, **The Meaning of a Joint Closely Held Business Investment**, uses the definition of control as defined in FASB Statement 94, **Consolidations of All Majority--Owned Subsidiaries**. However, that definition does not apply to entities that do not have voting shares. The authors believe, in that situation, the guidance in FASB Statement No. 57, **Related-Party Disclosures**, on control should be followed. That is, one party controls another when the controlling party can significantly influence the management or operating policies of an entity to the extent that the entity may be prevented from fully pursuing its own intent.*

*See Appendix A for the definition of "period of professional engagement."

Joint Interest in Vacation Home

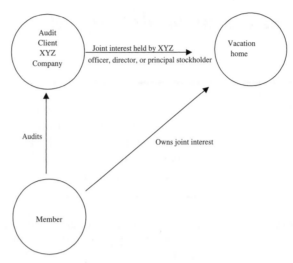

If the member's interest in the vacation home is material to the member's personal assets, the CPA firm is not independent with respect to XYZ Company **(even if the vacation home is used solely for the personal interests of the owners).** (If XYZ Company is a SEC registrant, the joint interest in the vacation home is precluded without regard to materiality.)

Investment with General Partner of Private Entity

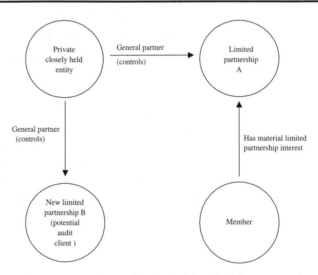

The general partner (private closely held entity) has control over Limited Partnership A. This is considered a joint, closely held business investment; therefore, since the member has a material closely held investment with the general partner, the member and CPA firm would not be independent with respect to New Limited Partnership B.

NOTE: If the member's investment in Limited Partnership A was not material, independence would not be impaired with respect to Limited Partnership B. Under SEC rules, if Limited Partnership B was a SEC registrant, CPA firm would not be independent with respect to Limited Partnership B without regard to the materiality of the member's investment.

Section C: Cooperative Arrangements

Introduction	If (1) during the period of the professional engagement,* or (2) at the time of expressing an opinion, the CPA firm had any cooperative arrangement with the client that is **material** to the firm or the client, independence is impaired.
Basic Principle	If a CPA firm has a material cooperative arrangement with a client, independence is impaired, because advancement of the CPA firm's interest would, to some extent, be dependent upon advancement of the client's interest.
	NOTE: The SEC prohibits business relationships, such as cooperative arrangements, without regard to materiality.
What Is a Cooperative Arrangement?	A cooperative arrangement may exist when the CPA firm and the client join together to conduct a mutual business activity.
	The following examples illustrate cooperative arrangements that impair independence.

- Prime/subcontractor relationships to provide services/products to third parties.
- Joint ventures to develop or market services or products.
- Combining arrangements in which the CPA firm and the client bundle services/products and market those to third parties with reference to both parties.
- Arrangements under which the CPA firm acts as a distributor/marketer of the client's services/products or vice versa.

Joint Participations	Joint participation in a business activity with a client does not constitute a cooperative arrangement, **if all of the following conditions are met**:

1. The CPA firm and the client have separate contracts with the third party.
2. The CPA firm does not assume any responsibility for activities or results of the client.

See Appendix A for the definition of "period of professional engagement."

3. Neither the CPA firm nor the client has the authority to act as a representative or agent for the other.

NOTE: Many business arrangements with clients will not generate an independence problem from an AICPA perspective, because they can be structured as a joint participation, not a cooperative arrangement. However, the SEC considers whether, in the particular circumstances, the member and the client have a mutuality or identity of interest that to a reasonable observer would impair independence.

A Reminder About Contingent Fees in Joint Participations

Rule 302, *Contingent Fees* (ET 302.01) (see Chapter 29), prohibits contingent fees for any professional service for a client when the member performs for that client

1. Audits or reviews of financial statements,
2. Compilations of financial statements (when a third party is expected to use the report and the report does not disclose a lack of independence), and
3. Examinations of prospective financial statements.

A Reminder About Commissions in Joint Participations

Rule 503, *Commissions and Referral Fees* (ET 503.01) (see Chapter 32), prohibits the receipt of a commission for recommending or referring

1. Any product/service to a client, or
2. Any product/service supplied by a client

when any audit, review, or compilation (without lack of independence paragraph) of a financial statement or examination of prospective financial statements is performed for the client.

Section D: Lease Arrangements

Introduction

The AICPA and SEC have different requirements concerning lease arrangements between a member or a member's firm and a client.

Basic Principle

A lease arrangement with a client will impair independence if the lease is a capital lease (AICPA) or if the lease is material to the member or the member's firm (SEC).

AICPA Position

According to the AICPA, a member or a member's firm that leases property to or from a client

1. Impairs its independence if the lease meets the criteria for a capital lease (FASB Statement No. 13, *Accounting for Leases*, paragraph 6.a.i), unless the lease is considered a loan from a financial institution (Chapter 15, Loans to and from Clients).
2. Does not impair its independence if the lease meets the criteria for an operating lease (FASB Statement No. 13, paragraph 6.a.ii), the terms and conditions of the lease are comparable with similar leases, and all amounts are paid in accordance with lease terms.

SEC Position

The SEC does not apply the above decision criteria. Instead, the SEC considers a lease to or from a client that is **material** to the CPA firm as impairing independence.

Example of a material lease

CPA Firm had its office in a building that was owned by XYZ Company, an audit client. The CPA Firm was the only tenant other than the client and occupied approximately twenty-five percent of the available office space. According to the SEC, independence was impaired because a reasonable third party would question the CPA Firm's objectivity.

Rental of Block Computer Time

The SEC also addresses other rental relationships with clients. For example, the SEC considers a CPA firm's rental of block computer time to a client, except in emergency or temporary situations, to be a business relationship beyond the customary professional relationship. Therefore, independence is impaired.

Authoritative Sources

1. Interpretation 101-1, *Interpretation of Rule 101*, (ET 101.02.A.3).
2. Interpretation 101-12, *Independence and Cooperative Arrangements With Clients* (ET 101.14).
3. SEC *Codification of Financial Reporting Policies,* Business Relationships (sec 602.02.g).
4. Ethics Ruling No. 69, *Investment With a General Partner* (ET 191.138-.139).
5. Ethics Ruling No. 80, *The Meaning of a Joint Closely Held Business Investment* (ET 191.160-.161).
6. Ethics Ruling No. 91, *Member Leasing Property to or from a Client* (ET 191.182-.183).
7. Ethics Ruling No. 92, *Joint Interest in Vacation Home* (ET 191.184-.185).

15 LOANS TO AND FROM CLIENTS

Introduction	Independence is impaired, if (1) during the period of the engagement,[*] or (2) at the time of expressing an opinion, a member or member's firm had

1. Any loan (e.g., including any loan commitment, loan guarantee, letter of credit, or a line of credit),
2. To or from any client, or
3. Any officer, director, or principal stockholder of that client.

This chapter focuses primarily on the exceptions to the rule above.

Basic Principle	All loans to or from clients **without regard to materiality** (unless the loan is from a financial institution and meets certain conditions), impair independence.

Exceptions	Exceptions relate **only** to financial institutions. There are two categories of financial institution loan exceptions

1. Grandfathered loan, and
2. Other permitted loans.

*NOTE: The mere servicing of a member's loan by a client financial institution does **not** impair independence.*

Definition of Grandfathered Loans	Grandfathered loans must be

1. From a financial institution, **and**
2. Made under normal lending procedures, terms, and requirements.

[*]*See Appendix A for the definition of "period of professional engagement."*

NOTE: "Normal lending procedures, terms, and requirements" is defined as procedures, terms, and requirements that are reasonably comparable to those relating to loans of a similar character made to other borrowers during the loan commitment period. In making comparisons with other loans, the member should consider all loan provisions, including

- *Credit standing.*
- *Amount of loan in relation to collateral.*
- *Repayment terms.*
- *Interest rate, including points.*
- *Closing costs.*
- *General availability of loans to the public.*

Conditions for Grandfathered Loans

A grandfathered loan must meet **one** of the following conditions:

1. Was in existence as of January 1, 1992.
2. Was obtained from a financial institution before independence was required.
3. Was obtained from a nonclient financial institution that was later sold to a client.
4. Was obtained from a client financial institution by the borrower prior to his or her becoming a member (as defined in Chapter 8).

NOTE: In applying the grandfathered loan exemptions, the date of the loan commitment or line of credit extension governs, not the closing date or date funds were obtained. If subsequent to the relevant date in 1. through 4. above, any of the terms (e.g., maturity date, interest rate, revised collateral or covenants) are changed from the original loan agreement, the loan is no longer grandfathered.

Other Requirements for Grandfathered Loans

To avoid a loss of independence, grandfathered loans must be current at all times, and fall into one of the following categories:

1. A home mortgage, including a home equity loan.
2. A secured loan having

   a. Collateral value greater than or equal to the loan balance, or
   b. If collateral value is less than the loan balance, the unsecured portion must not be material to the member's net worth.

3. An unsecured loan that is not material to the member's net worth.

Other Permitted Loans

Other than grandfathered loans, a member may have other permitted loans from a financial institution that will not impair independence.

Other permitted loans must be obtained under the financial institution's normal lending procedures, terms, and requirements, and be kept current as to all terms.

Types of Other Permitted Loans

Other permitted loans must fall within one of the following categories:

1. Automobile loans.
2. Lease collateralized by an automobile.
3. Loans fully secured by the cash surrender value of a life insurance policy.
4. Loans full collateralized by cash deposits at the same financial institution (e.g., passbook loans).
5. Credit cards and cash advances where the aggregate outstanding balance is reduced to $5,000 or less by the payment due date.

Loan from a Nonclient Subsidiary of Client

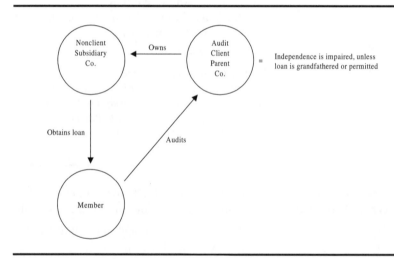

Loan from a Nonclient Parent of a Client Subsidiary

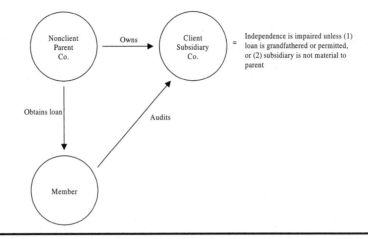

Member Connected with Entity Having a Loan to or from Client

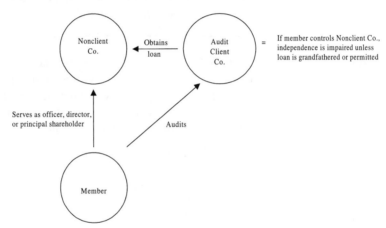

*NOTE: The member may be independent under the rule on loans to and from clients, but have a conflict of interest under Interpretation 102-2, **Conflicts of Interest** (ET 102.03). See Chapter 6.*

Authoritative Sources

1. Interpretation 101-1, *Interpretation of Rule 101* (ET 101.02.A.4).
2. Interpretation 101-5, *Loans from Financial Institution Clients and Related Terminology* (ET 101.07).
3. Ethics Ruling No. 67, *Servicing of Loan* (ET 191.134-.135).
4. Ethics Ruling No. 98, *Member's Loan From a Nonclient Subsidiary or Parent of an Attest Client* (ET 191.196-.197).
5. Ethics Ruling No. 110, *Member is Connected with an Entity That Has a Loan To or From a Client* (ET 191.220-.221).

16 A MEMBER'S EMPLOYMENT BY, AND CONNECTIONS WITH CLIENTS

In This Chapter	*For information on*	*See section*
	General Principles, Prohibitions, and Exceptions	A
	Specialized Industry Clients	B

Overview

Section A discusses how independence is impaired when a member is employed by or connected with a client and presents two exceptions to the general principles where independence may not be impaired. Section A also discusses the effect on independence when a client employee becomes an owner, partner, or shareholder in the CPA firm.

Section B discusses how a member can maintain independence when joining a credit union or trade association client. Also, Section B discusses how a member who is an owner or lessee in a common interest realty association can maintain independence with respect to that association.

Section A: General Principles, Prohibitions, and Exceptions

Introduction

A member or a member's firm may not be independent because of their (1) employment by (e.g., as a director or an officer), or (2) connection with (e.g., as a promoter or underwriter) a client.

Section A also discusses the effect on independence when

- A member participating in the engagement considers or accepts employment with the client during the engagement, and
- A client employee becomes an owner, partner, or shareholder in the CPA firm.

Basic Principle

Independence is impaired whenever the member

- Is virtually a part of the client's management or under management's control.
- Performs management functions as an employee or makes management decisions.
- Is connected with the client as a promoter, underwriter, voting trustee, director or officer.

Prohibited Relationships

Prohibited relationships apply to (1) the period covered by the financial statements, (2) the period of the professional engagement, and (3) at the time of expressing an opinion.*

Connection with the client as promoter, underwriter, or voting trustee is prohibited.

Employment by the client as director, officer, employee, or in any management position is prohibited.

In addition, the member or member's firm can not serve as a trustee of the client's (1) pension trust, or (2) profit sharing trust, without losing independence with respect to the client and the trust.

NOTE: A member serving on a client's deferred compensation committee is not independent because this constitutes performance of a management function.

---

*See Appendix A for the definition of "period of professional engagement."

Exceptions for Advisory Boards and for Certain Not-for-Profit Organizations

A member may serve on an advisory board of a client without impairing independence provided **all** of the following conditions are met:

1. The responsibilities are in fact advisory,
2. The advisory board neither makes, nor appears to make, management decisions, and
3. The advisory board and the client's board of directors (or those having equivalent authority to make decisions) are distinct groups, with minimal, if any, common membership.

Example

A member serving on a curricula advisory board of a college that is an audit client of the firm may not impair independence.

A member may also be a purely **honorary** director or trustee of a charitable, religious, civic, or similar organization and remain independent with respect to such organization.

To remain independent, the member must

1. Hold a directorship or trusteeship that is purely **honorary**,
2. Not vote on board matters,
3. Not otherwise, participate in board or management functions, and
4. If named in letterheads and externally circulated materials of the organization be identified as an honorary director or honorary trustee.

NOTE: A member serving on the board of directors of a nonprofit social club (e.g., a golf or tennis club) is not independent, because the organization is not a charitable, religious, civic, or similar organization.

Members on Board of a Federated Fund-Raising Organization

A member may serve as a director or officer of a local United Way (or similar organization) and be independent with respect to those charities that receive funds from the federated organization. However, if the federated organization exercises managerial control over a given charity, the member is not independent.

*NOTE: If the member concludes that a conflict of interest exists under Interpretation 102-2, **Conflicts of Interest** (ET 102.03), independence is impaired. See Chapter 6.*

Member Considering or Accepting Employment with a Client (AICPA Rule)	During the performance of an engagement, a member participating in the engagement may (1) be offered employment by the client, or (2) seek employment with the client.

In this situation to avoid any appearance that integrity, or objectivity has been impaired, the member must remove himself or herself from the engagement until the offer is rejected, or employment is no longer being sought.

If a CPA firm becomes aware that a member participated in the engagement while (1) employment was being considered, or (2) after it had been accepted, the CPA firm should consider what additional procedures, if any, should be performed.

NOTE: Once a member is asked to consider employment with the client during the engagement, it is not sufficient to ask the client to defer discussion until the report is issued. Moreover, if a member has no interest in pursuing employment opportunities with the client, the member should promptly notify the client. There would be no impairment of independence. A CPA firm should have explicit policies requiring the member to immediately notify the CPA firm, if a member is asked by a client to consider employment.

Considering or Accepting Employment with a Client (ISB Rule)

A CPA firm may not be independent if a firm professional (FP) considers or is employed by an audit client. If FP has

1. Knowledge of, and
2. Relationships with the firm,

that could adversely influence the audit, independence is impaired unless the firm implements the following safeguards.

Considering Employment-- Safeguards

1. The firm requires FP to promptly notify the firm of the conversations about possible employment with the client.
2. If employment negotiations are in process, the firm immediately removes FP from the audit.
3. The firm reviews FP's work on the audit to determine its adequacy.

Accepting Employment-- Safeguards

1. The audit engagement team considers whether the audit plan needs to be modified to reduce the risk of circumvention.
2. If FP will have significant interaction with the audit team, the firm takes steps to ensure that the existing audit team has the stature and objectivity to deal with FP.

3. If FP joins the client (a) within one year of leaving the firm and (b) has significant interaction with the audit team, the next annual audit is separately reviewed by a professional uninvolved in the audit. The purpose of the review is to determine if the audit team exercises appropriate skepticism in evaluating representations and work of FP. The extent of the review depends in part on the position that FP has at the audit client.

4. The firm requires (a) prompt liquidation of all capital balances, (b) settlement of all retirement balances (unless they are immaterial to the firm and fixed as to amount/payment), and (c) settlement of immaterial retirement balances if within five years of leaving the firm, FP's name as an officer or employee of the audit client is required to be disclosed by the SEC in a proxy statement or an annual report.

NOTE: The definition of retirement balances used above excludes a defined contribution plan (e.g., a 401(K)) if the firm has no funding obligation after FP leaves the firm. The above ISB requirements are effective for employment with audit client situations arising after December 31, 2000.

Client Officer or Employee Is Employed by CPA Firm

According to both the SEC and the AICPA, independence will not be impaired when a former officer or employee of the client becomes an owner, partner, or shareholder in the CPA firm, **provided**

1. Such individual completely disassociates himself or herself from the client (including its affiliates), and
2. Does not participate in auditing the client's financial statements that cover any of the employment period.

Steps Involved in Disassociating from Client

To completely disassociate from the client, the member should

- Terminate the relationship with the client.
- Dispose of any direct or material indirect interest in the client.
- Collect or repay any client loans unless permitted or grandfathered as defined in Chapter 15, Loans to and from Clients.
- Withdraw from a client-sponsored health or welfare plan, unless the client is legally required to let the member participate (e.g., a COBRA plan).
- Stop contributing to client-sponsored benefit plans.
- Liquidate or transfer all vested pension benefits as soon as possible.

NOTE: A member may not be able to liquidate or transfer pension benefits on a timely basis because

- *A significant penalty is imposed, or*
- *The administrative requirements of the plan do not permit timely liquidation or transfer.*

If either of these conditions prevent liquidation or transfer, independence would not be considered impaired as long as the member does not participate in the engagement.

Service on the Board of Directors of a Nonclient Bank

The AICPA discourages a member from serving as a director of a nonclient bank, if the member has clients (requiring independence or otherwise) that are customers of the bank.

The AICPA discourages bank directorships to avoid situations in which the member would have

- A conflict of interest under Interpretation 102-2 (ET 102.03), as discussed in Chapter 6, or
- A problem with confidential client information under Rule 301 (ET 301.01), as discussed in Chapter 28.

NOTE: A more appropriate way for the member to serve the nonclient bank would be as a consultant to the board of directors.

Section B: Specialized Industry Clients

Introduction

A member may join a client credit union, own or lease in a common interest realty association, or become a member of a client trade association and maintain independence if certain conditions are followed.

Membership in a Client Credit Union

A membership in a client credit union does not impair independence provided that **all** of the following conditions are met:

1. A member and his partners and employees must individually qualify to join the credit union, other than by qualifying because of the services provided by the member's firm.
2. The member's vote and other activities must not significantly influence operating, financial, or operating policies of the credit union.
3. Any loans from the credit union must meet the conditions discussed in Chapter 15.
4. Any deposits must be fully insured and any uninsured deposits must be immaterial to the member and member's firm.

Association with a Common Interest Realty Association (CIRA)

A member or member's firm may be associated (e.g., owner or lessee) of a CIRA (e.g., cooperatives, condominiums, time-share developments, homeowner associations) and be independent with respect to the CIRA if **all** of the following conditions are met:

1. The CIRA performs functions similar to local governments (e.g., road maintenance).
2. The member's or member's firm annual assessment is not material to the member or the member's firm or the CIRA's operating budgeted assessments.
3. The liquidation of the CIRA or sale of its assets would not result in a distribution to the member or the member's firm.
4. Creditors, in the event of insolvency, would not have recourse to the member or the member's firm.
5. The member or the member's firm does not act in any capacity as management or an employee.

Membership in a Client Trade Association	If a member joins a trade association that is a client, independence is not impaired provided the member does not serve the association as an officer, director, or in any capacity equivalent to a member of management.

Trustee of a Charitable Foundation That Is Sole Beneficiary of Estate	A member becomes a trustee of a charitable foundation that is the sole beneficiary of the foundation's deceased organizer. The member is not independent with respect to the foundation or the estate.

Co-Fiduciary with Client Bank	A member, along with a client bank, serves as a co-fiduciary for an estate or trust. If the estate or trust assets are not material to the total assets of the bank or its trust department, independence is not impaired with respect to the bank.

Authoritative Sources

1. Interpretation 101-1, *Interpretation of Rule 101* (ET 101.02.B.1 and 2).
2. Interpretation 101-4, *Honorary Directorships and Trusteeships of Not-for-Profit Organization* (ET 101.06).
3. SEC *Codification of Financial Reporting Policies*, Director, Officer, Employee (sec 602.02.d).
4. ISB Standard No. 3, *Employment with Audit Clients.*
5. Ethics Ruling No. 2, *Association Membership* (ET 191.003-.004).
6. Ethics Ruling No. 11, *Member as Executor or Trustee* (ET 191.021-.022).
7. Ethics Ruling No. 12, *Member as Trustee* (ET 191.023-.024)
8. Ethics Ruling No. 14, *Member on Board of Federated Fund-Raising Organization* (ET 191.027-.028).
9. Ethics Ruling No. 16, *Member on Board of Directors of Nonprofit Social Club* (ET 191.031-.032).
10. Ethics Ruling No. 19, *Member on Deferred Compensation Committee* (ET 191.037-.038).
11. Ethics Ruling No. 31, *Performance of Services for Common Interest Realty Associations (CIRAs), Including Cooperatives, Condominium Associations, Planned Unit Developments, Homeowners Associations, and Timeshare Developments* (ET 191.061-.062).

12. Ethics Ruling No. 38, *Member as Co-Fiduciary With Client Bank* (ET 191.075-.076).
13. Ethics Ruling No. 64, *Member on Board of Organization for Which Client Raises Funds* (ET 191.128-.129).
14. Ethics Ruling No. 72, *Member on Advisory Board of Client* (ET 191.144-.145).
15. Ethics Ruling No. 75, *Member Joining Client Credit Union* (ET 191.150-.151).
16. Ethics Ruling No. 77, *Individual Considering or Accepting Employment with the Client* (ET 191.154-.155).
17. Ethics Ruling No. 82, *Campaign Treasurer* (ET 191.164-.165).
18. Ethics Ruling No. 85, *Bank Director* (ET 191.170-.171).
19. Ethics Ruling No. 93, *Service on Board of Directors of Federated Fund-Raising Organization* (ET 191.186-.187).

17 EMPLOYMENT OF A SPOUSE, DEPENDENT, OR CLOSE RELATIVE BY A CLIENT

In This Chapter

For information on	See section
Employment of a Spouse or Dependent	A
Employment of a Close Relative	B

Overview

Section A discusses independence issues that arise when a client employs a spouse, cohabitant, or dependent. SEC rules are significantly different in this situation as compared to AICPA requirements.

Section B discusses independence issues that arise when (1) an individual participating in the engagement, (2) a proprietor, partner, or shareholder in a significant participating office of the CPA firm, or (3) a member, as defined by the SEC, has a close relative who is employed by the client.

Section A: Employment of a Spouse, or Dependent by a Client

Introduction

Independence may be impaired because a client employs a spouse, cohabitant, or dependent (1) during the period of the professional engagement*, or (2) at the time of expressing an opinion in a position of

- Significant influence over operating, financial, or accounting policies,
- Audit-sensitivity, or
- That appears to enable the employee to mold the shape of the financial statements (SEC Rule).

Basic Principle

If a person in a member's immediate family is employed by a client in a position of influence over the financial statements or in an audit-sensitive position, the member's independence is impaired.

Spouse, Cohabitant, or Dependent Employee Has Significant Influence Position

If the member's spouse, cohabitant, or dependent has a position with the client that allows "significant influence" over operating, financial, or accounting policies, the CPA firm is not independent.

For purposes of a "significant influence" position under AICPA rules, a member is defined as

1. Any professional individual participating in the engagement, or
2. Any proprietor, partner, or shareholder who

    a. Is located in an office participating in a significant portion of the engagement, or
    b. Has the ability to exercise influence over the engagement, or
    c. Has any involvement with the engagement.

NOTE: This is an exception to the definition of member explained in Chapter 8 and is only for the purpose of evaluating employment relationships.

---

*See Appendix A for the definition of "period of professional engagement."

Spouse, Cohabitant, or Dependent Employee Has Audit-Sensitive Position

A position is "audit-sensitive" (even though not of "significant influence"), if the person's activities are (1) an element of, or (2) subject to, significant controls over financial reporting.
For purposes of an "audit-sensitive" position, a member is defined as an individual participating in the engagement.

Examples of audit-sensitive positions are

- Cashier
- Internal auditor
- Accounting supervisor
- Purchasing agent
- Inventory warehouse supervisor

*NOTE: A spouse of a member may be employed by a private company as an accountant. The member's independence is not impaired, if the spouse performs the same functions that the member could perform under Interpretation 101-3, **Performance of Other Services** (ET 101.05), which is discussed in Chapter 13.*

SEC Rules on Employment of Spouse, Cohabitant, or Dependent

SEC rules are more stringent in that employment of a spouse, cohabitant, or dependent person by a client is generally ascribed to the member (as defined by the SEC in Chapter 8) without regard to participating office locations, ability to exercise significant influence over the engagement, or involvement with the engagement. If such person occupies a position with the client that appears to provide the opportunity to mold the shape of the financial statement, the CPA firm is not independent.

Example

A tax partner in a CPA firm's New York practice office has a spouse who is chief financial officer of ABC Co. located in Washington, DC. If XYZ Co., an audit client of the firm's D.C. office acquires ABC Co., the CPA firm will lose its independence unless the tax partner resigns from the CPA firm or the spouse resigns from ABC Co. Under AICPA rules, the CPA firm may be independent without either individual resigning.

Section B: Employment of a Close Relative by a Client

Introduction

If during (1) the period of the professional engagement, or (2) at the time of expressing an opinion (or issuing a review report)*

- An individual participating in the engagement,
- A proprietor, partner, or shareholder in an office of the CPA firm participating in a significant portion of the engagement, or
- Under SEC requirements, a member (as defined by the SEC),

Has a close relative that is employed by the client, the CPA firm may not be independent.

Basic Principle

If a member's close relative is employed by a client in a position of significant influence or audit-sensitivity, the member's independence may be impaired.

Definition of Close Relative

Nondependent close relatives are not members as defined above. However, in certain circumstances their employment by a client may impair independence.

Close relatives are the member's

- Nondependent children (including grandchildren and stepchildren)
- Brothers and sisters
- Grandparents, parents, and parents-in-law
- Spouses of any of the above

The SEC definition of close relatives expands the above to include a spouse's brothers and sisters and their spouses.

Example

A member's spouse has a brother whose wife is CFO of a client. According to the SEC, the member is not independent. Under AICPA requirements, the member would be independent.

See Appendix A for the definition of "period of professional engagement."

Individual Participating in the Engagement

Independence is impaired, if an individual participating in the engagement has a close relative that is employed by the client who

- Could exercise significant influence over the client's operating, financial, or accounting policies, or
- Is in an audit-sensitive position (see Section A for meaning of audit-sensitive).

Proprietor, Partner, or Shareholder

Independence is impaired if a proprietor, partner, or shareholder of the CPA firm is located in an office participating in a significant portion of the engagement has a close relative that is employed by the client who could exercise significant influence over the client's operating, financial, accounting policies.

Member (as Defined by SEC)

The SEC rule for a member (as defined in Chapter 8 for a SEC engagement) having a close relative that is employed by a client presumes an impairment of independence. The SEC makes this presumption without regard to whether the member is located in a significant participating office of the CPA firm.

The SEC mitigates the above presumption when there is adequate geographical separation of the member from (1) the close relative, and (2) the audit engagement that precludes the possibility of contact and influence.

Example of SEC's Mitigating Position

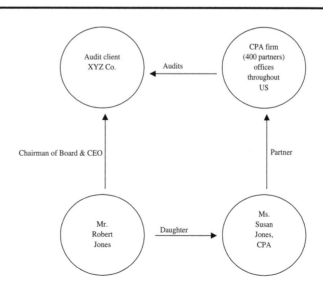

The SEC concluded that CPA Firm was independent, because Susan Jones' close relative (her father, Robert Jones), although having significant influence over XYZ Co., was (1) geographically separated (Ms. Jones' office was over 500 miles from Mr. Jones' office), and (2) Ms. Jones would not be involved in the audit.

Authoritative Sources

1. Interpretation 101-9, *The Meaning of Certain Independence Terminology and the Effect of Family Relationships on Independence* (ET 101.11, as revised May 2000).
2. SEC *Codification of Financial Reporting Policies,* Family Relationships (sec 602.02.h).
3. Ethics Ruling No. 6, *Member's Spouse as Accountant of Client* (ET 191.011-.012).

18 GIFTS AND PRIVILEGES

Introduction	If a member accepts (1) more than a token gift or (2) other unusual consideration from a client, the appearance of independence may be impaired.
Basic Principle	The receipt of gifts or other unusual consideration from clients leaves the recipient open to allegations that they are obligated to the client; thus, the appearance of independence may be impaired.
Prohibited Transfers	A member should not accept more than a token gift from a client. Also, a member should not accept lavish entertainment from a client. Likewise, a member should not purchase client products or services at discounts that are not available to the general public.

NOTE: An individual recipient cannot mitigate the appearance of a lack of independence by disclosing the gift or privilege to the CPA firm. Therefore, CPA firms should have a policy that prohibits acceptance of gifts greater than a defined token amount (e.g., $100).

Exercise Caution in Accepting or Returning Gifts	In practice, the prohibition against accepting gifts has to be interpreted sensibly and, if returned, handled diplomatically. Clients could be offended by the sudden rejection of, for example, a wedding present given to an individual in an act of friendship and without an ulterior motive.

Authoritative Source

1. Ethics Ruling No. 1, *Acceptance of a Gift* (ET 191.001-.002).

19 ACTUAL OR THREATENED LITIGATION

Introduction

In some circumstances, independence may be considered to be impaired as a result of litigation or the expressed intention to bring litigation.

The litigation may be between a client and the member or between third parties (such as investors or creditors) and the client company and its management or the member.

Basic Principle

Independence may be impaired whenever the member and the client company or its management are in threatened or actual positions of *material adverse interests* by reason of threatened or actual litigation.

Litigation impairs independence whenever it would reasonably be expected to *alter substantially the normal relationship* between the client's management and the auditor.

Rationale

To render an informed, objective opinion on a client's financial statements, the relationship between management and the member must be characterized by complete candor and full disclosure regarding all aspects of the client's operations.

The member must be able to exercise unbiased professional judgments on financial reporting decisions made by management.

When the member and the client management are placed in adversarial positions, the member's objectivity may be affected by self-interest or management's candor and willingness to make disclosure may be impaired.

Litigation Between Client and Member

Independence would be considered to be impaired in the following circumstances:

- Present management brings litigation alleging deficiencies in the member's audit work.
- The member brings litigation against present management alleging management's fraud or deceit.
- Present management expresses an intent to bring litigation alleging deficiencies in audit work and the auditor concludes it is probable a claim will be filed.

Independence would not be considered to be impaired in the following circumstance:

- Litigation (threatened or actual) relates to an engagement that does not require independence, such as tax work, *and*
- The alleged damages are not material to the member's firm or the client company.

Litigation by Third Parties

A member may become involved in litigation (primary litigation) in which the member and the client company or its management and others are mutual defendants, such as a class-action suit on behalf of stockholders against management, the auditors, and underwriters in a securities offering.

Independence would not ordinarily be considered impaired in the following circumstances:

- The client, its management, or its directors file cross-claims against the auditor to protect a right to legal redress in the event of an adverse decision in the primary litigation. (Except when there is a significant risk of settlement of the cross-claim in an amount material to the member's firm or the client.)
- Underwriters or others assert cross-claims against the member, but the company and present management do not.

If a person who files cross-claims against a member is also an officer or director of other clients of the member, independence would not usually be impaired with respect to those other clients.

Example

A class-action suit is filed against the auditor and Company A and its directors and management. The directors of Company A file cross-claims against the auditor. One of the directors is also a member of the board of Company B, which is also an audit client of the auditor. The auditor's independence with respect to Company B is not impaired.

Litigation by Third Parties in the Name of the Client

A third-party litigant, such as an insurance company, may bring litigation against the member in the name of the client under subrogation rights.

When the client is only the nominal plaintiff, the member's independence would not normally be affected.

However, adverse interests, and hence impaired independence, may exist if the member's defense alleges fraud or deceit by present management.

SEC Position on Impairment of Appearance of Independence

The SEC considers whether the particular circumstances of the situation, including the nature of the claims and defenses made, may impair independence.

The naming of auditors and clients as codefendants in a civil suit would not in and of itself impair independence.

The appearance of independence, however, could be adversely affected by situations in which management and the auditor are bound closely together by common allegations against them.

> **Example**
>
> In one situation, management and the auditors were charged with agreeing together to withhold information from stockholders and the SEC staff.
> This situation creates such a commonality of legal interest with the client that it is doubtful whether the auditors could be considered independent.

Effect of ADR Techniques

Alternative dispute resolution techniques (ADR) are used to resolve disputes without litigation.

An agreement to use ADR techniques signed in advance of a dispute, or the start of an ADR proceeding under such an agreement, would not ordinarily impair independence because such a proceeding is normally designed to facilitate negotiation.

If an ADR proceeding is started that is similar to an adversarial action, such as binding arbitration, independence would be impaired.

Termination of Impairment

An impairment of independence arising from threatened or actual litigation is usually eliminated when a final resolution is reached and there are no longer matters at issue between the member and the client.

Authoritative Sources

1. Interpretation 101-6, *The Effect of Actual or Threatened Litigation on Independence* (ET 101.08).
2. SEC *Codification of Financial Reporting Policies,* Litigation (sec 602.02.i.ii).
3. Ethics Ruling No. 95, *Agreement with Attest Client to Use ADR Techniques* (ET191.190-.191).
4. Ethics Ruling No. 96, *Commencement of ADR Proceedings* (ET 191.192-.193).

20 INDEMNIFICATION AGREEMENTS

Introduction

Indemnification agreements between the member and client may

1. Indemnify the member from certain damages, losses, or costs resulting from client acts or misrepresentations, or
2. Indemnify the client from certain liabilities and costs resulting from acts of the member.

The first situation impairs independence from an SEC perspective and may also impair independence based on AICPA rules. The second situation impairs independence from both an SEC and an AICPA perspective. This section defines and discusses indemnification agreements.

Basic Principle

Indemnification agreements reduce a member's objectivity and thereby impair independence. With one limited exception (discussed below), they impair independence.

Definition of Indemnification

An indemnification agreement is a contract between two parties whereby one party agrees to compensate or reimburse a second party for certain losses or expenses incurred.

Indemnification of the Member by the Client

The AICPA permits a member to include an indemnification clause in an engagement letter without impairing independence **provided** the indemnification is restricted to knowing misrepresentations made by the client's management.

The SEC considers indemnification to be against public policy. Therefore, the member, inserting such a clause in an engagement letter, would not be independent. According to the SEC, indemnity agreements remove one of the major stimuli to objective and unbiased consideration of problems encountered in an engagement. Existence of such an agreement may result in the use of less extensive procedures or a failure to carefully appraise information disclosed during the engagement.

Indemnification of the Client by the Member

If a member (e.g., as a condition of obtaining or retaining a client), agrees that the member or the member's firm will indemnify the client for damages, losses, or claims arising from litigation, or claims, or settlements that relate to client acts, the member is not independent under AICPA or SEC rules.

Authoritative Sources

1. SEC *Codification of Financial Reporting Policies, Indemnification by Client,* (sec 602.02.i.i).
2. Ethics Ruling No. 94, *Indemnification Clause in Engagement Letters* (ET 191.188-.189).
3. Ethics Ruling No. 102, *Member's Indemnification of a Client* (ET 191.204-.205).

21 OUTSOURCING OF THE INTERNAL AUDIT FUNCTION AND OTHER EXTENDED AUDIT SERVICES

Introduction	A member or member's firm may be asked to assist in performance of a client's internal audit function or to otherwise extend audit services beyond the requirements of GAAS.

Definition of Extended Audit Services	Extended audit services involve performing audit procedures that are generally of the type considered to be extensions of audit scope applied in the audit of financial statements.

Examples

Extended audit services might include confirming receivables, analyzing fluctuations in account balances, and testing and evaluating the effectiveness of controls.

Basic Principle	Independence would not be considered to be impaired provided that the member does not act or appear to act in a capacity equivalent to a member of client management or as an employee.

Essential Understanding with Client	A member should be satisfied that the client's management, board of directors, and audit committee understand

- The member may not perform management functions or make management decisions.
- The member may not act or appear to act in a capacity equivalent to that of an employee.
- Client management is responsible for establishing and maintaining internal control, including responsibility for ongoing monitoring.

- Client management is responsible for directing the internal audit function.

NOTE: It is preferable that the understanding be documented in an engagement letter.

Requirements for Responsibilities of the Client's Management

The client should be responsible for

- Designating a competent individual (or individuals) to be responsible for the internal audit function.
- Determining the scope, risk and frequency of internal audit activities.
- Evaluating the findings and results arising from internal audit activities.
- Evaluating the adequacy of the audit procedures performed and audit findings by obtaining reports from the member and other means.

NOTE: These requirements can normally be met by the client appointing an employee as director of internal audit who is, or reports to, a senior member of management. The director of internal audit would then establish audit scope and report on audit results to the board or audit committee.

Other Responsibilities of the Member

The member should

- Direct, review and supervise day-to-day performance of the audit procedures.
- Report to the individual responsible for the internal audit function information that allows the individual to evaluate audit scope and findings.
- Assist that individual, as requested, in

  - Performing preliminary audit risk assessments.
  - Preparing audit plans.
  - Recommending audit priorities.

Examples of Activities that Would Impair Independence

- Performing ongoing monitoring activities or control activities that

  - Affect the execution of transactions (such as assistance in authorization of transactions).
  - Ensure that transactions are properly executed or accounted for.

- Performing routine activities in operating or production processes equivalent to an ongoing compliance or quality control function.
- Determining which recommendations for improving controls should be implemented.
- Reporting to the board or audit committee on behalf of management or the individual responsible for internal audit.
- Authorizing, executing, or consummating transactions.
- Otherwise exercising authority on behalf of the client.
- Preparing source documents of transactions.
- Having custody of assets.
- Approving or being responsible for the overall internal audit work plan.
- Being connected with the client in any capacity that is or appears to be equivalent to a member of management or employee.

Examples

The appearance of an unacceptable connection with the client would be created by

- Being listed as an employee in directories or other client publications.
- Permitting oneself to be referred to by title or description as supervising or being in charge of the internal audit function.
- Using the client's letterhead or internal correspondence forms in communications.

Examples of Permissible Related Activities

- Performing separate evaluations of the effectiveness of a client's internal control, including separate evaluations of the client's ongoing monitoring activities.
- Performing an attestation engagement to report on the client's assertion regarding the effectiveness of its internal control over financial reporting as long as management does not rely on the member's work as the primary basis for its assertion.
- Providing operational auditing services to review business processes, as selected by the client, and assess their efficiency and effectiveness.
- Performing very frequent, but separate, evaluations of the effectiveness of the ongoing control and monitoring activities built in to the client's normal recurring activities.

NOTE: In all of these examples, the member would need to observe the previously explained requirements relating to responsibilities of client management versus the member's responsibilities and communicate an understanding of these matters to the client's management, board, and audit committee.

Authoritative Sources

1. Interpretation 101-13, *Extended Audit Services* (ET 101.15).
2. Ethics Ruling No. 103, *Member Providing Attest Report on Internal Controls* (ET 191.206-.207).
3. Ethics Ruling No. 104, *Member Providing Operational Auditing Services* (ET 191.208-.209).
4. Ethics Ruling No. 105, *Frequency of Performance of Extended Audit Procedures* (ET 191.210-.211).

22 INDEPENDENCE REQUIREMENTS FOR STATE AND LOCAL GOVERNMENTAL AUDITS

Introduction

State and local governmental audits are more likely to involve a principal auditor and other auditors than audits of commercial entities. Federal circulars and state and local statutes frequently require participation by small and minority-owned CPA firms in the audit of entities and units that are part of the government's general-purpose financial statements.

This chapter provides guidance on the independence requirements for different auditors that may be involved in the audit of the general-purpose financial statements of a state or local government.

The chapter also discusses the General Accounting Office's independence requirements and the AICPA ethics rulings that address governmental audits.

NOTE: This chapter assumes that you have a knowledge of GAAP for state and local governmental entities.

Categories of Auditors

There are four categories of auditors that may be involved in the audit of a state or local government's general-purpose financial statement

1. Principal auditor.
2. Other auditor of a **material** fund type, fund, account group, component unit, or related (disclosed or footnoted) organization.
3. Other auditor of **immaterial** fund type(s), account group(s), component unit(s), or related (disclosed) organization(s) that are **material** in the aggregate.
4. Other auditor of **immaterial** fund type(s), account group(s), component unit(s), or related (disclosed) organization(s) that are **immaterial** in the aggregate.

Principal Auditor of the General-Purpose Financial Statements	The principal auditor (category 1) of the government's general-purpose financial statements must be independent of

1. The primary government (including all of its fund types, funds, and account groups).
2. All component units of the reporting entity.
3. All other entities that are required to be disclosed in notes to the general-purpose financial statements under GASB Statement No. 14, *The Financial Reporting Entity*, except for disclosed organizations for which the primary government is not financially accountable for, and the required financial statement note does not include financial information.

Other Auditor of a *Material* Fund Type, Fund, Account Group, Component Unit, or Disclosed Organization	The category 2, other auditor, must be independent of

1. The fund type, fund, account group, component unit, or disclosed organization being audited.
2. The primary government.
3. Any other fund type, fund, account group, component unit, or disclosed organization of the financial reporting entity that is financially accountable to such entity or unit, or can significantly influence the entity or unit audited.

Other Auditor of *Immaterial* Fund Type(s), Account Group(s), Component Unit(s), or Related Organization(s) That Are *Material* When Aggregated	The category 3, other auditor, must be independent of the

1. Entities/units being audited, and
2. The primary government.

Other Auditor of *Immaterial* **Fund Type(s), Fund(s), Account Group(s), Component Unit(s), or Disclosed Organization(s) That Are** *Immaterial* **in the Aggregate**	The category 4, other auditor, must be independent of the
	
	1. Entities/units being audited, and
	2. Must not be associated with the primary government in any capacity as a
	
	   • Promoter, underwriter, or voting trustee.
	   • Director, officer, employee, or member of management.
	   • Trustee of any pension fund.

GAO's Independence Requirements	The GAO in its *Governmental Auditing Standards* (i.e., the Yellow Book) requires public accountants to follow the AICPA's independence requirements and the requirements of the relevant state board of accountancy. In addition, the GAO indicates that personal and external impairments (e.g., external restrictions on audit scope or on the time allowed to complete an audit) cause a loss of independence. *NOTE: Personal impairments include (1) preconceived ideas toward individuals, groups, organizations, or objectives of a particular program that could bias the audit, and (2) biases, including those induced by political or social convictions, that result from employment in, or loyalty to, a particular group, organization, or level of government.*

Member Serves as an Elected Legislator	If a member serves as an elected city legislator independence is impaired with respect to the city even though the city manager is elected (rather than appointed) by the legislature.

Auditor Serves on Advisory Unit	An auditor's independence with respect to a county is not impaired as a result of serving on a citizen's committee that is studying
	
	   • Possible changes in the form of county government, or
	   • The financial status of the state when the client is a county in that state.

Member as a Bondholder   A member who owns an immaterial amount of municipal bonds is not independent with respect to the municipality.

Authoritative Sources

1. Interpretation 101-10, *The Effect on Independence of Relationships with Entities Included in the Governmental Financial Statements* (ET 101.12).
2. Governmental Auditing Standards, *Standards for Audit of Governmental Organizations Programs, Activities, and Functions, 1994 Revision* Chapter 3, "General Standards," paragraph 3.15.
3. Ethics Ruling No. 10, *Member as Legislator* (ET 191.019-.020).
4. Ethics Ruling No. 20, *Member Serving on Governmental Advisory Unit* (ET 191.039-.040).
5. Ethics Ruling No. 29, *Member as Bondholder* (ET 191.057-.058).

23 INDEPENDENCE REQUIREMENTS FOR AUDITS OF EMPLOYEE BENEFIT PLANS

Introduction

This chapter explains the independence requirements established by the Department of Labor (DOL) Regulation 2509.75-9, *Interpretive Bulletin Relating to Guidelines on Independence of Accountant Retained by Employee Benefit Plan*. DOL has independence requirements that are stricter than AICPA rules. This chapter also presents the AICPA ethics rulings that address audits of employee benefit plans and highlights differences between the DOL and those rulings.

Basic Principle

An auditor's independence with respect to an employee benefit plan is impaired whenever the auditor has a financial interest in or relationship with the plan or plan sponsor.

DOL's Definition of "Member"

According to the DOL, member includes

1. All owners, partners, or shareholders in the CPA firm.
2. All professional employees participating in the audit.
3. All professional employees located in an office of the CPA firm participating in a significant portion of the audit.

When a Member Is Not Independent

DOL indicates that a member is not independent if (1) during the period covered by the financial statements, (2) during the period of engagement,* or (3) at the date of the audit report, the member or the member's firm

1. Had, or was committed to acquire a direct or material indirect financial interest in the plan or plan sponsor,

See Appendix A for the definition of "period of professional engagement."

2. Was connected with the plan or plan sponsor as a promoter, underwriter, or investment advisor, or
3. Was employed by the plan or plan sponsor as a voting trustee, director, or employee.

If the member maintains financial records for the plan, DOL regulations also state that the member is not independent.

NOTE: The meaning of "maintenance of financial records" is unclear. Some DOL officials maintain that posting a general ledger from client-prepared underlying records and preparing participant account balances (i.e., bookkeeping) for a defined benefit plan impairs independence. The AICPA rules allow members to provide bookkeeping services, which is not equivalent to maintaining financial records, and remain independent (See Chapter 13). The DOL has not clarified what maintenance of financial records means.

Member Provides Appraisal or Valuation Services

DOL regulations do not discuss whether providing appraisal or valuation services (relating to real estate or securities that do not have a market price) impairs independence. DOL officials have publicly expressed concern about members providing such services to benefit plans.

NOTE: A member, if asked to provide appraisal or valuation services to a plan, should consider obtaining DOL's opinion on the matter in advance. Chapter 36 provides information on how to contact the DOL about independence questions.

Member Serves As Director of Plan Sponsor

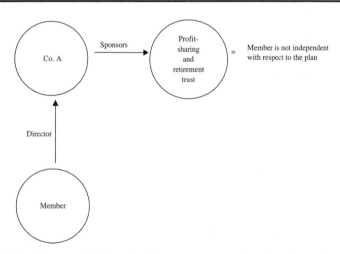

NOTE: Member would be involved in management functions that affect the plan; therefore, independence is impaired.

Member Provides Asset Management or Investment Services to Plan

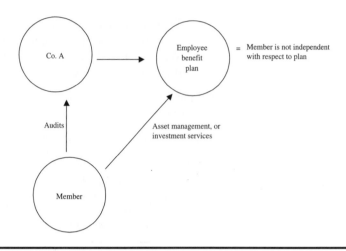

Member's Relationships with Participating Employer(s) in a Multiemployer Benefit Plan

Member's independence is not impaired with respect to a multiemployer benefit plan unless the member has a direct or indirect financial interest or other relationship that would give the member significant influence over one or more of the employers (plan sponsors).

*NOTE: The DOL does not permit any direct or material indirect financial interest in **any** plan sponsor of a multiemployer plan.*

Member, Spouse, or Cohabitant Participates in Health and Welfare Plan of Client

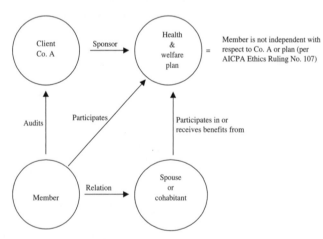

NOTE: However, if member's spouse or cohabitant participates in the Plan by being employed by Co. A, the member would be independent provided that

    1.   The member is independent with respect to Co. A, given the spouse's or cohabitant's position (Chapter 17), and

2. *The Plan is normally offered to all employees of Co. A that are in equivalent positions.*

Although the AICPA has not officially changed Ruling 107 (the health and welfare plan exception) to apply to spouses and dependents rather than spouses and cohabitants, as it has done for Ruling 108 (the retirement and savings plan exception), the authors believe that the AICPA may incorporate such changes into Ruling 107 and other rulings in the future.

Member or Spouse Participates in a Benefit Plan That Is Sponsored by a Client or Invests in Sponsor/Client or Another Client

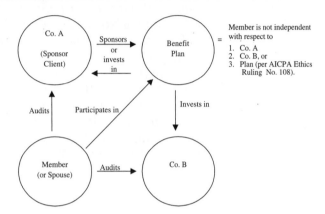

NOTE: However, if the member's spouse or dependent participates in the Plan as an employee of Co. A or Co. B, the member would be independent provided that

1. *The member is independent with respect to Co. A or Co. B, given the spouse's or dependent's position (Chapter 17).*
2. *The plan is normally offered to all employees in equivalent positions.*
3. *The member does not participate in the engagement.*
4. *The member is not in a position to influence the engagement, meaning that the member does not have direct management responsibility for, or does not provide direct technical consultation, quality control, or oversight of, the engagement or engagement team.*

A Member's relationship with a cohabitant may be the same as that of a spouse.

Authoritative Sources

1. Department of Labor, *Interpretive Bulletin Relating to Guidelines on Independence of Accountant Retained by Employee Benefit Plan* (Reg. 2509.75-9).
2. Ethics Ruling No. 21, *Member as Director and Auditor of the Entity's Profit Sharing Trust* (ET 191.041-.042).
3. Ethics Ruling No. 60, *Employee Benefit Plans--Member's Relationships with Participating Employers* (ET 191.119-120).
4. Ethics Ruling No. 107, *Participation in Health and Welfare Plan of Client* (ET 191.214-.215).
5. Ethics Ruling No. 108, *Participation of Member or Spouse in Retirement, Savings, or Similar Plan Sponsored by, or That Invests in, Client* (Revised) (ET 191.216-.217).
6. Ethics Ruling No. 111, *Employee Benefit Plan Sponsored by Client* (ET 191.222-.223).

24 INDEPENDENCE REQUIREMENTS FOR AGREED-UPON PROCEDURES (AUP) ENGAGEMENTS[1]

The definitions of members and their firms as presented in Chapter 8 does not apply to

1. SAS No. 75, *Engagements to Apply Agreed-Upon Procedures to Specified Elements, Accounts, or Items of a Financial Statement,*[2] and
2. Agreed-upon procedures engagements performed under the SSAEs.

If an agreed-upon procedures report issued under SAS No. 75 or the SSAEs states that (1) its use is restricted to identified parties, and (2) the member (as defined below) believes that the report will be restricted to those parties, the concept of "engagement team" independence applies.

---

[1] *On April 15, 2000, the Professional Ethics Division of the AICPA issued an Exposure Draft which would revise Interpretation 101-11 under Rule 101:* **Independence and the Performance of Professional Services Under the Statements on Standards for Attestation Engagements** *and Statement on Auditing Standards No. 75,* **Engagements to Apply Agreed-Upon Procedures to Specified Elements Accounts, or Items of a Financial Statement***. The revision would permit a member to perform certain specific engagements under an engagement-team criterion of independence provided the firm has established appropriate safeguards to ensure that the engagement team is adequately protected from outside influences that may affect their independence or objectivity. Under the revised standard, the firm, all individuals who participate in the acceptance or performance of the engagement, and those individuals who are in a position to influence the engagement are required to be independent. All other members of the firm would not be required to be independent, provided the firm has established appropriate safeguards. Please check the John Wiley & Sons, Inc. website at www.wiley.com/ethics for more information.*

[2] *In October 2000, the Auditing Standards Board issued SAS 93,* **Omnibus Statement on Auditing Standards--2000***. This SAS withdraws SAS 75,* **Engagements to Apply Agreed-Upon Procedures to Specified Elements, Accounts, or Items of a Financial Statement***. SAS 75 will no longer be necessary when SSAE 10,* **Attestation Standards: Revision and Recodification***, is issued. Among other things, SSAE 10 amends the attestation standards to remove the requirement for a written assertion as a condition for performance for agreed-upon procedures engagements. The withdrawal of SAS 75 is concurrent with the effective date of SSAE 10, which is effective for agreed-upon procedures engagements for which the subject matter or assertion is as of or for a period ending on or after June 1, 2001, with earlier application permitted.*

Basic Principle	The concept of independence differs in an AUP engagement as compared to other attestation services. In an AUP engagement, independence applies to "engagement team" members, which is less inclusive than members in other attest services.

Restricted Use AUP Reports	Engagement team independence applies to SAS No. 75 agreed-upon procedures reports that contain the following paragraph:

> This report is intended solely for the information and use of the specified parties listed above and is not intended to be, and should not be, used by anyone other than these specified parties.

In addition, engagement team independence applies to agreed-upon procedures reports issued under the SSAEs for

1. Prospective financial statements.
2. Compliance with specified requirements of laws and regulations.
3. Effectiveness of internal control over compliance.
4. Reports issued under SSAE No. 4, *Agreed-Upon Procedures Engagements.*

The SSAE reports have to contain the following paragraph:

> This report is intended solely for the use of (list or refer to specified users) and should not be used by those who have not agreed to the procedures and taken responsibility for the sufficiency of the procedures for their purposes.

NOTE: Restricted-use reports under SAS No. 75 and the SSAEs continue to be restricted even if they are made a matter of public record.

Meaning of "Member" or AUP Engagements	If any of the following individuals participate in (1) acceptance or (2) performance of the AUP engagement, they are "engagement team" members.

Category 1
- Owners
- Partners
- Shareholders
- Full-time and part-time professional employees
- Consultants
- Individuals who provide supervisory services

Category 2

The term member of the AUP engagement team also includes

- Spouses (and cohabitants), whether or not dependent, of any Category 1 individual.
- Dependents, whether or not related, of any Category 1 individual.

Prohibited Relationships

If any individual in Categories 1 or 2 above or the CPA firm has any of the illustrative prohibited relationships listed below (1) during the period of the AUP engagement or (2) at the time report is issued, the CPA firm is not independent.

Prohibited relationships

1. Had or was committed to acquire a direct or material indirect financial interest (Chapter 9).
2. Was a trustee or executor/administrator of any trust/estate that had or was committed to acquire a direct or material indirect financial interest (Chapter 9).
3. Had any material joint, closely held business investment with the client or any officer, director, or principal stockholder (Chapter 14).
4. Had any loan (except those exempted) to or from the client or any officer, director, or principal stockholder (Chapter 15).
5. Was connected with the client as a promoter, underwriter, voting trustee, director, officer, employee, or in any managerial capacity (Chapter 16).
6. Was a trustee for any pension or profit-sharing trust of the client (Chapter 16).

"Members" Located in a Participating Office

If the following individuals are located in an office having significant participation in the AUP engagement, the term engagement team member also includes them.

- Owners
- Partners
- Shareholders
- Spouses and dependents (of the above), if they have (1) a position of significant influence or (2) a material financial interest in the client.

Development of Subject Matter and Gaining Financially from Outcome of the Engagement

Independence is impaired, if the CPA firm or any individual in category 1 above, or any owner, partner, or shareholder in an office with significant participation in the AUP engagement

1. Contributed to the development of the subject matter of the engagement, or
2. Stands to gain financially directly from the outcome of the engagement.

Likewise, independence is impaired, if any individual in category 1 above knows or could reasonably be expected to know that any owner, partner, or shareholder in any office of the CPA firm

1. Contributed to the development of the subject matter,
2. Stands to gain financially from the outcome of the engagement, or
3. Has a position of significant influence with the client.

Nondependent Close Relative Employed by, or Invested in, Client

Independence is impaired, if any individual in Category 1 above has a nondependent close relative (as defined in Chapter 17) who has

1. A position of significant influence with the client, or
2. A financial interest in the client that is material to the close relative.

Applicability of Interpretations of Rule 101

All of the interpretations of Rule 101 (ET 101.02) apply to AUP engagements except for Interpretation 101-9, *The Meaning of Certain Independence Terminology and the Effect of Family Relationships on Independence.*

In addition, Interpretation 101-6, *The Effect of Actual or Threatened Litigation on Independence* (Chapter 19), is not applicable unless

1. The litigation relates to the engagement, or
2. Is material to the CPA firm, or the client's financial statements.

Authoritative Sources

---

1. Interpretation 101-11, *Independence and the Performance of Professional Services under the Statements on Standards for Attestation Engagements and Statement on Auditing Standards No. 75, Engagements to Apply Agreed-upon Procedures to Specified Elements, Accounts, or Items of a Financial Statement* (ET 101.13).
2. Prohibited Relationships as described in Interpretation 101-1, *Interpretation of Rule 101* (ET 101.02).

25 ALTERNATIVE PRACTICE STRUCTURES

Overview

A traditional CPA firm engaged in auditing and other attestation services might be closely aligned with another organization, public or private, that performs other professional services (e.g., tax and consulting).

These types of alliances are sometimes called *Alternative Practice Structures* (APS)--a nontraditional structure for the practice of public accounting.

Section A: Model of an APS

Diagram of a Possible APS

The following diagram depicts typical relationships among a CPA firm providing attest services and an allied public company and its subsidiaries:

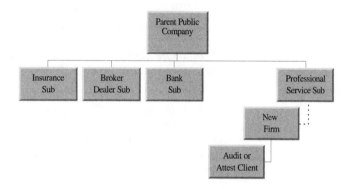

Background of Possible APS Model

An existing CPA firm is sold by its owners to another entity shown in the diagram as **Parent Public Co.**

Parent Public Co. has several existing subsidiaries shown as **Insurance Sub, Broker-Dealer Sub,** and **Bank Sub.** It also has formed a new subsidiary, **Professional Services Sub,** that provides *nonattest* professional services, such as tax, personal financial planning, and consulting.

The former owners and employees of the CPA firm that has been sold to Parent Public Co. became employees of Professional Service Sub, and provide nonattest services through that entity.

The owners separately form a new CPA firm shown as **New Firm** in the diagram that they own and control. New Firm provides audit and attest services to clients.

New Firm leases employees, office space and equipment and back-office functions, such as billing and advertising, from Parent Public Co. (In the diagram, a dotted line from New Firm to Professional Services Sub indicates this alliance between the entities.)

Section B: APS Independence Rules for Members

Definition of Member or Member's Firm in APS	**Member** in an APS includes any person (whether leased or employed) or entity that is defined as a member in Chapter 8 (Interpretation 101-9). New Firm is the *firm* in that definition.

Applicability of Independence Requirements	All the members and the firm (New Firm) are subject to all of the independence requirements (Rule 101 and its interpretations and rulings). *NOTE: This means that the independence requirements are applied in the traditional manner to the owners and employees of New Firm. The determination of whether an employee of New Firm is a member is not affected by whether the individual is leased from Professional Services Sub or employed directly by New Firm.*

Existence of More Than One New Firm	If there is more than one New Firm, then the owners of one New Firm generally would not be considered members with respect to audit or attest clients of Other New Firms. However, if owners of one New Firm **perform services** for Other New Firms or **have shared economic interests** with them, they would be considered members. **Example** If owners of New Firm perform services in Other New Firm, such owners are considered owners of both CPA firms for purposes of applying the independence requirements. Individuals with a managerial position (leased or otherwise) in one office of a New Firm might at times be considered to have a managerial position in another office of that or Other New Firms if work is done in more than one office. **Example** An audit manager leased from Professional Services Sub works on audits in two offices--one in each of two New firms. The audit manager is a member of both New Firms and has to be independent of audit and attest clients of both New Firms.

Section C: APS Independence Rules for Other-Than-Members

Introduction

Independence requirements normally extend only to those persons and entities included in the term "member or member's firm." In the case of an APS, that would be limited to New Firm and persons who own or are employed by New Firm, or who are controlled by one or more of those persons.

To ensure the protection of the public interest, additional restrictions are required for an APS.

Basic Principle

Persons or entities who can immediately and directly exert significant influence over New Firm owners and managerial employees are subject to all of the same independence requirements as a member.

NOTE: These persons and entities are called direct superiors and are defined more precisely later.

Other persons and entities in the APS that are not connected with a member or member's firm through direct reporting relationships are subject to some, but not all, independence requirements.

Definition of Direct Superiors and Applicable Independence Requirements

Persons subject to the same independence requirements as a member are persons so closely associated with

- An owner of New Firm, or
- A person with a managerial position in New Firm located in an office participating in a significant portion of the audit or attest engagement (whether leased or employed directly by New Firm)

That such *persons* can directly control the activities of the owner or managerial employee.

A person who can *directly control* is the immediate superior of the owner or managerial employee who has the power to direct activities of that person so as to be able to directly or indirectly derive a benefit from that person's activities.

Example

The chief executive of the office of Professional Service Sub where the owners and managerial employees of New Firm are employed is a *direct superior*. The chief executive has day-to-day responsibility for the activities of the owners and managerial employees of New Firm, and can recommend their promotions and compensation levels.

The chief executive is subject to all of the independence requirements with respect to New Firm's audit and attest services clients.

Definition of Indirect Superiors and Other Public Co. Entities

Indirect superiors are persons one or more levels above persons included in the definition of *direct superior*. (Members do not directly report to indirect superiors.)

Generally, indirect superiors start with persons in the organization structure to whom direct superiors report and go upline from that point.

Indirect superiors also include spouses, cohabitants, and dependent persons of those persons.

Example

The chief executive of Professional Services Sub reports to the senior vice president of Public Co. The senior vice president is an indirect superior. So is the senior vice president's spouse.

Other Public Co. Entities are Public Co. itself and all entities consolidated in Public Co.'s financial statements that are not included in the definition of member or subject to the same rules as a member.

Example

Broker-Dealer Sub and its officers are Other Public Co. Entities

---

Applicability of Independence Requirements to Indirect Superiors and Other Public Co. Entities

Indirect superiors and other Public Co. entities may not have a relationship contemplated by Interpretation 101-1.A (ET Section 101.2) with an audit or attest client of New Firm that is *material* to those persons or entities.

Interpretation 101.1.A is concerned with investments, loans, and similar matters (See Chapters 9, 10, and 15).

Materiality is based on the aggregate amount of financial relationships with the attest client assessed in relation to the person's net worth.

Example

  The senior vice president of Public Co., to whom the CEO of Professional Services Sub reports, owns equity and debt securities of one of New Firm's audit clients. If the combined amount of the senior VP's interest is material to that person's net worth, New Firm's independence is impaired.

If the financial relationships with New Firm's client are held by an Other Public Co. entity, then materiality is based on the amount of the aggregate interest in relation to the consolidated financial statements of Public Co.

Other Restrictions Applicable to Indirect Superiors and Other Public Co. Entities

Independence of New Firm with respect to an audit or attest client would also be impaired by the following relationships:

- Indirect superiors or other Public Co. entities have financial relationships that permit them to exert significant influence over the client.
- Other Public Co. entities or their employees are connected with the client as a promoter, underwriter, voting trustee, director or officer.

Except as noted above, services may be provided to a New Firm client without impairing independence that *would* impair independence if performed by a member.

Example

  Bank Sub provides trustee and asset custodial services to an audit client of New Firm. If New Firm provided these services, its independence would be impaired. However, provision of the services by Bank Sub does not impair New Firm's independence.

Other Restrictions Applicable to New Firm

New Firm (and its owners and employees) may not perform a service requiring independence for Public Co. or any of its subsidiaries or divisions.

Example

  New firm could not audit the consolidated financial statements of Public Co. or the individual financial statements of a subsidiary or division.

If an audit or attest client of New Firm holds an investment in Public Co. that is material to the client or allows the client to exercise significant influence, New Firm is not independent with respect to that client.

Example

Company A, an audit client of New Firm, acquires a 25% interest in Public Co. New Firm is not independent of Company A.

When making referrals of services among New Firm and any of the entities within Public Co., a member should consider Rule 102 on integrity, objectivity, and conflicts of interest and the related interpretations (see Chapter 6).

Example

An owner of New Firm is assisting an audit client in obtaining financing. Before referring that client to Bank Sub, the owner should consider the provisions of Interpretation 102-2, *Conflicts of Interest.*

Multidisciplinary Practices

Multidisciplinary practices (MDP) are arrangements in which CPAs share fees with attorneys or other professionals. They have gained increased attention since the American Bar Association's MDP commission issued a recommendation in support of MDP in June 1999. Currently, the SEC generally prohibits auditing firms from offering legal services to clients (sec 602.02.e.ii). However, some of the largest firms do offer legal services to their foreign audit clients. Guidance on this issue is being developed by the ISB.

Authoritative Source

---

1. Interpretation 101-14, *The Effect of Alternative Practice Structures on the Applicability of Independence Rules* (ET Section 101.16).

NOTE: At this time, some individual regulators have issued positions on APSs, and the SEC has commented on APS issues to CPA firms involved, and to the AICPA and the APS. However, the AICPA guidelines provide the only general guidance.

26 QUALITY CONTROL SYSTEMS FOR INDEPENDENCE

	For information on	See section
In This Chapter	A Firm's Quality Control Responsibilities	A
	A Member's Related Quality Control Responsibilites	B

Overview

A firm has a responsibility to ensure that its personnel comply with professional standards applicable to its accounting and auditing/attest practice.

To meet this responsibility, a firm designs and implements a system of quality control policies and procedures, including those related to maintaining independence, integrity, and objectivity.

A member has a responsibility to comply with professional standards and with the firm's policies and procedures related to ensuring compliance with professional standards.

Applicability

CPA firms or individual members that are enrolled in an AICPA-approved practice-monitoring program are obligated to adhere to quality control standards. In addition, the Principles of Professional Conduct (see Chapter 2) indicate that members should practice in firms that have in place quality control procedures to provide reasonable assurance that services are competently delivered and adequately supervised.

The Statements on Quality Control apply to a CPA firm's accounting, auditing, and attest practice.

Section A: A Firm's Quality Control Responsibilities

Element of Quality Control	A firm should establish policies and procedures to provide reasonable assurance that • Personnel maintain independence (in fact and appearance) in all required circumstances. • All professional responsibilities are performed with integrity. • Personnel maintain objectivity in discharging professional responsibilities.
Requirement to Adhere to Applicable Rules	A firm should require that all professional personnel adhere to the applicable independence rules, regulations, interpretations, and rulings of the • SEC, including ISB • AICPA • State CPA society • State board of accountancy • State statute • Other regulatory agencies (such as DOL and GAO)
Inform Personnel of Requirements and Specific Prohibitions and Restrictions	A firm should inform personnel of applicable requirements and of the following: • Investments that are not to be held. • Relationships that must not exist. • Transactions prohibited by firm policy. **Example** A firm can inform personnel of requirements through training, and of prohibited investments through maintaining and communicating a list of clients that require maintenance of independence (e.g., a restricted client list). A firm needs to keep the list current and communicate changes in it on a timely basis. *NOTE: The SECPS has adopted requirements on maintaining a database of restricted entities--those for which independence must be maintained.*

Affirmation of Compliance	A firm should periodically obtain written independence representations from all professional personnel that affirm that the individual

- Is familiar with the firm's policies and procedures related to independence, integrity, and objectivity.
- Held no prohibited investments during the period.
- Engaged in no prohibited relationships, activities, or transactions during the period.

Resolution and Documentation of Independence Questions	A firm should designate a competent person, or group, as responsible for resolving questions that arise on independence.

A firm should establish requirements for documentation of the resolution of independence questions, including sources consulted in and outside the firm.

Confirmation of Independence of Other Auditors	A firm when acting as principal auditor, should confirm the independence of another firm engaged to perform segments of an engagement.

Section B: A Member's Related Quality Control Responsibilities

Requirement to Be Informed

A member has a personal responsibility to be well-informed about applicable requirements as well as about firm policies and procedures.

> **Examples**
>
> A member can become well-informed by attending firm training, studying authoritative sources, and educational materials, such as this book.

Requirement to be Sensitive to Potential Impairment of Independence

A member has a responsibility to be sensitive to activities and relationships that might create a mutuality of interests with clients or conflicts of interest that might impair independence in fact or be seen by a reasonable observer as impairing independence in appearance.

Responsibility for Self-Assessment

A member has a responsibility to review continuously activities and relationships to assess whether the member has fulfilled

- The obligation to users of audit or attest work to apply objective judgment.
- The obligation to the firm to adhere to its established policies and procedures.
- The obligation to fellow professionals to avoid activities and relationships that would appear to a reasonable observer to impair independence.

Responsibility for Affirming Adherence to Requirements

A member has a responsibility to affirm honestly, in accordance with firm policies, adherence to requirements on independence, integrity, and objectivity after reviewing personal investments, relationships, and transactions.

Responsibility for Resolving Independence Issues

A member may determine the need to act to avoid or cure a departure from professional standards or firm policies and procedures. The member should act promptly and notify appropriate firm personnel designated with responsibility for resolving independence questions.

Example

> A member should dispose of a financial interest in a new client promptly. On learning a prohibited interest or relation with a client exists, a member should notify appropriate firm personnel.

Observing Restrictions on Outside Employment

A member has a responsibility to observe the restrictions a firm has placed on outside employment and avoid outside employment that might impair independence.

Example

> A tax manager is asked by a real estate developer audit client to accept part-time employment in advising its potential customers about tax advantages of real estate investments.

Most firms would not permit this type of outside employment even with a nonclient. Among other problems, it violates independence requirements with respect to the developer client, and might create other potential conflicts.

Authoritative Sources

1. Statement on Quality Control Standards (SQCS) No. 2, *System of Quality Control for a CPA Firm's Accounting and Auditing Practice* (QC Section 20).
2. AICPA *Guide for Establishing and Maintaining a System for Quality Control for a CPA Firm's Accounting and Auditing Practice.*

PART D

AICPA RULES OTHER THAN INDEPENDENCE, INTEGRITY, AND OBJECTIVITY

27 RULES 201, 202, AND 203–GENERAL STANDARDS, COMPLIANCE WITH STANDARDS, AND ACCOUNTING PRINCIPLES

In This Chapter

For information on	*See section*
General Standards Applicable to all Members	A
Compliance with Standards for Members in Public Practice	B
Representations About Accounting Principles Applicable to Members in Public Practice	C
Representations About Accounting Principles Applicable to Members Not in Accounting Practice	D

Overview

Section A discusses the general standards of professional competence, due professional care, planning and supervision, and sufficient relevant data that apply to all AICPA members.

Section B discusses the standards promulgated by bodies designated by Council for members in public practice.

Section C discusses representations by member in public practice when departures from generally accepted accounting principles exist.

Section D discusses representations in letters or other communications by members not in public practice when departures from generally accepted accounting principles exist.

NOTE: In the context of Rules 201, 202, and 203, as opposed to Rule 101 on independence (see Chapters 5 and 8), the term "member" is used in the limited sense of a member, associate member, or international associate of the AICPA.

Section A: General Standards Applicable to All Members

Rule 201	Rule 201 states that a member shall comply with the following standards and any interpretations issued by bodies designated by Council:

1. **Professional Competence.** A member must only perform services that the member or the member's firm can complete with professional competence.
2. **Due Professional Care.** A member must exercise due professional care when performing professional services.
3. **Planning and Supervision.** A member must adequately plan and supervise the performance of professional services.
4. **Sufficient Relevant Data.** The member must obtain sufficient relevant data to provide a reasonable basis for conclusions or recommendations when performing professional services.

When Rule 201 Applies	This rule applies to any professional service provided by an AICPA member, whether or not in public practice.

When the member in public practice performs an engagement governed by the Statements on Auditing Standards, the Statements on Standards for Attestation Engagements, Statements on Standards for Accounting and Review Services, or the Statements on Standards for Consulting Services, Rule 201 does not apply because the provisions of the rule are already incorporated in these standards.

Work involving consulting services, tax return preparation, tax planning/advice, tax research, personal financial planning, and bookkeeping is covered by Rule 201 whether performed by a member in, or not in, public practice.

The Meaning of Competence	When a member performs services or work covered by Rule 201, he or she must

- Have or obtain the requisite technical qualifications and knowledge.
- Apply knowledge and skill with reasonable care and diligence.

- Have the ability to supervise and evaluate the quality of the work (when applicable).
- Exercise sound judgment.

NOTE: If a member does not have the necessary competence (even with additional research or consultation), the member should suggest that someone else perform the work.

Retaining a Subcontractor to Assist a Member with a Consulting Service Engagement

When retaining a subcontractor, a member has a responsibility to ensure that the subcontractor has the

- Professional qualification,
- Technical skills, and
- Other resources required.

NOTE: The member may want to obtain references regarding the subcontractor's competency and reputation from other CPAs and other customers of the subcontractor.

Supervision of a Technical Specialist on a Consulting Engagement

A member must be qualified to supervise and evaluate the work of specialists that he or she employs.

NOTE: Supervision does not require that the member be qualified to perform each of the specialist's tasks. The member should be able to define the tasks and evaluate the end product.

Section B: Compliance with Standards for Members in Public Practice

Rule 202	Rule 202 states that a member who performs auditing, review, compilation, consulting services, tax, or other professional services shall comply with standards promulgated by bodies designated by Council.

Bodies Designated to Issue Standards

Designated body	*Standards*
1. Accounting and Review Services Committee (ARSC)	Statements on Standards for Accounting and Review Services (SSAR)
2. Auditing Standards Board	• Statements on Auditing Standards (SAS) • Statements on Standards for Attestation Engagements (SSAE) • Statements on Quality Control Standards (SQCS)
3. Consulting Services Executive Committee (CSEC)	Statements on Standards for Consulting Services (SSCS)
4. Tax Executive Committee	Statements on Standards for Tax Services (SSTS)

NOTE: Council resolutions give the first three bodies the authority to promulgate SSAE in their respective areas of responsibility.

Section C: Representations About Accounting Principles Applicable to Members in Public Practice

Rule 203	If the audited or reviewed financial statements or data contain any departure from an established accounting principle that has material effect on the statements or data taken as a whole, a member should not

1. Express an opinion or state that the entity's financial statements or other financial data are presented in conformity with generally accepted accounting principles.
2. State that he or she is not aware of any material modifications that should be made to such statements or data in order for them to be in conformity with generally accepted accounting principles.

The only exception to the rule is: If the statements or data contain a departure needed to prevent the statements from being misleading, the member will still be in compliance with Rule 203 if the member describes

- The departure,
- The approximate effects, if possible, and
- The reasons why compliance with the principle would result in a misleading statement.

Bodies Designated to Issue Established Accounting Principles

Designated body	*Standards*
1. Financial Accounting Standards Board (FASB)	• Statements of Financial Accounting Standards and Interpretations • Accounting Principles Board Opinions • AICPA Accounting Research Bulletins
2. Governmental Accounting Standards Board (GASB)	• Statements of Governmental Accounting Standards (issued in July 1984, and thereafter) • GASB Interpretations
3. Federal Accounting Standards Advisory Board (FASAB)	• Statements of Federal Accounting Standards

Rule 203 Departures from Established Accounting Principles--Audit Engagements

An auditor is permitted to express an unqualified audit opinion on financial statements that contain a material departure from pronouncements covered by Rule 203 in those unusual circumstances when literal application of that pronouncement would result in misleading financial statements.

NOTE: The authors believe circumstances that could cause adherence to a Rule 203 pronouncement to produce misleading financial statements would be extremely rare. Only a handful of such reports have ever been issued.

Rule 203 Departures from Established Accounting Principles--Review Engagements

An accountant is permitted to indicate that he or she is not aware of any material modifications when the reviewed financial statements contain a material departure from a pronouncement covered by Rule 203 in those unusual circumstances when literal application of that pronouncement would result in misleading financial statements.

NOTE: The authors believe circumstances that could cause adherence to a Rule 203 pronouncement to produce misleading financial statements would be extremely rare.

Preparation and Transmittal of Financial Statements

If a member is a stockholder, partner, director or employee for an entity other than his or her CPA firm and the member prepares financial statements for distribution to third parties, the transmittal letter should

- Indicate the member's relationship with the other entity, and
- Not imply the member is independent.

Rule 203 applies if the member states that the financial statements are prepared in conformity with GAAP.

*NOTE: Although the **Code of Professional Conduct** does not require that the transmittal be in writing, the authors recommend that the such communications be in writing.*

Example

> XYZ Company
> 123 Santa Fe Way
> Anytown, US
>
> I have prepared the attached XYZ Company balance sheet for the period ending December 31, 20X1. Please call me if you have any questions.
>
> Sincerely,
>
> *Dan M. Guy*
>
> Dan M. Guy, CPA
> Controller

NOTE: The authors believe that the member should not use his or her CPA firm letterhead (or other firm identification) in any such transmittal document.

Applicability of Rule 203 to Litigation Support Services

Rule 203 applies to a member performing litigation support services.

Section D: Representations about Accounting Principles Applicable to Members Not in Public Practice

Representations about GAAP	Rule 203 (see Section C) applies to members not in public practice when they represent in a letter or other communication that financial statements are in conformity with GAAP.

Types of Representations Covered	Letters, reports or other communication about financial statements include

- A client entity's representations and reports to its auditor.
- Reports to regulatory agencies and creditors.

Authoritative Sources

1. Appendix A, *Council Resolution Designating Bodies to Promulgate Technical Standards.*
2. Rule 201, *General Standards* (ET 201.01).
3. Rule 202, *Compliance with Standards* (ET 202.01).
4. Rule 203, *Accounting Principles* (ET 203.01).
5. Interpretation 201-1, *Competence* (ET201.02).
6. Interpretation 203-1, *Departures from Established Accounting Principles* (ET 203.02).
7. Interpretation 203-2, *Status of FASB, GASB, and FASAB Interpretations* (ET 203.03).
8. Interpretation 203-4, *Responsibility of Employees for the Preparation of Financial Statements in Conformity with GAAP* (ET 203.05).
9. Ethics Ruling No. 8, *Subcontractor Selection for Management Consulting Services Engagements* (ET 291.015-.016).
10. Ethics Ruling No. 9, *Supervision of Technical Specialists in Management Consulting Services Engagements* (ET 291.017-.018).
11. Ethics Ruling No. 10, *Preparation and Transmittal of Financial Statements by a Member in Public Practice* (ET 291.019-.020).
12. Ethics Ruling No. 11, *Applicability of Rule 203 to Member Performing Litigation Support Services* (ET 291.021-.022).

28 RULE 301–CONFIDENTIAL CLIENT INFORMATION

Basic Rule

Rule 301 prohibits a member in public practice from disclosing confidential client information without the client's specific consent.

What Is Not Prohibited by the Rule

Rule 301 does not

1. Release a member from his or her professional obligations under Rule 202, *Compliance with Standards*, and Rule 203, *Accounting Principles* (see Chapter 27).
2. Affect compliance with

   a. A subpoena or summons.
   b. Applicable laws and regulations.

NOTE: Confidentiality of client information is a professional rule but must be distinguished from privileged communication. Therefore a member may be compelled by subpoena or summons to disclose confidential client information. However, certain communications between CPAs and their tax clients are protected by a privilege of confidentiality under Section 7525 of the Internal Revenue Code. In addition, some states statutes may include a privilege of confidentiality for accountant/client communications.

3. Prohibit professional practice reviews under the authority of

   a. The AICPA.
   b. A state society.
   c. A state board of accountancy.

4. Prevent a member from initiating an ethics complaint or responding to an ethics inquiry from

   a. The AICPA's Professional Ethics Division.
   b. The AICPA's Trial Board.
   c. A state society or state board investigative or disciplinary body.

Applicability to Purchase or Merger of an Accounting Practice

This rule affects a review of a practice for a purchase, merger or sale. The member must take precautions, such as obtaining a confidentiality agreement from the prospective purchaser, to protect the confidential information.

Members Shall Not Use Client Information for Their Own Advantage

Members

- Involved in professional practice reviews.
- Involved in ethics complaints or ethics inquiries.
- Reviewing a practice in connection with a prospective purchase or merger.

May not

- Disclose confidential client information obtained during these reviews or investigations
- Use such information for their own benefit.

Members involved in professional practice or investigative or disciplinary hearings, however, are not restricted from appropriately exchanging information in connection with these reviews or investigations.

Changing CPAs to Hide Information

Rule 301 is not intended to help an unscrupulous client hide illegal acts or other information by changing CPAs.

Example

A member withdraws from an engagement after discovering irregularities in the client's tax return. If the successor accountant contacts the member, the member should, at a minimum, suggest that the successor ask the client to allow the member and successor to talk freely. This notifies the successor of some conflict. *The member withdrawing from the engagement should seek legal advice as to his or her status and obligations in this situation.*

SEC Rules on Insider Trading

The SEC prohibits illegal insider trading under the Securities Exchange Act of 1934.

Illegal insider trading can occur when

- Buying or selling a security while possessing material, nonpublic information about the security, or
- Communicating (tipping) such information to others who trade the securities.

Insider trading violates the law if the person who trades or communicates the information violates his or her fiduciary duty or other relationship of trust and confidence.

Examples of Insider Trading Cases Brought by the SEC

The SEC has brought insider cases against

- Corporate officers, directors and employees who traded the corporation's securities after learning significant confidential corporate information.
- Friends, business associates and family members who traded securities after receiving information from corporate officers, directors or employees.
- Law, banking, brokerage, and printing firm employees who were given confidential information to provide services to the corporation whose securities they traded.
- Government employees who had access to confidential information.
- Others who took advantage of confidential information from their employers.

Specific Activities That Would and Would Not Violate Client Confidentiality

Type of activity	*See section*
Permitted Use of Outside Bureaus or Agencies	A
Distribution of, or Revealing, Information to Others	B
Investment Advisory or Management Consulting Services	C
Service on the Board of a Nonclient Bank	D

Section A: Use of Outside Bureaus or Agencies

Use of Outside Bureaus or Agencies

A member may use

- Outside services to process clients' tax returns (e.g., perform calculations and print the return).
- A records retention agency to store clients' records, working papers, etc.

Member Must Take Precautions to Preserve Confidentiality

Whether using an outside service bureau or a records retention agency, the member is responsible for taking all necessary precautions to preserve the confidentiality of client information.

Section B: Distribution of, or Revealing Information

Disclosure to Insurance Carrier or Attorney Permitted

A member may give confidential client information, without the client's permission, to

- A professional liability insurance carrier solely to help defend the member against actual or potential claims.
- The member's attorney or a court to initiate, pursue, or defend himself or herself in legal or alternative dispute resolution proceedings.

Revealing Names of Clients

A member may disclose the names of clients without the client's specific consent unless disclosing the client's name would reveal confidential information.

Example

A member's practice is limited to bankruptcy matters. Disclosing a client's name may suggest that client is experiencing financial difficulties. This may be confidential client information and therefore disclosing the name of the client is prohibited.

NOTE: The ethical responsibility for confidentiality does not override the legal duty imposed by law or regulation to report matters to government authorities. Therefore, the member must comply with applicable federal or state laws.

Revealing Client Information to Competitors

A client may be engaged to perform services that involve examining confidential information about competitors. The member would be prohibited under Rule 301 from revealing confidential information.

Example

A municipality in a particular state enforces a personal property tax on business inventories, fixtures and equipment and machinery. The municipality uses a CPA Firm A to examine the books and records of businesses to verify the amount declared. CPA Firm A will examine sales, purchases, gross profit percentages, and inventories as well as fixed asset accounts. Company Z is one of the companies examined, and retains CPA Firm B as its CPA.

Firm B objects to Firm A's examination on the grounds that information gathered on Company Z, the client, could be inadvertently conveyed to Company Z's competitors by Firm A. Firm A would be allowed to perform the engagement, as long as all parties complied with the prohibition against revealing client information.

Request from Trade Association

A trade association is compiling a report containing profit or loss percentages of companies for distribution to its members. The trade association requests such information from the member about his or her clients. If the member has the clients' permission, he or she may comply with this request.

Disclosure of Confidential Client Information in a Divorce

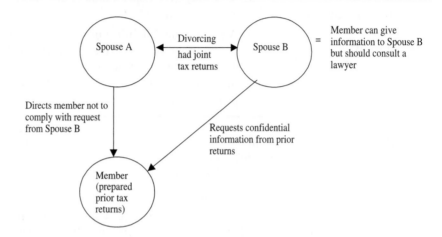

Rationale: Since Spouse B is a client with respect to prior tax returns, the member is not prohibited by Rule 301 from giving information to Spouse B. The member, however, should review the legal implications with an attorney.

Section C: Investment Advisory or Management Consulting Services

Member Providing Investment Advisory Services to Company Executives	A member may accept an engagement in which the member is retained by a company to provide personal financial planning or tax services for its executives if the member can perform these investment advisory services with objectivity. (The executives are aware of the company's relationship with the member and have agreed to the arrangement.) The member must carefully consider

- Rule 102, *Integrity and Objectivity* (ET 102.01) (Chapter 6) since the member may find, in performing these services, that the member may recommend actions to the executives that are unfavorable to the company.
- Rule 301, *Confidential Client Information* (ET 301.01) since the member has a responsibility to keep client information confidential. In this case, the clients are both the company and the executives.

The member should consider informing the company and the executives of possible results of the engagement.

Disclosing Information Obtained from Nonclient Sources	A member performing management consulting services may not reveal information from outside nonclient sources without permission. Rule 301 prohibits disclosing confidential information from clients, and therefore does not directly apply. However, Rule 501, *Acts Discreditable,* does apply. See Chapter 30 on Rule 501 for related guidance.
Disclosing Knowledge Obtained from a Different Client Engagement	A member who has knowledge and expertise gained from previous client engagements, which results in special competence in a particular field, can provide that knowledge and expertise to another client as long as the details of a previous client's engagement are not disclosed.

Example

A prospective client, Company B, has asked a member's firm to study the desirability of its using a newly developed electronic ticketing system for his business. The member has performed a recent study for another client, Company A, that leads the member to believe that the ticketing system would not be desirable for Company B. The member should communicate reservations about the ticketing system provided that the details of Company A's engagement are not disclosed. If, however, Company B would clearly know the origin of the information and such information is sensitive, the member should not accept the engagement without the approval of Company A.

Section D: Service on the Board of Directors of a Nonclient Bank

Service on the Board of Directors of a Nonclient Bank

The AICPA discourages a member from serving as a director of a non-client bank, if the member has clients (requiring independence or otherwise) that are customers of the bank.

The AICPA discourages bank directorships to avoid situations in which the member would have

- A conflict of interest under Interpretation 102-2 (ET102.03) as discussed in Chapter 6, or
- A problem with confidential client information under Rule 301 (ET 301.01) as discussed in Chapter 28.

NOTE: A more appropriate way for the member to serve the nonclient bank would be as a consultant to the board of directors.

Authoritative Sources

1. Rule 301, *Confidential Client Information* (ET 301.01).
2. Interpretation 301-3, *Confidential Information and the Purchase, Sale or Merger of a Practice* (ET 301.04).
3. The Securities Exchange Act of 1934, *Insider Trading*, Section 21 (d) (2).
4. Ethics Ruling No. 1, *Computer Processing of Clients' Returns* (ET 391.001-.002).
5. Ethics Ruling No. 2, *Distribution of Client Information to Trade Associations* (ET 391.003-.004).
6. Ethics Ruling No. 3, *Information to Successor Accountant about Tax Return Irregularities* (ET 391.005-.006).
7. Ethics Ruling No 5, *Records Retention Agency* (ET 391.009-.010).
8. Ethics Ruling No. 6, *Revealing Client Information to Competitors* (ET 391.011-012).
9. Ethics Ruling No. 7, *Revealing Names of Clients* (ET 391.013-.014).
10. Ethics Ruling No. 14, *Use of Confidential Information on Management Consulting Service Engagements (*ET 391.027-.028).

11. Ethics Ruling No. 15, *Earlier Similar Management Consulting Service Study with Negative Outcome* (ET 391.029-.030)
12. Ethics Ruling No. 16, *Disclosure of Confidential Client Information* (ET 391.031-.032).
13. Ethics Ruling No. 18, *Bank Director* (ET 391.035-.036).
14. Ethics Ruling No. 20, *Disclosure of Confidential Client Information to Professional Liability Insurance Carrier* (ET 391.039-.040).
15. Ethics Ruling No. 21, *Member Providing Services for Company Executives* (ET 391.041-.042).
16. Ethics Ruling No. 23, *Disclosure of Confidential Client Information in Legal or Alternative Dispute Resolution Proceedings* (ET 391.045-.046).

29 RULE 302–CONTINGENT FEES

In This Chapter	This chapter applies only to members in public practice. It contains the following sections

For information on	*See section*
AICPA Requirements	A
State Requirements	B

Overview

The AICPA once prohibited contingent fees for all professional services. The AICPA has retained the prohibition for any professional service when the CPA also provides audit, certain attestation services, or compilation services to the client as described in Section A.

Some state boards still prohibit contingent fees (see Section B). Other organizations, such as the SEC, generally have not taken exception to the AICPA rules except for its application to affiliates of audit clients (see page 29-6).

Section A: AICPA

Basic Rule	Rule 302 prohibits contingent fees **for any professional service performed for a client** when the member in public practice (or member's firm) also performs for that client

1. An audit or a review of a financial statement.
2. An examination of prospective financial information.
3. A compilation of a financial statement expected to be used by third parties except when the compilation report discloses a lack of independence.

These services are referred to in this chapter as disqualifying services.

NOTE: The guidance on contingent fees is similar to that for commissions and referral fees. The reader may also want to consider the guidance in Chapter 32, Rule 503--Commissions and Referral Fees.

Rationale

The basic purpose of this rule and Rule 503 on commissions is to ensure the member's objectivity and to avoid a conflict of interest in performing the service.

Period of Applicability

This prohibition applies during

- The period in which the member is engaged to perform any of these disqualifying services, and
- The period covered by any historical financial statements involved in these services.

Basic Rule--Prohibition on Tax Return Preparation or Claim for Refund For a Contingent Fee

Rule 302 also prohibits a member in public practice from preparing for a contingent fee

- An original or amended tax return, or
- A claim for a tax refund.

This includes giving advice on determining some portion of a return or claim for refund for events that have occurred at the time the advice is given.

Definition of a Contingent Fee

A contingent fee is a fee for performing any service in which the amount of the fee (or whether a fee will be paid) depends on the results of the service.

NOTE: A member's fees may vary depending on the complexity of services rendered.

Exceptions to Definition

Solely for applying this rule, fees are not considered contingent if they are

- Fixed by the courts or other public authorities.
- In tax matters, determined based on the results of judicial proceedings or the findings of governmental agencies.

Example

A member performs services for a client in bankruptcy. The judge awards a fee to the member. Such fee is not considered a contingent fee.

A fee is considered to be based on the findings of governmental agencies if the member can demonstrate, at the time that fees are set, that the member's client reasonably expects substantive consideration from an agency. The expectation is not reasonable when original tax returns are being prepared.

Definition of the Receipt of a Contingent Fee

A contingent fee is deemed to be received when

- The performance of the related services is complete, and
- The contingent fee is determined.

NOTE: This means that the contingent fee does not have to have been paid by the client to be deemed to have been received by the member's firm.

Examples of Permitted Contingent Fees

The following are some examples of tax services for which contingent fees would be permitted

- Representing a client

  - In a tax return examination by a revenue agent
  - By helping to influence tax legislation, or
  - By helping to get a private letter ruling.

- When established procedures are available for review of refund requests, requesting such a refund for

  - Interest or penalty overpayments or
  - Deposits of taxes not properly recorded.

- Requesting a reduction in the assessed value of property under an established taxing authority's review process for hearing such arguments.
- Filing an amended return claiming a refund

  - Based on an issue that is the subject of a test case for another taxpayer or for which a position is being developed by a taxing authority.
  - For an amount that is greater than the threshold for review set by the Joint Committee on Internal Revenue Taxation (last set at $1 million at March 1991) or state taxing authority.

*NOTE: The key consideration is that the contingent fee is based on an amount **not** determined by the member.*

Example of Contingent Fees Not Permitted

The following is an example of a circumstance in which a contingent fee would be not be permitted

- Preparing an amended income tax return for a client for a refund of taxes because a deduction was inadvertently omitted in the original return. There is no question as to the propriety of the deduction; rather the claim is filed to correct an omission.

Receipt of Contingent Fees by Member's Spouse

A member's spouse may provide services to a member's attest client for a contingent fee if

- The activities of the member's spouse are separate from the member's practice.
- The member is not significantly involved in those activities.

The member should consider whether a conflict of interest exists (see Chapter 6, Requirements for Integrity and Objectivity (Including Freedom from Conflicts of Interest).

Investment Advisory Services for Attest Client

A member may only provide investment advisory services for a client for a fee based on a percentage of the client's investment portfolio if

- The member does not perform any disqualifying services for the client, or
- All of the following conditions are met

  - The fee is determined as a specified percentage of the client's investment portfolio.

- The dollar amount of the portfolio on which the fee is based is determined at the beginning of each period and is adjusted during the period only for additions and withdrawals.
- The fee arrangement is not renewed more often than on a quarterly basis.

NOTE: Since the dollar amount is set at the beginning of the period and adjusted only for client additions and withdrawals, but not for increases or decreases based on the portfolio's investment performance, the CPA's fee is not contingent on the portfolio's performance.

When performing such services, the member should consider Rule 101, *Independence*. See the guidance in Chapter 5, Basic Concepts of Rule 101–Independence, and Rule 102–Integrity and Objectivity, and Chapter 13, Performance of Other Services for Clients.

Investment Advisory Services for Nonattest Client

A member or member's firm may provide investment advisory services for a contingent fee to

- The owners, officers, or employees of an attest client.
- A nonattest client employee benefit plan sponsored by an attest client.

The member should, however, consider his or her obligations under

- Interpretation 102-2, *Conflicts of Interest* (Chapter 6) and
- Rule 301, *Confidential Client Information* (Chapter 28).

*NOTE: The SEC, DOL, and ISB do **not** agree with the AICPA's view that the following are separate clients from the attest entity:*

- *The owners, officers, or employees of an attest client*
- *A nonattest client employee benefit plan sponsored by an attest client.*

The position of these agencies is that services that would impair independence for the plan would generally have the same effect with respect to the sponsor. See Subsection L of Chapter 13, Performance of Other Services for Clients.

Section B: State Rules

State Rules

CPAs must also consider state laws concerning contingent fees. As of September 30, 2000, forty-two jurisdictions provide for the acceptance of contingent fees and twelve jurisdictions prohibit them. Several states are considering different proposals during this year. A chart containing information about contingent fees is updated regularly on the AICPA website at www.aicpa.org/states/uaa/commfees.htm.

Appendix B contains information on how to contact state boards and state societies.

The Uniform Accountancy Act

The Uniform Accountancy Act, sponsored by NASBA and developed along with the AICPA, permits contingent fees on behalf of nonattest clients. The language is taken from the AICPA's *Code of Professional Conduct*.

Authoritative Sources

1. Rule 302, *Contingent Fees* (302.01).
2. Interpretation 302-1, *Contingent Fees in Tax Matters* (ET 302.02).
3. Ethics Ruling No. 17, *Definition of the Receipt of a Contingent Fee or a Commission* (ET 391.033-.04).
4. Ethics Ruling No. 19, *Receipt of Contingent Fees or Commissions by Member's Spouse* (ET 391.037-.038).
5. Ethics Ruling No. 24, *Investment Advisory Services* (ET 391.047-.048).
6. Ethics Ruling No. 25, *Commission and Contingent Fee Arrangements with Nonattest Client* (ET 391.049-.050).

30 RULE 501–ACTS DISCREDITABLE

	For information on	*See section*
In This Chapter	Guidance for all Members	A
	Guidance for Members in Public Practice	B

Overview of Rule 501

Rule 501 prohibits acts discreditable to the profession. Section A discusses discreditable acts that apply to all members.

Section B discusses discreditable acts that apply to members in public practice.

Section A: Guidance For All Members

Basic Rule	Rule 501 prohibits acts discreditable to the profession.
Employment Discrimination and Harassment	A member who violates any state or federal antidiscrimination law, including laws prohibiting sexual or other forms of harassment, commits a discreditable act.
	Violation of the law is determined by the courts and is deemed to occur after the member has waived or lost the right to appeal.
False or Misleading Information Resulting from Member's Negligence	The following, when committed through the member's negligence, are discreditable acts:
	• Making false or misleading entries, or not correcting such entries if the member has the authority to do so.
	• Signing a materially false or misleading document.
	• Allowing or directing others to make such entries or sign such documents.
Soliciting or Disclosing CPA Exam Questions and Answers	A member who solicits or knowingly discloses Uniform CPA Exam questions without written authorization of the AICPA commits a discreditable act.
	NOTE: This restriction applies to the questions from the Uniform CPA Examination for May 1996 and after. Prior to the May 1996 exam, CPA exam questions and unofficial answers were made available to the public. Beginning in May 1996, the examination became secure. Questions and unofficial answers are no longer published.
Failing to File a Tax Return or Pay Tax Liability	A member who fails to file tax returns or remit payroll or other taxes collected for others on a timely basis may be considered to have committed a discreditable act.

Section B: Guidance For Members in Public Practice

Subsection A : Retaining Client Records

Basic Principle

A member who retains client records after the client requests them commits a discreditable act. This is true even if state statutes grant the member a lien on certain records in his or her possession.

NOTE: Some states have rules on retaining client records. Practitioners should consult their state laws and regulations for additional guidance. See Appendix B for information on contacting state boards and state societies.

Definition of Client Records

A client's records are defined as any accounting or other records belonging to the client that were given to the member by, or on behalf of, the client. They do not include a member's workpapers.

Member's Workpapers Include PBCs

A member's workpapers include, but are not limited to, analyses and schedules prepared by the client (PBCs) at the request of the member. These are the member's property and are not considered client records.

Engagement Terminated Prior to Completion

If the engagement is terminated by either the member or the client prior to completion, a member is required to return only records provided by the client.

Example

A member is preparing a client's tax return. The client terminates the engagement before completion. The member is not required to give the client the tax return. The member is only required to return client records.

Engagement Completed

If the engagement is complete, the member should return client records.

If asked, the member should also give the client information in the member's workpapers that is not in the client's books and records, and without which the client's financial information is incomplete.

Examples include

- Adjusting, closing, combining or consolidating journal entries.
- Information normally contained in books of original entry and general or subsidiary ledgers.
- Tax or depreciation carryforward information.

The member may require that the client pay all fees before the member provides such information.

Format of Requested Information

The member should provide the information described above in the medium requested, but only if it already exists in that format. For example, the member does not need to convert hardcopy information to an electronic form if it does not exist in that form.

Additional Requests for Information

Once the member has given client records and the additional completing information described above to an appropriate client representative, the member need not provide such information again either to the representative or other individuals associated with the client.

The client representative is the person, such as a general partner or majority shareholder, that has been held out as the client's representative.

Example

Two individuals associated with a client company are currently on opposing sides in an internal dispute. Both individuals have made separate requests for client records and other information that is required under Rule 501 to be provided. Individual A is a majority shareholder and has been dealing with the member as the company's representative. The member need only provide client records and appropriate information once to Individual A.

Removal of Client Files from an Accounting Firm

If a member who is not an owner of the firm is terminated, the member may not take or keep originals or copies of proprietary information or information from client files without the firm's permission, unless permitted by a contractual agreement.

Subsection B: Failing to Follow Requirements for Government Audits or Requirements of Regulatory Agencies

Standards or Requirements for Government Audits

A member who audits a recipient of government monies or government units must comply with GAAS as well as other relevant guidance for governmental audits. Such guidance includes

- Government audit standards
- Guides
- Procedures
- Statutes
- Rules
- Regulations

A member who accepts such an engagement and fails to comply with relevant guidance commits a discreditable act, unless the member discloses the lack of compliance and reasons for it in his or her report.

Requirements of Governmental Bodies, Commissions or Other Regulatory Agencies

A member who performs attest or similar services for entities subject to the jurisdiction of governmental bodies, commissions, or other regulatory agencies must comply with applicable GAAS as well as the requirements of those bodies.

Examples of such bodies include

- The Securities and Exchange Commission (SEC).
- The Federal Communications Commission (FCC).
- State insurance commissions.
- Other regulatory agencies that have established such requirements.

A material departure from such requirements is a discreditable act, unless the member discloses that such requirements were not followed and the reasons for not following the requirements in his or her report or such information is disclosed in the financial statements.

In addition, a member should follow the requirements of such organizations, as well as GAAP, if the member prepares financial statements or related information, such as management's discussion and analysis, for the purpose of reporting to such bodies.

*NOTE: This guidance applies to members **not** in public practice as well as members in public practice.*

Subsection C: Nonclient Confidentiality

Basic Principle

If a member obtains information from a nonclient source with the understanding that the source and details not be disclosed, the member may not reveal this information without permission.

NOTE: Confidential client information is discussed in Chapter 28.

Terms of Engagement Should Address Nonclient Confidentiality

In an engagement such as a feasibility study in which it appears that the member will rely on confidential information from nonclient sources, the terms of the engagement should state that the member's outside confidential sources will not be divulged even if they might affect the outcome of the engagement.

Terms of Engagement Are Silent

If the terms of the engagement are silent and the member needs to use outside confidential sources, the member should obtain the client's approval to present recommendations without disclosing confidential information.

If client does not agree, the member should withdraw rather than breach confidence or improperly limit the information in his or her final recommendation.

Subsection D: Collection of Notes Issued in Payment

Collection of Notes

If a member's firm has a delinquent client, and the firm made arrangements with a bank to collect notes issued by a client as payment for outstanding fees and notifies the client, this would not violate any part of the *Code of Professional Conduct*.

NOTE: See also Chapter 12, Unpaid Fees.

Authoritative Sources

1. Rule 501, *Acts Discreditable.* (ET 501.01)
2. Interpretation 501-1, *Retention of Client Records* (ET 501.02).
3. Interpretation 501-2, *Discrimination and Harassment in Employment Practices* (ET 501.03).
4. Interpretation 501-3, *Failure to Follow Standards and/or Procedures or Other Requirements in Governmental Audits* (ET 501.04).
5. Interpretation 501-4, *Negligence in the Preparation of Financial Statements or Records* (ET 501.05).
6. Interpretation 501-5, *Failure to Follow Requirements of Governmental Bodies, Commissions, or Other Regulatory Agencies in Performing Attest or Similar Services* (Revised) (ET 501.06).
7. Interpretation 501-6, *Solicitation or Disclosure of CPA Examination Questions or Answers* (ET 501.07).
8. Interpretation 501-7, *Failure to File Tax Return or Pay Tax Liability* (ET 501-8).
9. Ethics Ruling No. 2, *Collection of Notes Issued in Payment* (ET 591.003-.004).
10. Ethics Ruling No. 14, *Use of Confidential Information on Management Consulting Service Engagements* (ET 391.027-.028).
11. Ethics Ruling No. 182, *Termination of Engagement Prior to Completion* (ET 591.363-.364).
12. Ethics Ruling No. 189, *Request for Client Records and Other Information* (ET 591.377-.378).
13. Ethics Ruling No.191, *Member Removing Client Files from an Accounting Firm* (ET 591.381-.382).

31 RULE 502–ADVERTISING AND OTHER FORMS OF SOLICITATION

Overview

Rule 502 prohibits false or misleading advertising by members.

Section A contains guidance on acceptable and unacceptable forms of advertising and solicitation by CPAs.

Section B provides additional guidance for CPAs from Treasury Department Circular 230 and the Investment Advisers Act.

Finally, although Rule 502 applies to members in public practice, Section C provides guidance on applying this rule in situations that members not in public practice might encounter.

Section A: AICPA Guidance for Members in Public Practice

Basic Rule	Rule 502 prohibits members in public practice from the following when soliciting clients:

- False, misleading, or deceptive advertising.
- Coercion.
- Over-reaching or harassing conduct.

Definition of False, Misleading or Deceptive Advertising

Examples of prohibited false, misleading or deceptive advertising or solicitation include those that

- Create false expectations of favorable outcomes.
- Imply that the member can influence a body or official such as a court or regulatory agency.
- Represent that services will be performed for a fee when the member knows at the time of representation that the fee is likely to be substantially increased.
- Make representations that would deceive or be likely to be misunderstood.

Permitted Forms of Advertising

As a result of a consent agreement between the AICPA and the Federal Trade Commission (FTC), CPAs may now use forms of advertising such as the following *as long as they are not false, misleading or deceptive*:

- In-person solicitation of clients.
- Comparative advertising.
- Self-laudatory advertising.
- Testimonials or endorsements.

Engagements Obtained through Third Parties

Members may obtain clients or customers through the efforts of third parties, as long as the member determines that the promotional efforts of the third parties do not violate the *Code of Professional Conduct*.

Rationale for Engagements Obtained through Third Parties	Members who receive benefits from the actions of third parties must not do through the third parties what they are prohibited from doing themselves.
Use of CPA and Attorney Titles	A member who is both licensed as an attorney and a CPA may simultaneously practice accounting and law. The member may use either a single or separate letterhead, as long as • The member's use of the CPA designation complies with Rule 502. • The member conforms with the rules of the applicable Bar Association.
Use of AICPA PFS Designation	A member who holds the AICPA's Personal Financial Specialist (PFS) designation may use it after his or her name. If all partners or shareholders currently hold the designation, "Personal Financial Specialists" may be used on a firm's letterhead and in marketing materials.
Member Interviewed by the Press	When interviewed by a writer or reporter, the member should comply with the *Code of Professional Conduct* and not provide the press with any information for publication that the member himself or herself could not publish.
Serving as Course Instructor	A member who conducts a course should be sure that the promotions for the course do not violate Rule 502. The promotional material may include information on the instructor's background, such as the degrees he or she holds, professional society affiliations, and the name of the firm.
Member's Association with Newsletters and Publications	A newsletter, tax booklet, or similar publication not prepared by the member may be attributed to the member or the member's firm if the member concludes that the information attributed to the member or firm is not false, misleading, or deceptive.

Section B: Other Regulatory Guidance for Members in Public Practice

Treasury Department Circular 230	Treasury Department Circular 230, *Regulations Governing the Practice of Attorneys, Certified Public Accountants, Enrolled Agents, and Enrolled Actuaries and Appraisers Before the Internal Revenue Service,* prohibits CPAs, as well as other professionals, from • Making false or misleading claims • Making an uninvited solicitation of employment in matters related to the IRS.
SEC Regulations	The SEC regulates advertising by investment advisers. Rule 206(4)-1 of the Investment Advisers Act, *Advertisements by Investment Advisers*, describes advertising practices that the SEC considers fraudulent, deceptive or manipulative. Advertising, as defined for this purpose, means any written communication addressed to more than one person, or any notice or announcement in a publication or by radio or television, which offers any investment advisory service with regard to securities.
State Regulations	State laws may contain additional requirements on advertising and solicitation. See Appendix B for information on how to contact state boards and state societies.

Section C: Guidance for Members Not in Public Practice

Use of CPA by Controller of Bank	A member who is the controller of a bank may use the CPA title on bank stationery or in paid advertisements that list the bank's officers and directors.
Member Interviewed by the Press	When interviewed by a writer or reporter, the member should comply with the *Code of Professional Conduct* and not provide the press with any information for publication that the member himself could not publish.
Serving as Course Instructor	A member who conducts a course should be sure that the promotions for the course do not violate Rule 502. The promotional material may include information on the instructor's background, such as the degrees he or she holds and professional society affiliations.

Authoritative Sources

1. Rule 502, *Advertising and Other Forms of Solicitation* (ET 502.01).
2. Interpretation 502-2, *False, Misleading or Deceptive Acts in Advertising or Solicitation* (ET 502.03).
3. Interpretation 502-5, *Engagements Obtained through Efforts of Third Parties* (ET 502.06).
4. Rule 206(4)-1of the Investment Advisers Act, *Advertisements by Investment Advisers*
5. Treasury Circular 230, *Regulations Governing the Practice of Attorneys, Certified Public Accountants, Enrolled Agents, and Enrolled Actuaries and Appraisers Before the Internal Revenue Service.*
6. Ethics Ruling No. 33, *Course Instructor* (ET 591.065-.066).
7. Ethics Ruling No. 38, *CPA Title, Controller of Bank* (ET 591.075-.076).

8. Ethics Ruling No. 78, *Letterhead: Lawyer-CPA* (ET 591.155-.156).
9. Ethics Ruling No. 108, *Member Interviewed by the Press* (ET 591.215-.216).
10. Ethics Ruling No. 176, *Member's Association with Newsletters and Publications* (ET 591.351-.352).
11. Ethics Ruling No. 183, *Use of the AICPA Personal Financial Specialist Designation* (ET 591.365-.366).

32 RULE 503–COMMISSIONS AND REFERRAL FEES

In This Chapter

This chapter applies only to members in public practice. It contains the following sections:

For information on	See section
AICPA Requirements	A
State Requirements	B

Overview

The AICPA once prohibited commissions and referral fees for all professional services. The AICPA has retained the prohibition for any professional service when the CPA also provides audit, certain attestation, or compilation services to the client as described in Section A.

Some state boards still prohibit commissions and referral fees (see Section B). Other organizations, such as the SEC, generally have not taken exception to the AICPA rules except for its application of certain rules to affiliates of audit clients (see page 32-5).

Section A: AICPA Requirements

Basic Rule

Rule 503 prohibits a member in public practice from receiving a commission or referral fee from a client when the member or member's firm performs for that client

1. An audit or a review of a financial statement.
2. An examination of prospective financial information.
3. A compilation of a financial statement expected to be used by third parties except when the compilation report discloses a lack of independence.

These services are referred to in this chapter as disqualifying services.

*NOTE: The **Code of Professional Conduct** does not define commissions or referral fees. Some states define commissions and referral fees. For example, the New York State Society's Professional Ethics Committee defines a commission as "compensation, except for a referral fee, for recommending or referring any product or service to be supplied by another person." Referral fees are defined as "compensation for recommending or referring any service of a CPA to any person."*

Prohibitions

A member who performs any of the disqualifying services listed in the *Basic Rule* may not receive a commission for recommending or referring

- Any product or service **to a client.**
- Any product or service supplied **by a client.**

NOTE: This prohibition includes both commissions paid to the member by a client and commissions paid by a third-party supplier of products or services. The guidance on commissions and referral fees is similar to that for contingent fees. The reader may also want to consider the guidance in Chapter 29, Rule 302--Contingent Fees.

Period of Applicability

This prohibition applies during

- The period in which the member is engaged to perform any of these disqualifying services, and
- The period covered by any historical financial statements involved in the disqualifying services.

Rationale

The basic purpose of this rule is to ensure the member's objectivity and to avoid a conflict of interest in performing the service.

Basic Rule--
Disclosure of
Permitted
Commissions

A member whose firm does not perform any disqualifying services for a client may receive a commission or referral fee for other types of services, such as personal financial planning, from that client. The member should disclose the commission **to the party to whom the product or service was recommended or referred.**

Documenting
Disclosure of
Commissions

A number of states require that a CPA issue a separate disclosure document to the party to whom the product or service was recommended.

NOTE: Even if not required by state law or regulation, the authors believe that this is a good practice.

Example Written
Disclosures of
Permitted
Commissions

One example of a state that requires a written disclosure statement for permitted commissions is California. Some of the California State Board of Accountancy requirements for this statement are

- A description of the product(s) or service(s) recommended to the client.
- The identity of the third party that will provide the product or service.
- The business relationship of the member to the third party.
- A description of any fee or commission that may be received by the member.
- The dollar amount or value of the fee or commission payment(s) or the basis on which the payment(s) shall be computed.

When the product or service cannot be specifically identified at the time of the initial disclosure, the member must provide this information in a supplemental disclosure within thirty days of the receipt of the fee or commission.

In addition, the disclosure must

- Be on letterhead of the member's firm and signed by the member.
- Be signed and dated by the client.

- Contain an acknowledgment by the client that the client has read and understands the information contained in the disclosure.
- Be retained by the member for a period of five years.

The member client should send a copy of the disclosure document to the client.

Disclosure of Permitted Referral Fees

Any member who accepts a referral fee for recommending or referring any service of a CPA or who pays a referral fee to obtain a client shall disclose this fact to the client.

NOTE: The member may not perform any disqualifying services for the client and accept a referral fee. Referral fees may be treated differently under state laws from commissions. While some of the guidance in the Code of Professional Conduct mentions both commissions and referral fees, many state laws (e.g., California) expressly prohibit CPAs from accepting a commission or fee solely for referring a client to a third party.

Definition of Receipt of Commission

A commission is considered received when

- The performance of the related services is complete, and
- The fee or the commission is determined.

Example

A member sells a life insurance policy to a client in 20X1. The member's commission payments are determined to be a fixed percentage of future years' renewal premiums. The commission is considered received in the year the policy is sold, (i.e., 20X1), no matter when payments are actually received.

Referral of Products of Others

A member cannot permit others, such as a distributor or agent, to do things that would violate the Code if the member did them. The member is held responsible for the actions of distributors or agents.

Example 1

CPA has Audit Client A. Audit Client A asks CPA to recommend a computer wholesaler for Client A's purchase of new computers. CPA may not receive a commission from the wholesaler for the recommendation.

Example 2

CPA has Audit Client A. Audit Client A asks CPA to recommend a source for Client A's purchase of new computers. CPA refers Client A to distributor B. Client A buys the computer, which distributor B obtains from a wholesaler. CPA may not receive a commission from the wholesaler, even though the referral was actually to the distributor.

Receipt of Commissions by Member's Spouse

A member's spouse refers products or services for a commission to a client for whom the member's firm performs disqualifying services. Rule 503 is not violated if

- The activities of the member's spouse are separate from the member's practice, and
- The member is not significantly involved in those activities.

The member should consider whether a conflict of interest exists (see Chapter 6).

Commission Arrangements with Nonattest Client

A member or member's firm may refer products or services of a nonclient or a nonattest client for a commission to

- The owners, officers or employees of an attest client.
- A nonattest client employee benefit plan sponsored by an attest client.

The member should disclose the commission to the owner, officers, or employees, or to the employee benefit plan.

The member should also consider

- Interpretation 102-2, *Conflicts of Interest* (Chapter 6), and
- Rule 301, *Confidential Client Information* (Chapter 28).

*NOTE: The SEC, DOL, and ISB do **not** agree with the AICPA's view that the following are separate clients from the attest entity:*

- *The owners, officers, or employees of an attest client*
- *A nonattest client employee benefit plan sponsored by an attest client*

The position of these entities is that services that would impair independence for the plan would generally have the same effect with respect to the sponsor. See Subsection L of Chapter 13, Performance of Other Services for Clients.

Sales of Products to Clients

A member may purchase a product from a third-party supplier and resell the product to a client, since the profit on the sale does not constitute a commission. The purchase of the product involves the member taking title to the product and having the associated risks of ownership.

Billing for Subcontractor's Services

A member has contracted with a computer hardware maintenance service to provide support for a client's computer operations. The member may bill the client a higher service fee than that charged to the member by the service provider. The increased fee is not a commission.

Section B: State Requirements

State Rules

CPAs must also consider state laws concerning commissions. As of September 30, 2000, forty-two jurisdictions provide for the acceptance of commissions and twelve jurisdictions prohibit them. Several states are considering amending their requirements and continuing the trend in recent years to permit such fee arrangements or permit them under limited circumstances. A chart containing information about commissions is updated regularly on the AICPA website at www.aicpa.org/states/uaa/commfees.htm.

Appendix B contains information on how to contact state boards and state societies.

The Uniform Accountancy Act

The Uniform Accountancy Act, sponsored by NASBA and developed along with the AICPA, permits commissions with disclosure on behalf of nonattest clients. The language is taken from the AICPA's *Code of Professional Conduct*.

Authoritative Sources

1. Rule 503, *Commissions and Referral Fees*. (ET 503.01).
2. Ethics Rulings No. 184, *Definition of the Receipt of a Contingent Fee or a Commission* (ET 591.367-.368).
3. Ethics Ruling No. 185, *Sale of Products to Clients* (ET 591.369-.370).
4. Ethics Ruling No. 186, *Billing for Subcontractor's Services* (ET 591.371-.372)
5. Ethics Ruling No. 187, *Receipt of Contingent Fees or Commissions by Member's Spouse* (ET 591.373-.374)
6. Ethics Ruling No. 188, *Referral of Products of Others* (ET 591.375-.376).
7. Ethics Ruling No. 192, *Commission and Contingent Fee Arrangements with Nonattest Client* (ET 59.383-.384).
8. California Board of Accountancy Regulations, Section 56, *Commissions--Basic Disclosure Requirement*.

33 RULE 505–FORM OF ORGANIZATION AND NAME

In This Chapter

This chapter applies only to members in public practice. It contains the following sections:

For information on	*See section*
Permitted Forms of Organization	A
Misleading Firm Name	B
Members Who Own a Separate Business	C

Overview

Rule 505 applies to both the form and the name of the organization for members in public practice. Section A provides guidance on permitted forms of organization, which must be allowed by law or regulation and also meet the requirements set by the AICPA Council.

Section B provides guidance on determining what is and is not acceptable for a firm name.

Section C provides guidance for a member in public practice who participates in a separate business that performs professional services for which standards are promulgated by bodies designated by Council (e.g., accounting, tax, consulting).

Section A: Permitted Forms of Organization

Basic Rule

Rule 505 states that a member may practice public accounting only in a permitted form of organization. A permitted form of organization must

- Be allowed by law or regulation, and
- Meet the requirements set by the AICPA Council.

Applicability of Rule 505 to Firms Performing Attest Services

A member in public practice in any firm or organization that does any of the following must comply with the requirements of the AICPA *Council Resolution Concerning Rule 505-Form of Organization and Name* (the Council Resolution).

- Performs audits or other engagements under SAS.
- Performs reviews under SSARS.
- Performs examinations of prospective financial information under SSAE.
- Holds out as a firm of CPAs or uses the term "certified public accountant(s)" or the designation CPA in connection with its name.

Applicability of Rule 505 to Firms Performing Compilations

A member who performs compilations under SSARS but practices in a firm or organization that does not meet the definition of a firm or organization as described in, "Applicability of Rule 505 to Firms Performing Attest Services," must comply with the following requirements:

- A CPA must have ultimate responsibility for the firm's compilation services and for each business unit performing compilations. (Non-CPA owners could not ultimately be responsible for these services.)
- A CPA must individually sign any compilation report. The report may not be signed in the firm's name.

For example, John Jones, CPA, an employee of XYZ Wholesale Company, may sign the report, but not under the firm name of XYZ Wholesale Company.

Applicability of Rule 505 to Firms Not Performing Attest or Compilation Services

Firms not performing attest or compilation services may take any legally permissible form.

Requirements of the Council Resolution

The requirements of the Council Resolution are

1. CPAs must own a majority of the financial interests and voting rights.

    A nonCPA owner must be actively providing services to the firm's clients as his or her principal occupation. Investors or commercial enterprises not actively providing services to the firm's clients as their principal occupation may not be owners.

2. A CPA must have ultimate responsibility for

    - All the services provided by the firm, and
    - Each functional and geographic business unit that performs attest or compilation services, or any other engagements under SAS and SSARS. Non-CPA owners cannot be ultimately responsible for any of these services or engagements.

3. Non-CPAs who become owners after adoption of the Council Resolution must have a baccalaureate degree.

NOTE: Beginning in 2010, non-CPAs who become owners should also have 150 semester hours of education from an accredited college or university.

4. Non-CPA owners cannot hold themselves out as CPAs, but are be permitted to use the following titles:

    - Principal
    - Owner
    - Officer
    - Member
    - Shareholder
    - Any other title permitted by state law

5. Non-CPA owners must follow the *Code of Professional Conduct*. AICPA members may be held responsible under the *Code* for acts of co-owners.

6. Non-CPA owners must complete the same work-related CPE requirements as AICPA members.

NOTE: AICPA bylaws require that, effective January 1, 2001, all AICPA members, both in public practice and not in public practice, shall complete 120 hours (or its equivalent) of continuing professional education for each three-year period.

7. Owners shall at all times own their equity and be the beneficial owners of their equity. If the owner stops being actively involved in the firm, his ownership must be transferred to the firm or other qualified owners within a reasonable amount of time.

8. Non-CPA owners cannot be members of the AICPA.

Applicability to Alternative Practice Structures

A traditional CPA firm engaged in auditing and other attestation services might be closely aligned with another organization, public or private, that performs other professional services.

These types of alliances are sometimes called *Alternative Practice Structures* (APS)--a nontraditional structure for the practice of public accounting.

Examples of APSs include American Express Tax and Business Services and Century Business Services.

An APS is in compliance with the financial interests provision (requirement 1) of the Council Resolution if

- CPA owners of the attest firm remain financially responsible under applicable state laws or regulations for the attest work performed.
- The firm is in compliance with the other requirements of AICPA's bylaws, the Council Resolution, and the *Code of Professional Conduct.*

NOTE: A June 2000 change to AICPA Bylaws 2.2 and 2.3 requires that members practicing public accounting in firms not enrolled in an AICPA-approved practice-monitoring program must enroll individually in a peer review program if they perform services, such as compilations, that are subject to peer review. For a model of an APS and for information on APS independence rules, see Chapter 25, Alternative Practice Structures.

Employment by, or Partnership with, Non-CPAs

A member employed in a public accounting firm made up of one or more non-CPA practitioners must comply with the *Code of Professional Conduct.*

If the member becomes a partner in the firm, he or she is responsible for the compliance with the *Code of Professional Conduct* of all persons associated with him or her.

NOTE: The authors believe that if the member becomes a shareholder in the firm, the same guidance would apply.

Example

A member in partnership with a noncertified public accountant would be held accountable if the noncertified partner violated the *Code of Professional Conduct*.

A member who is in a partnership with non-CPAs may sign a report with his or her signature and the designation "Certified Public Accountant" under the firm name. However, it must be clear that the partnership itself was not held out as being composed of CPAs.

Example

Schaller, Nichols, and Guy, Public Accountants
Dan Guy, CPA

Audit with Former Partner

A member's firm, which has been dissolved previously, consisted of one partner certified as a CPA and one noncertified partner. One account has been retained which the two practitioners plan to continue to work on together. Although it is proper for the audit to be carried out jointly by the two partners, the opinion should be presented on plain paper and signed in a manner similar to the following:

Dan Guy, Certified Public Accountant
Linda Nichols, Accountant

This form of signature assures the client that both partners participated in the audit, but leaves no doubt as to whether a partnership existed.

State Requirements

Many states now allow CPAs to practice as limited liability companies (LLC), limited liability partnerships (LLP) and general corporations. According to the AICPA's *Digest of State Issues*, as of January 2000

- Fifty-one jurisdictions have passed LLC legislation.
- Fifty-three jurisdictions have passed LLP legislation.
- At least two states have passed bills to allow CPAs to form general corporations.
- Forty-three states have explicitly amended their accountancy statute to provide for these forms of practice.

Also, NASBA's Uniform Accountancy Act (UAA) has sections that allow non-CPAs to have ownership interests in CPA firms if certain conditions are met. A number of states are currently evaluating whether to adopt the UAA.

Section B: Misleading Firm Name

Basic Rule

Rule 505 prohibits members from practicing public accounting under a misleading firm name.

- A successor firm *may* include the names of one or more past owners in the firm name.

Example

A firm is composed of four members who practice under the name of the managing partner. The managing partner is elected to high public office and leaves the partnership. The three remaining members may continue to practice under the managing partner's name followed by the designation "and Company."

- A firm **may not** designate itself as "Members of the American Institute of Certified Public Accountants" unless **all** of its CPA owners are AICPA members

Associations of Accountants who Are Not Partners

Members who are not partners should not use a joint letterhead showing the names of both members even if they

- Share an office,
- Have the same employees,
- Have a joint bank account, and
- Work together on each other's engagements.

Rule 505 would be violated if any reports were issued under the joint letterhead.

NOTE: The public might assume that a partnership exists when in fact none exists.

Association of Firms That Are Not Partners

Three firms who wished to form an association, but not a partnership, would not be able to use a title such as "Smith, Jones, and Associates." Each firm should use its own name on its letterhead and list the other two firms as correspondents.

Practice of Public Accounting under Name of Association or Group Prohibited	Several CPA firms, who remain separate and distinct, but form an association or group which would have joint advertising, training, professional development, and management assistance, are not allowed to practice public accounting under the name of the association or group.

Practicing under the name of an association or group may confuse the public about the relationship among firms. |
| **Permitted Use of Firm Name Along with Name of Association or Group** | However, as long as the firm practiced only in its own firm name it could

• Indicate the association or group name elsewhere on the stationery.
• List the names of the other firms in the association or group on its stationery. |
Firm Name of Merged Partnerships	When two partnerships merge, it is permissible for the newly merged firm to practice under a title that includes the name of a partner who had retired from one of the two firms prior to the merger.
Nonproprietary Partner	A firm may **not** use a designation such as "nonproprietary partner" to describe a high-ranking staff person who was a former partner of merged firms but is not a partner in the merging firm. The use of the term "partner" should be limited to legal partners.
Partner Having Separate CPA Proprietorship	A member may be a partner of a firm of public accountants, none of which are certified as CPAs, and may retain his or her own practice as a CPA. However, clients and others should be advised of this dual position of the member to prevent misunderstanding.
Partnership Roster	A firm may use an established firm name in a different state even if there is some difference in the roster of partners. The firm must otherwise comply with Rule 505, *Form of Organization and Name*.
State Requirements	States may also have regulations concerning the use of the name of the practice. For example, some states prohibit use of a name that implies the existence of a partnership when there is none. See Appendix B for information on contacting state boards and state societies.

Section C: Members Who Own a Separate Business

Applicability of Rules of Conduct to Members Who Own a Separate Business

A member in public accounting who owns an interest in a separate business that performs any of the following services is required to comply with the *Code of Professional Conduct*:

- Accounting
- Tax
- Personal financial planning
- Litigation support services
- Services for which standards are promulgated by bodies designated by Council (e.g., consulting).

NOTE: The following engagements are covered by standards issued by bodies designated by Council:

- *Audits and examinations*
- *Reviews*
- *Compilations*
- *Agreed-upon procedures*
- *Consulting services*
- *Tax*

Example

A member in public practice plans to form a separate business to perform centralized billing services for local doctors. Although the member maintains that this service is similar to one offered by a local bank and therefore not the practice of public accounting, the service is a type performed by public accountants. Therefore, the member could proceed with the business only if he or she complied with the *Code of Professional Conduct*, particularly Rule 502, *Advertising and Other Forms of Solicitation* (Chapter 31) and Rule 505, *Form of Organization and Name*.

Member Controls Business

If the member controls the separate business, either individually or collectively with the firm or members of the firm, then all owners and employees of the separate business must comply with all provisions of the *Code of Professional Conduct*. The business is included in the definition of member for the purpose of applying the independence rules (see Chapter 8).

Member Does Not Control Business

If the member, individually or collectively with the firm or members of his or her firm, does not control the separate business, the provisions of the *Code of Professional Conduct* apply to the member but not to the entity, its other owners, and employees.

Example

A separate business enters into a contingent fee arrangement with an attest client of the member. If the member controls the separate business, such an arrangement would not be permitted (see Chapter 29, Contingent Fees). If the member does not control the separate business, the separate business would be permitted to enter into the arrangement.

Authoritative Sources

1. Bylaw Section 230R, *Implementing Resolutions under Section 2.3 Requirements for Retention of Membership, Continuing Professional Education for Members.*
2. Rule 505, *Form Of Organization And Name* (ET 505.01).
3. Appendix B--Council Resolution Concerning Rule 505, *Form of Organization and Name.*
4. Interpretation 505-2, *Application of Rules of Conduct to Members Who Own a Separate Business* (ET 505.03).
5. Interpretation 505-3, *Application of Rule 505 to Alternative Practice Structures* (ET 505.04).
6. Ethics Ruling No. 3, *Employment by Non-CPA Firm* (ET 591.005-.006).
7. Ethics Ruling No. 134, *Association of Accountants Not Partners* (ET 591.267-.268).
8. Ethics Ruling No. 135, *Association of Firms Not Partners* (ET 591.269-.270).
9. Ethics Ruling No. 136, *Audit with Former Partner* (ET 591.271-.272).
10. Ethics Ruling No. 137, *Nonproprietary Partners* (ET 591.273-.274).
11. Ethics Ruling No. 138, *Partner Having Separate Proprietorship* (ET 591.275-.276).
12. Ethics Ruling No. 140, *Political Election* (ET 591.279-.280).
13. Ethics Ruling No. 141, *Responsibility for Non-CPA Partner* (ET 591.281-.282).
14. Ethics Ruling No. 144, *Title: Partnership Roster* (ET 591.287-.288).

15. Ethics Ruling No.145, *Firm Name of Merged Partnerships* (ET 591.289-.290).
16. Ethics Ruling No.177, *Data Processing: Billing Services* (ET 591.353-.354).
17. Ethics Ruling No.179, *Practice of Public Accounting Under Name of Association or Group* (ET 591.357-.358).
18. Ethics Ruling No. 190, *Non-CPA Partner* (ET 591.379-.380).

PART E

OTHER ETHICS GUIDANCE

34 STATEMENTS ON STANDARDS FOR TAX SERVICES AND INTERPRETATIONS (SSTS)

What are the SSTS?

The Statements on Standards for Tax Services (SSTS) supersede and replace the Statements on Responsibilities in Tax Practice (SRTP). They are enforceable standards of conduct for tax practice under the *Code of Professional Conduct.*

Applicability

The standards apply to all members when

- Recommending tax return positions, and
- Preparing or signing tax returns, including claims for refunds.

Effective Date

The SSTS have been approved by the Tax Executive Committee, were published in the October issue of the *Journal of Accountancy*, and became binding on members as of October 31, 2000.

In This Chapter

Section A: SSTS No. 1, *Tax Return Positions*

**Basic Rule--
Recommending
Tax Positions,
Preparing or
Signing a Return**

SSTS No.1 prohibits members from

1. Recommending a tax position unless the member believes that the position has a realistic possibility of being sustained administratively or judicially if challenged.

   NOTE: This is referred to as the realistic possibility standard. See Interpretation No. 1-1.

2. Knowingly preparing or signing a return that takes a position that the member would not recommend under 1. above.

NOTE: The taxpayer has the final responsibility for positions taken on the return.

In some cases, a member may conclude that a position does not meet the standard in 1. The taxpayer, however, may still wish to take the position. If the member concludes that the tax position is not frivolous, the member may

- Recommend the tax return position as long as the member advises the taxpayer to disclose the position, or
- Prepare or sign a return that reflects such a tax position as long as the position is disclosed.

**Basic Rule--Advising
Taxpayer of
Penalties**

When recommending tax return positions and preparing or signing a return, a member should, when relevant, advise the taxpayer of

- Potential penalties for a tax position, and
- The possibility of avoiding penalties through disclosures.

NOTE: Such advice may be given orally. Although a member should advise the taxpayer with respect to disclosure, the taxpayer is responsible for deciding whether and how to disclose.

Basic Rule-- **Prohibited** **Positions**	If a position is • Designed to exploit the likelihood of audit or detection, or • Only an arguing position for negotiating with a taxing authority The member should not recommend such a position, or prepare or sign a return that takes such position.
Basic Rule--The **Propriety of Being** **an Advocate for a** **Taxpayer**	A member should be an advocate for the taxpayer when recommending a tax return position that complies with SSTS No. 1.
Appropriate **Disclosure**	Appropriate disclosure is determined by • The facts and circumstances of a particular case, and • The authorities regarding disclosure in the applicable taxing jurisdiction.
Definition of a **Taxpayer**	A taxpayer is defined as a client, a member's employer, or any other recipient of tax services.
Tax Returns Include **Information** **Returns**	A tax return is primarily a taxpayer's representation of facts. Under the SSTS, *tax return* includes information return.
Definition of Tax **Return Position**	A tax return position is • A position taken in a tax return on which the member has specifically provided advice to the taxpayer, or • A position about which a member knows the material facts and, on the basis of those facts, concludes whether the position is appropriate.
Definition of **Frivolous Position**	A frivolous position is one that is knowingly advanced in bad faith and is patently improper.

Section B: Interpretation No. 1-1, *Realistic Possibility Standard*

Basic Rule

To meet the realistic possibility standard, the member should believe that, based on a reasonable interpretation of the tax law, the position

- Is justified by existing law, or
- Can be supported by a good-faith argument for extending or changing existing law through the courts.

A member should not take into account the likelihood of audit or detection when determining whether this standard has been met.

Relationship to Other IRS Standards

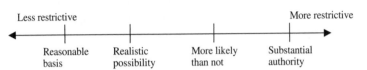

The realistic possibility standard is

- Less stringent than the Internal Revenue Code's substantial authority standard and the "more likely than not" standard that apply to substantial underpayments of tax liability.
- Stricter than the Internal Revenue Code's reasonable basis standard.

Authorities for Determining Realistic Possibility Standard

In determining whether a tax return meets the realistic possibility standard, a member is not limited to authorities considered when determining whether substantial authority exists under the Internal Revenue Code. The member may also rely on

- Well-reasoned treatises.
- Articles in recognized professional tax publications.
- Other commonly used reference tools and sources of tax analyses.

Determining whether a Realistic Possibility Exists

In determining whether a realistic possibility exists, a member should

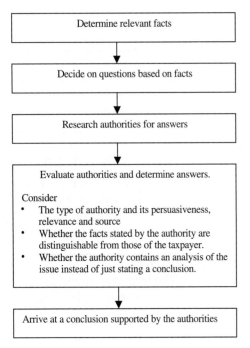

Determine relevant facts

Decide on questions based on facts

Research authorities for answers

Evaluate authorities and determine answers.

Consider
- The type of authority and its persuasiveness, relevance and source
- Whether the facts stated by the authority are distinguishable from those of the taxpayer.
- Whether the authority contains an analysis of the issue instead of just stating a conclusion.

Arrive at a conclusion supported by the authorities

Section C: SSTS No. 2, *Answers to Questions on Returns*

Basic Rule	SSTS No. 2 states that a member, before signing as preparer of a tax return, should make a reasonable effort to get information from the taxpayer needed to answer all questions on the return.

Rationale

A member should try to obtain all answers because

- A question and answer may be important in determining the taxable income or loss, or the tax liability.
- As preparer, the member must often sign a declaration that the return is true, correct, and complete.

Definition of Questions

The term "questions" includes any request for information. The request need not be stated as a question. Questions are found

- On the return,
- In the instructions, or
- In the regulations.

Omitting an Answer

Reasonable grounds for omitting an answer might include

- The information is not easily obtained and the answer does not significantly impact taxable income or loss, or the tax liability shown on the return.
- The meaning of the question is uncertain in relation to the particular return.
- The answer is very lengthy. In this case, the member should put a statement on the return saying that data will be supplied upon examination.

An answer should not be omitted simply because it may not be in the taxpayer's favor.

If the taxpayer has a good reason for omitting an answer, the taxpayer does not have to include an explanation of such reason in the return. However, the taxpayer should consider whether the return would be incomplete because of the omission.

Section D: SSTS No. 3, *Certain Procedural Aspects of Preparing Returns*

Basic Rule--Relying on Information from Taxpayer

SSTS No. 3 states that while a member may rely without verification on information provided by the taxpayer or third parties, the member should question such information if it appears incorrect, incomplete or inconsistent.

Example

A taxpayer gives a member an unsupported list of dividends and interest. The member may rely on the list as long as it does not seem to be incorrect, incomplete, or inconsistent.

NOTE: Even though a member is not required to examine underlying documents, a member should encourage the taxpayer to provide appropriate supporting data.

Example

A member should encourage a taxpayer to provide supporting documents to allow the member to thoroughly consider income and deductions from security transactions and from pass-through entities, such as estates, trusts, partnerships, and S corporations.

Basic Rule-- Responsibility for Conditions for Deductibility

If a taxpayer must meet certain conditions to support tax treatment of an item, the member should inquire to determine if the condition has been met.

Example

A deduction may require that books and records be maintained, or that supporting documents exist. The member should ask the taxpayer about such records and determine that the condition for the deduction is met.

Basic Rule--Prior Year Returns and Other Relevant Information

A member should

- Consider tax returns from prior years wherever possible.
- Consider relevant information from another taxpayer's return if known to the member and necessary for preparing the original taxpayer's return. The member should comply with any confidentiality rules or laws that would apply to such information.

Section E: SSTS No. 4, *Use of Estimates*

Basic Rule

SSTS No. 4 states that, unless prohibited by law or rule, a member may use a taxpayer's estimates if

- Obtaining exact data is impractical, and
- The member determines that estimates are reasonable based on the facts and circumstances known to the member.

However, SSTS No. 4 also states that estimates should not be presented so as to imply greater accuracy than exists.

Appraisals or Valuations

Appraisals or valuations are not considered estimates under the SSTS.

Specific Disclosure of Estimates

Although it is usually not necessary to disclose that an estimate was used, such disclosure should be made in certain circumstances to avoid misleading taxing authorities as to the degree of accuracy. Such circumstances may exist when the taxpayer

- Has died or is ill at the time the return is due.
- Has not received a Schedule K-1 for a pass-though entity at the time the tax return is due.
- Has pending litigation that might affect the return (e.g., bankruptcy).
- Has lost relevant records because of a fire or computer failure.

Section F: SSTS No. 5, *Departure from a Position Previously Concluded in an Administrative Proceeding or Court Decision*

Basic Rule

SSTS No. 5 allows a member to recommend a position, or sign or prepare a return containing a position, that differs from a position determined in an administrative proceeding or court decision for a taxpayer's prior return.

NOTE: An exception occurs when a taxpayer is bound to a specified treatment for later years, such as by a formal closing agreement.

Definition of Administrative Proceeding

Administrative proceeding includes an examination by a taxing authority or an appeals conference for a return or claim for refund.

Definition of Court Decision

Court decision refers to a decision by any court having jurisdiction over tax matters.

Examples of When a Different Tax Treatment May Be Recommended in Subsequent Years

Normally, if the tax treatment of an item is determined in an administrative proceeding or court decision for the prior year's return, the member would recommend the same treatment in the current year. However, there may be circumstances in which different tax treatments would be warranted. Examples of such circumstances include

- Although taxing authorities tend to act consistently on items covered in prior administrative proceedings, the authorities are not bound to do so. A taxpayer is similarly not bound to the tax treatment of an item consented to in an earlier administrative proceeding.
- The prior decision may have been made without supporting documentation that is now available.
- A taxpayer may have settled or not appealed the court decision even though the position met the standards in SSTS No. 1, *Tax Return Positions*.
- Court decisions, rulings, or authorities that support the taxpayer's position now exist that did not exist during the prior proceeding.

Section G: SSTS No. 6, *Knowledge of Error: Return Preparation*

Basic Rule--Actions on Becoming Aware of an Error

SSTS No. 6 states that if a member becomes aware of an error in a previously filed return or that a return was not filed, the member should

- Promptly inform the taxpayer.

   NOTE: It is the taxpayer's responsibility to decide whether to correct the error.

- Recommend corrective actions.

   NOTE: Such recommendations may be communicated orally.

Basic Rule-- Correcting the Error and Notifying Tax Authority

The member may not notify the taxing authority without the taxpayer's permission, except when required by law.

NOTE: The taxpayer, not the member, is responsible for deciding whether to correct the error.

If the taxpayer fails to correct a prior year error, and asks the member to prepare this year's return, the member should consider whether to continue the relationship with the client in the current year. If the member does prepare the current year's return, the member should take steps to avoid repeating the error.

NOTE: A member should consider consulting his or her own legal counsel before deciding upon recommendations to the taxpayer and whether to continue a professional relationship with the taxpayer. When there is a possibility that the taxpayer could be charged with fraud or other criminal misconduct, the taxpayer should be advised to consult his or her legal counsel before taking any action.

Definition of Error

An error includes

- Any position, omission, or method of accounting that does not meet the standards of SSTS 1, *Tax Return Positions,* when the return is filed.
- A position in a prior year's return that no longer meets the standards of SSTS 1 because of retroactive application of laws, court decisions, or administrative pronouncements.

An error does not include an item that does not have a significant effect on the taxpayer's tax liability.

Applicability

SSTS No. 6 applies whether or not the member prepared or signed the return that contains the error.

Section H: SSTS 7, *Knowledge of Error: Administrative Proceedings*

Basic Rule--Actions on Becoming Aware of an Error

SSTS No. 7 states that if the member is representing a taxpayer in an administrative proceeding and becomes aware of an error in the return, the member should

- Notify the taxpayer without delay.
- Recommend corrective action.

NOTE: Such recommendation may be communicated orally.

Basic Rule-- Notifying Taxing Authority of Error

Although the member can only notify the taxing authority with the taxpayer's permission, except when required by law, the member should seek such permission from the taxpayer. If the taxpayer refuses, the member should consider withdrawing and discontinuing the relationship with the taxpayer.

NOTE: A member should consider consulting his or her own legal counsel before making recommendations to the taxpayer and deciding whether to continue a professional relationship with the taxpayer. When there is a possibility that the taxpayer could be charged with fraud or other criminal misconduct, the taxpayer should be advised to consult his or her legal counsel before taking any action.

Definition of Administrative Proceeding

An administrative proceeding includes an examination by a taxing authority or an appeals conference, but does not include a criminal proceeding.

Applicability

This SSTS applies whether or not the member prepared or signed the return that contains the error. Special considerations may apply when a member has been engaged by legal counsel to assist in matters relating to counsel's client.

Section I: SSTS No. 8, *Form and Content of Advice to Taxpayers*

Basic Rule

A member should

- Use his or her good judgment to make sure that tax advice reflects the professional competence of the member and serves the taxpayer's needs.
- Assume that tax advice provided to a taxpayer will the affect the reporting of matters or transactions in the taxpayer's tax returns and should therefore follow SSTS No. 1, *Tax Return Positions*, when giving advice.

A member is not required to

- Follow a standard format or guidelines when providing advice to a taxpayer, either written or orally.
- Communicate with a taxpayer when subsequent developments affect advice previously given unless

  1. The member is assisting a taxpayer in implementing procedures or plans associated with the advice provided.
  2. The member specifically agrees to undertake this obligation.

NOTE: Taxpayers should be made aware that tax advice reflects professional judgment based on an existing situation and that subsequent developments could affect previous advice. A member has no duty to keep informed of the effect of subsequent developments on his or her advice. However, if a member continues to be engaged by a taxpayer and is aware of subsequent events that would have affected advice previously given, the authors recommend that the member notify the client.

Applicability

This Statement does not cover a member's responsibilities when it is expected that third parties are likely to rely on the advice.

Confidentiality

The member should consider applicable confidentiality rules when providing tax advice.

Form of Advice to the Taxpayer

In deciding on the form of advice to the taxpayer, a member should consider

- How important is the transaction? How large are the amounts involved?
- Is the inquiry specific or general in nature?
- How much time is available to develop advice and submit a recommendation?
- What are the technical complications presented?
- What authorities and precedents exist on this subject?
- How sophisticated is the client in tax matters?
- Should a lawyer be consulted?

Authoritative Sources

1. Statements on Standards for Tax Services No. 1, *Tax Return Positions.*
2. Statements on Standards for Tax Services No. 2, *Answers to Questions on Returns.*
3. Statements on Standards for Tax Services No. 3, *Certain Procedural Aspects of Preparing Returns.*
4. Statements on Standards for Tax Services No. 4, *Use of Estimates.*
5. Statements on Standards for Tax Services No. 5, *Departure from a Position Previously Concluded in an Administrative Proceeding or Court Decision.*
6. Statements on Standards for Tax Services No. 6, *Knowledge of Error: Return Preparation.*
7. Statements on Standards for Tax Services No. 7, *Knowledge of Error: Administrative Proceedings.*
8. Statements on Standards for Tax Services No. 8, *Form and Content of Advice to Taxpayers.*
9. Interpretation No. 1-1, *Realistic Possibility Standard.*

35 STATEMENTS ON STANDARDS FOR CONSULTING SERVICES

Introduction

Consulting services differ fundamentally from attest services.

- In an attest service, the practitioner expresses a conclusion about the reliability of another party's assertion.
- In a consulting service, the practitioner develops the findings, conclusions, and recommendations presented. The nature and scope of work is determined by agreement between the practitioner and client, and is usually performed only for the use and benefit of the client.

To provide guidance on consulting services, the AICPA issued a Statement on Standards for Consulting Services (SSCS).

Applicability

This Statement on Standards for Consulting Services, *Consulting Services: Definitions and Standards*, applies to any AICPA member who holds out as a CPA while providing consulting services.

NOTE: See Chapter 13 for SECPS restrictions on consulting services for audit clients.

General Standards

Practitioners who perform consulting services must comply with the general standards of the profession described in Rule 201. Rule 201 states that a member shall comply with the following standards and any interpretations issued by bodies designated by Council:

1. **Professional Competence.** A member must only perform services that the member or the member's firm can complete with professional competence.
2. **Due Professional Care.** A member must exercise due professional care when performing professional services.
3. **Planning and Supervision.** A member must adequately plan and supervise the performance of professional services.
4. **Sufficient Relevant Data.** The member must obtain sufficient relevant data to provide a reasonable basis for conclusions or recommendations when performing professional services.

NOTE: See Chapter 27 for additional information on Rule 201.

Additional Standards for Consulting Services

Practitioners must also comply with the following additional general standards for consulting services.

1. **Client interest.** A member should serve the client interest by working to accomplish the objectives established in the understanding with the client while maintaining integrity and objectivity.
2. **Understanding with client.** The member should establish an understanding with the client about

   - The responsibilities of the parties.
   - The nature, scope, and limitations of services to be performed.

   This understanding

   - May be written or oral.
   - Should be modified if circumstances significantly change during the engagement.

   NOTE: See Chapter 13, Performance of Other Services for Clients, for additional requirements regarding an understanding with the client when consulting services are performed for an audit/attest client.

3. **Communication with client.** The member should inform the client of

   - Any conflicts of interest under Rule 102 (see Chapter 6),
   - Significant reservations concerning the scope or benefits of the engagement, and
   - Significant engagement findings or events.

Constraints Limit Services to Be Provided	Professional judgment is necessary in applying SSCS. The understanding with the client may establish constraints on the services to be provided. However, even when the agreed-upon scope of services has limitations, the member is *not* required to decline or withdraw from a consulting engagement. The member is required to inform the client of any significant reservations caused by the limitation.

Example

> The understanding with the client may limit the practitioner's efforts to gather important relevant data. The member should explain the effect of this limitation to the client.

Consulting Services for Attest Client	The SSCS states that performing consulting services for an attest client does not, in itself, impair independence. However, members and their firms must comply with all applicable independence standards when performing attest services, such as those of the

- AICPA
- State Boards,
- State societies, and
- Other regulatory agencies, including the SEC and Independence Standards Board.

Definition of Consulting Process	The consulting process refers to the analytical approach applied in performing a consulting service. It typically involves some combination of the following:

- Determining the client's objective
- Fact-finding
- Defining problems or opportunities
- Evaluating alternatives
- Formulating proposed actions
- Communicating results
- Implementing
- Following up

Definition of Consulting Services	Consulting services are professional services that use the practitioner's technical skills, education, observations, experiences, and knowledge of the consulting process.

See Exhibit 1 for types of consulting services.

Definition of Consulting Services Practitioner

A consulting services practitioner is

- Any AICPA member holding out as a CPA while performing consulting services for a client, or
- Any other individual performing consulting services for a client for an AICPA member or member's firm holding out as a CPA.

Authoritative Source

1. Statement on Standards for Consulting Services, *Consulting Services: Definitions and Standards.*

Exhibit 1--Types of Consulting Services

Service	*Description*	*Examples*
Consultations	The practitioner provides advice in a short time frame, based primarily on existing personal knowledge about • The client, • The circumstances, • The technical matters involved, • Client representations, and • The mutual intent of the parties.	• Reviewing and commenting on a client-prepared business plan • Suggesting computer software for further investigation by the client.
Advisory Services	The practitioner develops findings, conclusions, and recommendation for the client to consider and use in decision making.	• Operational review and improvement study. • Analysis of an accounting system. • Assistance with strategic planning. • Definition of requirements for an information system.
Implementation Services	The practitioner puts an action plan into effect. Client personnel and resources may be combined with the practitioner's to accomplish the implementation objectives. The practitioner is responsible to the client for the conduct and management of engagement activities.	• Providing computer system installation and support. • Executing steps to improve productivity. • Assisting with the merger of organizations.
Transaction Services	The practitioner provides services related to a specific client transaction, usually with a third party.	• Insolvency services. • Valuation services. • Preparation of information for obtaining financing. • Analysis of a potential merger or acquisition. • Litigation services.
Staff and Other Support Services	The practitioner provides appropriate staff and other support to perform client-specified tasks. The staff provided by the member may be directed by the client as needed.	• Data processing facilities management. • Computer programming. • Bankruptcy trusteeship. • Controllership activities.
Product Services	The practitioner provides the client with a product and related professional services to support the product's installation, use, or maintenance.	• Sale and delivery of packaged training programs. • Sale and implementation of computer software. • Sale and installation of systems development methodologies.

36 AN INTERPRETATIVE OUTLINE OF IFAC'S *CODE OF ETHICS FOR PROFESSIONAL ACCOUNTANTS*[1]
(Revised January 1998)[2]

INTRODUCTION TO THE CODE

The International Federation of Accountants

The International Federation of Accountants (IFAC) is a nonprofit, nongovernmental, nonpolitical international organization of accounting bodies designed to develop and enhance the worldwide accountancy profession.

The Ethics Committee

The Ethics Committee reports to IFAC's Board. The Committee has responsibility, among other things, to develop the *Code of Ethics for Professional Accountants (Code)*. The Committee is required to consult with and to advise the Board[3] on all ethics issues and to develop guidance on such issues for the Board's approval. Before the Committee can present an exposure draft amending or creating new guidance to the Board, the Committee must have approval of at least three-fourths of the Committee members.

---

[1] *Reprinted with permission from the **Guide to International Standards on Auditing and Related Services**, by Dan M. Guy and Douglas R. Carmichael. Published by Practitioners Publishing Company, Fort Worth, Texas.*

[2] *IFAC has issued an Exposure Draft, **Independence–Proposed Changes to the Code of Ethics for Professional Accountants**. This Exposure Draft features a new conceptual framework approach to independence. The proposed rules set out a framework describing the factors that could threaten a reporting accountant's independence and the safeguards that could be put in place to preserve independence. In addition, the Exposure Draft includes a series of specific cases and suggest how the risk to independence can be minimized. Please check for updates to this section on the John Wiley & Sons, Inc. website at www.wiley.com.*

[3] *The Board consists of the President, the Deputy President, and representatives from eighteen countries, which are elected for two and one-half year terms. The Board supervises the general IFAC work program, the budget, and certain committees and projects.*

Applicability of the *Code*	The IFAC *Code* recognizes that the task of developing detailed ethical requirements, implementing those requirements, and enforcing a code of ethics is primarily the responsibility of the member bodies of each country. However, some IFAC member bodies adopt the *Code* as the ethical requirements in their countries. In situations when a national requirement is in conflict with a provision of the *Code*, the national requirement should be followed.

When a professional accountant performs services in a country other than his or her home country, an important question is which ethical requirements (the IFAC *Code,* the country where the services are applied, or the home country) apply? In this situation, the professional accountant should refer to Section 6 below on "Cross-Border Activities."

Objectives of the *Code*

The objectives apply to all professional accountants, whether they are in public practice, industry, commerce, the public sector, or education. However, the objectives are not used to solve specific ethical problems.

To achieve the highest standards of professionalism, professional accountants should adhere to the following objectives:

- *Credibility*
  In the whole of society there is a need for credibility in information and information systems.

- *Professionalism*
  There is a need for individuals who can be clearly identified by clients, employers and other interested parties as professional persons in the accountancy field.

- *Quality of Service*
  There is a need for assurance that all services obtained from a professional accountant are carried out to the highest standards of performance.

- *Confidence*
  Users of the services of professional accountants should be able to feel confident that there exists a framework of professional ethics that governs the provision of those services.

Fundamental Principles of Ethics

The fundamental principles apply to all professional accountants, whether they are in public practice, industry, commerce, the public sector, or education. Like the objectives, the fundamental principles are not used to solve specific ethical problems. The fundamental principles are

- *Integrity*

  A professional accountant should be straightforward and honest in performing professional services.[4]

- *Objectivity*

  A professional accountant should be fair and should not allow prejudice or bias, conflict of interest or influence of others to override objectivity.

- *Professional Competence and Due Care*

  A professional accountant should perform professional services with due care, competence and diligence, and has a continuing duty to maintain professional knowledge and skill at a level required to ensure that a client or employer receives the advantage of competent professional service based on up-to-date developments in practice, legislation, and techniques

- *Confidentiality*

  A professional accountant should respect the confidentiality of information acquired during the course of performing professional services and should not use or disclose any such information without proper and specific authority or unless there is a legal or professional right or duty to disclose.

- *Professional Behavior*

  A professional accountant should act in a manner consistent with the good reputation of the profession and refrain from any conduct that might bring discredit to the profession.

- *Technical Standards*

  A professional accountant should carry out professional services in accordance with the relevant technical and professional standards. Professional accountants have a duty to carry out with care and skill, the instructions of the client or employer insofar as they are compatible with the requirements of integrity, objectivity and, in the case of professional accountants in public practice, independence. In addition, they

---

[4] *Professional service includes any service performed by a professional accountant that requires accountancy or related skills, including accounting, auditing, tax, consulting, and financial management services.*

should conform with the technical and professional standards promulgated by

- IFAC (for example, International Standards of Auditing),
- International Accounting Standards Committee,
- The member's professional body or other regulatory body, and
- Relevant legislation.

Organization of the Code

The *Code* is divided into three parts

- Part A applies to all professional accountants unless otherwise specified. Part A contains the following seven sections.

  1. Integrity and Objectivity
  2. Resolution of Ethical Conflicts
  3. Professional Competence
  4. Confidentiality
  5. Tax Practice
  6. Cross-Border Activities
  7. Publicity

- Part B applies only to those accountants in public practice. Part B contains the following seven sections.

  1. Independence
  2. Professional Competence and Responsibilities Regarding the Use of Nonaccountants
  3. Fees and Commission
  4. Activities Incompatible with the Practice of Public Accountancy
  5. Clients' Monies
  6. Relations with Other Professional Accountants in Public Practice
  7. Advertising and Solicitation

- Part C applies to employed professional accountants and may also apply, in appropriate circumstances, to accountants employed in public practice. Part C contains the following four sections.

  1. Conflict of Loyalties
  2. Support for Professional Colleagues
  3. Professional Competence (of Employed Professional Accountants)
  4. Presentation of Information

**Important
Definitions**

Auditor--This term is used and highlighted throughout the following discussion to refer to

1. All individuals performing services requiring independence.
2. All partners and proprietors in practice.
3. All professional employees working on the engagement.
4. All managerial employees located in an office participating in a significant part of the engagement.

Audit Firm or Practice--These terms refer to a sole practitioner, a partnership or a corporation of professional accountants that offer professional services to the public.

Professional Accountant--A term that includes those persons in public practice (a sole practitioner, partnership, or corporate entity), industry, commerce, the public sector or education.

Professional Accountant in Public Practice--A term that includes each partner or person occupying an equivalent or similar position, and each employee in a practice that provides **audit**, tax, or consulting services to a client. The term also includes professional accountants having managerial responsibilities in public practice.

Part A: Applicable to all Professional Accountants (including auditors, persons in industry, commerce, the public sector, and education)

Section 1

Integrity and Objectivity

All professional accountants/**auditors** must have integrity and objectivity. Integrity includes intellectual honesty, fair dealing, truthfulness, and freedom from conflicts of interest.

All professional accountants/**auditors** should avoid relationships that allow prejudice, bias, or other influences to override objectivity.

Professional accountants/**auditors** should neither accept nor offer gifts or entertainment that might reasonably be believed to have a significant and improper influence on professional judgment. What constitutes an excessive gift or entertainment varies from country to country, but professional accountants/**auditors** should avoid circumstances that would bring their professional reputation into dispute. **Auditors** should also refer to Section 8, *Acceptance of Goods, Services, and Gifts.*

Section 2

Resolution of Ethical Conflicts

Professional accountants/**auditors** should be constantly conscious of and be alert to factors that give rise to conflicts of interest. Examples of factors that give rise to conflicts of interest include

- A professional accountant **or auditor** may be asked to act contrary to technical or professional standards.
- A question of divided loyalty between the professional accountant's **or auditor's** superior and the required professional standards of conduct could occur.

Professional accountants/**auditors** should refer to Section 15 for guidance on how to resolve a conflict of interest matter.

Section 3

**Professional
Competence[5]**

Professional accountants/**auditors** should not portray themselves as having expertise or experience that they do not possess. Maintenance of professional competence requires that professional accountants/**auditors** have a continuing awareness of developments in the accounting profession, including relevant national and international pronouncements on accounting, auditing, and other relevant regulations and statutory requirements. In addition, the **auditor's** firm should adopt a quality control program.

Section 4

Confidentiality

Confidentiality covers (a) disclosure of information and (b) use (including the appearance of use) of information for personal advantage or for the advantage of another. Confidentiality does not apply to disclosure of information that is required to be disclosed by professional standards. Also, statute and common law govern confidentiality; therefore, its application is dependent on national or local law.

Professional accountants/**auditors** must respect the confidentiality of client or employer information. The duty of confidentiality continues even after the client/employer relationship with the accountant/**auditor** has ended.

The accountant/**auditor** should uphold the duty of confidentiality unless

1. The client/employer has given his or her permission to disclose the information.
2. There is a legal duty (for example, to disclose a violation of law to appropriate authorities) or a professional duty (for example, to comply with technical standards and ethical requirements, or to comply with quality review requirements of a national body) to disclose.

---

[5] *IFAC recommends that each member who is active as an accounting professional should participate in a minimum of thirty hours per year, or a minimum of ninety hours for every three-year period, of structured learning.*

Professional accountants/**auditors** are obligated to ensure that assistants under their control, and individuals that they have consulted with, adhere to confidentiality.

After deciding that confidential information should be disclosed but before disclosing such information, the professional accountant/**auditor** should consider

- Whether the information is based on known and substantiated facts.
- The appropriate recipients of the information.
- The legal consequences of disclosing the information.

Finally, the professional accountant/**auditor** should consider the need to consult with legal counsel and the relevant national professional body.

Section 5

Tax Practice

A professional accountant should follow the following principles in rendering tax services. A professional accountant (an **auditor** may also provide tax advice and prepare the tax return in addition to performing the audit of the client's financial statements)

1. Is entitled to advocate or advance the best position of the client or the employer.[6]
2. Should resolve doubt when there is reasonable support for the position in favor of the client or the employer.
3. Should make sure that the client or the employer is aware of the limitations of the tax advice and tax treatment.
4. Should not indicate to the client or the employer that the tax return preparation or advice given is beyond challenge.
5. Should advise the client or employer that they are responsible for the tax return.
6. Should record material advice given to a client or an employer in a letter or in a memorandum to the files.
7. Should not be associated with any tax return or related communication that

   a. Contains a false or misleading statement.

[6] *The term "client" applies to the professional accountant in public practice; whereas, the term "employer" applies to the employer of the employee professional accountant in industry, commerce, the public sector, or education.*

      b.   Contains statements or information that was furnished recklessly or without any knowledge of whether such information is true or false.

      c.   Omits or obscures information required to be submitted to tax authorities.

8. May use estimates in a tax return when such use is generally accepted or it is not practical to obtain exact data. When estimates are used, they should be

      a.   Presented as estimates.

      b.   Reasonable under the circumstances.

9. Should ordinarily rely on information furnished by the client or the employer if such information appears reasonable. However, where appropriate, encourage supporting data to be provided. In addition, the professional accountant should

      a.   Use the client's or the employer's prior years' returns when feasible.

      b.   Make inquiries when the information appears to be incorrect or incomplete.

      c.   Reference the books and records of the client or the employer.

10. Should promptly advise the client or the employer of any material errors or omissions in a tax return of a prior year or of a failure to file a required tax return. (The professional accountant has this responsibility even if he or she was not associated with the tax return of a prior year. However, the professional accountant is not obligated to inform the revenue authorities and should not do so without client or employer permission.)

11. If the client or the employer does not correct the matter in 10. above, should inform the client or the employer that the professional accountant cannot act for them in connection with the tax return or other related information. Also, consider whether continued association with the client or the employer is consistent with professional standards. (National or local requirements may require the professional accountant to inform the revenue authorities of this decision.)

Section 6

**Cross-Border
Activities**

When a professional accountant/**auditor** (a) performs services outside of his or her home country and (b) the ethical requirements of the two countries differ, the professional accountant/**auditor** should follow the **most demanding** standards considering:

1. IFAC's *Code.*
2. The ethical requirements of the other country.
3. The ethical requirements of the home country, **but only if they are required to be followed for services performed outside the home country.**

Section 7

Publicity

In marketing and promotion, professional accountants/**auditors** should not

1. Use means that bring the professional into disrepute.
2. Make exaggerated claims for the services that they provide, their qualifications, or their experiences.
3. Denigrate the work of other accountants.

Part B: Applicable to Professional Accountants in Public Practice (includes audit, tax, and consulting partners and persons occupying equivalent or similar positions, and each employee providing professional audit, tax, or consulting services)

Section 8

Independence

Auditors when undertaking an engagement that involves the expression on an opinion on financial information:

1. Should be independent (independence in fact), and
2. Should appear to be independent (independence in appearance).

Financial Involvement with, or in the Affairs of, Clients

If the **auditor** has any of the following involvements, he or she is not independent.

1. A direct financial interest in a client, including its parent, subsidiaries, and affiliates.
2. An indirect material financial interest in a client, for example, by being a trustee of any trust or executor or administrator of any estate if such trust or estate has a financial interest in a client.
3. Loans to or from the client or any officer, director, or principal shareholder of a client.
4. A financial interest in a joint venture with a client or employee(s) of a client.
5. A financial interest in a nonclient that has an investor or investee relationship with the client (as described below).

A. Direct and Indirect Financial Interests

The **auditor** is not independent if he or she has acquired, or is committed to acquire, a direct or indirect material financial interest in a client. A direct financial interest includes an interest held by the spouse or dependent child of the **auditor**. In some countries, the prohibition may extent to other close relatives.

For indirect financial interests of a trustee or estate, the materiality of the financial interest is paramount. That is, the shareholdings, if material to the size of the issued share capital of the client or if material to the total assets of the trust or estate, would impair the **auditor's** independent. The prohibition also covers situations when the **auditor's** spouse or dependent child serves as trustee, executor, or administrator of a trust or an estate.

If a direct or indirect financial interest is involuntarily acquired by inheritance, marriage, or by a merger or acquisition, the **auditor** should dispose of the interest at the earliest practicable date to avoid a loss of independence.

B. Loans to or from Clients

The **auditor** should not make a loan to a client or guarantee a client's debt or accept a loan from a client or a guarantee of the **auditor's** debt. However, (1) loans to or from banks or other similar financial institutions when made under normal lending procedures, terms, and requirements, (2) home mortgages, and (3) deposit accounts with banks and other similar financial institutions are excluded. The prohibition also covers loans and guarantees to or from clients and the **auditor's** spouse or dependent child.

C. Investor[7]--Investee[8] Relationships

Company A (an investor and a client) has a material investment in Company B (an investee and a nonclient). If the **auditor** has any direct or indirect material financial interest in Company B, he or she is not independent with respect to Company A.

Company X (an investor and a nonclient) has a material investment in Company Z (an investee and a client). If the **auditor** has any direct or indirect material financial interest in Company X, he or she is not independent with respect to Company Z.

D. Client--Nonclient Joint Ventures

Company G (a client) and Company T (a nonclient) have a joint venture--Company S. If the **auditor** has an immaterial financial interest in Company T, his or her independence would not be impaired with respect to Company G provided that the **auditor** could not significantly influence Company T.

Appointments in Companies

The **auditor** is not independent if, during the period under audit or immediately preceding an assignment, he or she was

---

[7] *An "investor" is a parent, general partner, or natural person or corporation that has the ability to significantly influence an investee*

[8] *An "investee" is a subsidiary or an entity subject to the significant influence of an investor.*

1. A member of the board, an officer, or an employee of the client.
2. A partner or an employee of a member of the board, an officer, or an employee of the client.

The *Code* suggests that the period "immediately preceding an assignment" should not be less than two years or as required by legislation.

Provision of Other Services to **Audit** Clients

The **auditor's** independence is not impaired by providing advisory services (accounting services, consulting, and tax services) to audit clients, provided there is no involvement in or responsibility assumed for management decisions.

The **auditor** may also prepare accounting records and financial statements (a frequently requested service in small client entities) and maintain his or her independence by observing the following requirements:

1. Do not have any relationship or combination of relationships with the client or any conflict of interest that would impair integrity or independence.
2. The client must accept responsibility for the financial statements.
3. Do not assume the role of employee or of management conducting client operations.
4. Do not eliminate the need to perform audit tests because of the work done preparing accounting records.

Ideally, the staff assistants assigned to the preparation of accounting records should not participate in the audit.

Personal and Family Relationships

If an **auditor,** who is a sole practitioner, partner, or an employee engaged on the assignment, is the spouse or dependent child of the client or a relative living in the client's common household, independence is impaired. In some countries, the range of relationships that impairs independence is wider. In fact, the *Code* indicates that it is up to each IFAC member body to determine what personal and family relationships impair independence.

Fees

If recurring total fees, coming from one client or group of connected clients, are the only or a substantial part of the **audit** firm's gross income, the **auditor** should carefully consider if independence is impaired. Likewise, if fees due from a client remain unpaid for an extended period, especially if prior year fees are not paid before the issuance of the current audit report, the **auditor's** independence may be impaired.

Allowances should be made for new **audit** firm practices and practices that are ceasing operations. Exemptions should also be made for the branch office of an **audit** firm where a given client's fees are a substantial part of the branch's fees. In the latter situation, a partner from another office should review the **audit**.

Contingent Fees

Professional services should not be provided to an **audit**, tax, or consulting client under a contingent fee arrangement in which no fee will be charged unless a specified finding or result is obtained. However, fees are not contingent if a court or other public authority fixes them. In countries where contingent fees are permitted by statute or by an IFAC member body, contingent fee engagements should be limited to those engagement where independence is not required (for example, tax services work would be an acceptable contingent fee arrangement, but a contingent fee **audit** engagement would not be acceptable).

Acceptance of Goods, Services, and Gifts

Professional accountants in public practice/**auditors** and their spouses and dependent children should not accept goods and services except on business terms available to others. Likewise, undue hospitality and gifts that are not commensurate with normal courtesies should not be accepted.

Ownership of Capital and Voting Rights

Ideally, a firm's capital should be owned entirely by professional accountants in public practice/**auditors**. However, others may own a portion of a firm's capital provided that professional accountants in public practice own the majority of capital and voting rights.

Former Partners

A partner in a firm may leave the firm and accept an appointment with an **audit** client. The firm may maintain its independence if the following conditions are met:

1. Payments made to the former partner for his or her interest and for any unfunded vested retirement benefits are fixed as to dates and amounts.
2. The payments in l. above do not cause substantial doubt about the firm's ability to continue as a going concern.
3. The former partner does not participate or appear to participate in the firm's business or professional activities. (The provision of office space to the former partner constitutes an appearance to participate.)

Actual or Threatened Litigation

Litigation involving the professional accountant in public practice/**auditor** and the client may impair the accountant's/**auditor's** independence and objectivity. The commencement or threat of litigation (1) by a client against the accountant/**auditor**, (2) by the accountant/**auditor** against the client alleging fraud or deceit by the client's officers, (3) or by others alleging substandard **audit** performance impairs independence. In these situations, the **auditor's** ability to report fairly and impartially on the client's financial statements and the willingness of the client to disclose information to the **auditor** may be affected. The *Code* recognizes that it not possible to specify precisely the point where it is improper for the **auditor** to report; therefore, the **auditor** should consider the circumstances from an independence-in-appearance perspective.

*Long Association of Senior Personnel with **Audit** Clients*

Long involvement of a senior **auditor** with an **audit** client could be perceived as a threat to objectivity and independence; therefore, the **audit** firm should provide for rotation of senior **auditors** serving the client. When not practical, review procedures or external-consulting arrangements should be established to guard against any reduction in objectivity and independence.

Section 9

Professional Competence and Responsibilities Regarding the Use of Nonaccountants	Professional accountants in public practice/**auditors** should refrain from agreeing to perform services for which they are not competent unless competent advice and assistance are obtained. Assistance may be obtained from experts such as other accountants, lawyers, actuaries, engineers, geologists, valuation specialists. When using these other experts, the professional accountant must take steps to see that such experts are aware of the fundamental ethical principles (see page 2). In supervising these experts, the professional accountant may

1. Ask the experts to read the appropriate ethical codes.
2. Require written confirmation of the experts' understanding of the ethical requirements.
3. Provide consultation when potential conflicts arise.

If the professional accountant is not satisfied that the ethical requirements will be followed, the engagement should not be accepted or, if in process, terminated.

Section 10

Fees and Commissions	*Professional Fees*

The fees that professional accountants in public practice/**auditors** charge should reflect the value of the services performed. In determining the fees to be charged, the professional accountant in public practice/**auditor** should consider the

1. Skill and knowledge required for the service.
2. Level of training and experience needed.
3. Time spent or to be spent.
4. Degree of responsibility required.

A professional accountant in public practice/**auditor** should not quote a fee for current or future services when it is likely at the time of making the quote that such fee will be substantially increased.

The professional accountant in public practice/**auditor** in quoting a fee should be satisfied that the fee provides for

1. Performing quality work.

2. Using due care to comply with all professional standards and quality control procedures.

The professional accountant in public practice/**auditor** should also be satisfied that the client is not misled about the scope of services that will be provided and the basis for charging future fees.

The professional accountant is public practice/**auditor** should make sure that the client understands the basis on which fees are calculated and the billing arrangements. This understanding should be obtained before the commencement of the engagement. Preferably, the understanding should be in writing.

Commissions

A professional accountant in public practice/**auditor** should not pay a commission to obtain a client or accept a commission for referral of a client, including payment and receipt of fees between professional accountants when no services are performed.

In addition, a professional accountant in public practice/**auditor** should not accept a commission for the referral of products or services of others.

In countries where commissions are permitted either by statute or member body, such arrangements should be limited to engagements not requiring independence. For engagements where commissions are acceptable, the professional accountant in public practice should disclose the commission to the client.

Arrangements for the purchase of an accounting practice, or portions thereof, are not considered to be commissions.

Section 11

Activities Incompatible with the Practice of Public Accountancy

A professional accountant in public practice/**auditor** should not concurrently engage in any business, occupation, or activity that impairs integrity, objectivity, independence, or the reputation of the profession.

Also, the simultaneous engagement in another business, occupation, or activity that does not allow the delivery of professional services in accordance with the fundamental ethical principles is inconsistent with the practice of public accountancy.

Section 12

Clients' Monies[9]

In some countries national law does not permit a professional accountant in public practice/**auditor** to hold clients' monies. Where it is permitted, the professional accountant in public practice/**auditor** should not hold clients' monies if he or she believes that such monies were obtained from, or are to be used in, illegal activities.

When holding clients' monies, the professional accountant in public practice/**auditor** should

1. Keep such monies in one (a general clients' monies account) or more bank accounts, separately from personal or firm monies.
2. Deposit such monies without delay to the appropriate bank account.
3. Place such monies in an interest-bearing account with the concurrence of the client within a reasonable time if it is likely that monies will remain in the account for a significant period of time.
4. Draw from the client bank account only on the instructions of the client.
5. Use such monies only for the purpose for which they are intended.
6. Pay firm fees due from a client from the bank account only after notifying the client of the amount and the client agrees to the withdrawal.
7. Credit all interest earned on clients' monies to client accounts.
8. At all times, be ready to account for clients' monies to the client.
9. Provide a statement of account to the client at least once a year.
10. Safeguard documents that can be converted to money against unauthorized use.

---

[9] *Clients' monies are defined as any monies, including document of title to money or documents that can be converted to money such as bills of exchange, promissory notes, or bearer bonds, received by a professional accountant in public practice/**auditor** to be held or paid out according to client instructions.*

Section 13

Relations with Other Professional Accountants in Public Practice

Accepting New Assignments

There are three ways a receiving accountant/**auditor**[10] may be involved in accepting new assignments in this section

1. The client's business expansion results in branches or subsidiary companies at locations where an existing accountant/**auditor**[11] does not practice and the existing accountant/**auditor** in consultation with the client or the client requests a receiving accountant/**auditor** to perform work at such locations.
2. The client needs special services or skills that the existing accountant/**auditor** does not have and the existing accountant/**auditor** in consultation with the client or the client requests a receiving accountant/**auditor** to perform such specialized services.
3. The client request a receiving accountant's/**auditor's** opinion (a second opinion) on the application of an accounting principle or an **audit** or reporting matter relative to specific circumstances or transactions.

In each of the three situations above, there is an assumption that the existing accountant/**auditor** will continue to provide existing professional services to the client. In these three situations, the receiving accountant/**auditor** should

1. When asked to provide services or advice, make inquiries as to whether the potential client has an existing accountant/**auditor**.
2. Limit the services provided to the specific referral from the existing accountant/**auditor** or the client unless otherwise requested by the client.
3. Support the existing accountant's/**auditor's** current relationship with the client.
4. Do not express any criticism of the professional services of the existing accountant/**auditor**.

---

[10] *A receiving accountant/**auditor** is a professional accountant in public practice/**auditor** to whom the client's existing accountant/**auditor** or the client has referred **audit**, accounting, tax, consulting, or similar appointments.*

[11] *An existing accountant/**auditor** is a professional accountant in public practice/**auditor** who currently holds an **audit**, accounting, tax, consulting, or similar appointment with a client.*

5. Regard a request from the client for services that are clearly distinct from the services being provided by the existing accountant/**auditor** or that are clearly distinct from the initial referral request for services as a separate request to provide services or advice.

6. Before accepting an assignment in 5 above, advise the client of the obligation to immediately communicate, preferably in writing, with the existing accountant/**auditor** to advise the existing accountant/**auditor** of the client's request and to ask for all relevant information, if any, needed to perform the assignment.

7. If the client insists that the communication in 6 above not be made, decide whether the client's reasons are valid (a mere disinclination by the client for the communication is not a satisfactory reason). For situations involving second opinions, there is a requirement for communication with the existing accountant/**auditor** in order for the receiving accountant/**auditor** to obtain a full understanding of the facts and circumstances. In addition, the receiving accountant/**auditor**, with the client's permission, is required to provide a copy of the final report to the existing accountant/**auditor**. If the client does not agree to these communications, the assignment should not be accepted.

8. Comply with the instructions received from the existing accountant/**auditor** or the client unless they conflict with relevant legal or other requirements.

9. Keep the existing accountant/**auditor** informed of the general nature of the services being performed.

In the three new assignment situations above, the existing accountant/**auditor** should maintain contact with the receiving accountant/**auditor** and cooperate with and assist them.

*Superseding Another Professional Accountant/**Auditor** in Public Practice*

Before accepting an appointment involving recurring professional services (**audit**, accounting, tax, consulting, or other), the proposed accountant/**auditor** should

1. Ascertain if the prospective client has advised the existing accountant/**auditor** of the proposed change.

2. Ascertain if the prospective client has given the existing accountant/**auditor** permission, preferably in writing, to discuss the client's affairs fully and freely.

3. Request permission from the prospective client to communicate with the existing accountant/**auditor**. If not permitted to communicate with the existing accountant/**auditor**, in absence of exceptional circumstances or obtaining the necessary facts by other means, decline the appointment.

4. Ask the existing accountant/**auditor**, preferably in writing, to

   a. Provide information about matters that are important in deciding whether to accept the appointment. (Unpaid fees do not preclude acceptance of the appointment.

   b. Provide all the necessary details needed to make a decision about acceptance.

5. If a response from the existing accountant/**auditor** is not received and there is no knowledge of exceptional circumstances about the engagement, communicate with the existing accountant/**auditor** by other means.

6. If information is not received from 5 above, send a letter to the existing accountant/**auditor**, stating an assumption that there is no professional reason why the appointment should not be accepted and that there is an intention to accept the appointment.

In situations where competitive bids are used, the accountant/**auditor** submitting a bid or tender should state in the submission that if the appointment results in the replacement of an existing accountant/**auditor**, acceptance of the appointment is contingent on performing the six steps above.

In responding to the proposed accountant/**auditor**, the existing accountant/**auditor** should

1. Ensure that the client has given permission to respond fully and freely to the proposed accountant/**auditor**.

2. Reply, preferably in writing, identifying reasons, if any, why the proposed accountant/**auditor** should not accept the appointment. If permission in 1 above is denied, communicate that to the proposed accountant/**auditor**.

3. Disclose all information needed by the proposed accountant/**auditor** relevant to his or her decision to accept or not accept the appointment.

4. Promptly transfer to the new accountant/**auditor** all books and papers of the client unless there is a legal right to withhold such information.

Section 14

Advertising[12] and Solicitation[13]

Member bodies determine whether advertising and solicitation are permitted. When advertising and solicitation are permitted by a member body, it should be

1. Presented in an objective manner.
2. Decent, honest, and truthful.
3. In good taste.

It should not

1. Create false, deceptive or unjustified expectations.
2. Imply the ability to influence any court, tribunal, regulatory agency, or similar body.
3. Consist of self-laudatory statements that are not fact-based.
4. Make comparisons with other professional accountants in public practice/**auditors.**
5. Contain testimonials or endorsements.
6. Contain representations that or likely to cause a reasonable person to misunderstand or be deceived.
7. Make unjustified claims to be an expert or specialist.

A professional accountant in public practice/**auditor** in a country where advertising is permitted should not advertise in newspapers or magazines published or distributed in a country where advertising is prohibited. Likewise, a professional accountant in public practice/**auditor** in a country where advertising is prohibited should not advertise in newspapers or magazines published in a country where advertising is permitted.

*Publicity by Professional Accountants in Public Practice/**Auditors** in a Country Where Advertising Is Not Permitted*

In a country where advertising is not permitted, publicity is acceptable provided that it

1. Is not false, misleading, or deceptive.
2. Is in good taste.
3. Is professionally dignified.
4. Avoids frequent repetition of, and undue prominence being given to, the name of the accountant/**auditor**.

---

[12] *Advertising is defined as the communication of information to the public about the services or skills provided by professional accountants in public practice/**auditors** with the objective of obtaining professional business.*

[13] *Solicitation is defined as an approach to a potential client for the purpose of obtaining professional business.*

The following topics discuss acceptable and unacceptable publicity in those countries where advertising is not permitted.

Appointments and Awards--These items should receive publicity, but the accountant/**auditor** should not make use of such opportunities for personal professional advantage.

Newspaper and Magazine Announcements--Such announcements may be used to inform the public of a new practice, partnership personnel changes, and address changes provided that they are limited to bare facts and that consideration is given to the area of distribution of the medium.

Seeking Employment or Professional Business--An accountant/**auditor** may use any medium to seek employment or a partnership. However, an accountant /**auditor**

1. May not publicize for subcontract work in a manner that seeks to procure professional business.
2. May publicize for subcontract work in the professional press but should omit his or her name, address, and telephone number.
3. May write a letter or make a direct approach to another accountant/**auditor** when seeking employment or business.

Directories (Non-Firm)--A professional accountant in public practice/**auditor** may be listed in a directory if the directory or the entry therein is not considered an advertisement. Entries should be limited to name, address, telephone number, professional description and other information needed to enable a user to contact the person or organization.

Brochures and Firm Directories--An accountant/**auditor** may issue these items to clients or others that request them provided that the brochure or firm directory

1. Is a factually and objectively worded account of services provided.
2. Contains only names of partners, office addresses, and names and addresses of associated firms and correspondents.

Books, Articles, Interviews, Lectures, Radio and Television Appearances--Accountants /**auditors** when engaged in any of these activities on professional subjects may state their name, professional qualifications, and the name of their firm. However, they should not identify the services that their firm provides.

Training Courses, Seminars, etc.--Accountants/**auditors** may invite clients, staff, or other professional accountants to their training courses or seminars. However, other persons should not be invited unless their request to attend is unsolicited.

Booklets and Documents Containing Technical Information--These items bearing the name of the accountant/**auditor** may be issued to staff, clients, other professional accountants, and others that request the information.

Stationery and Nameplates--These items should comply with the requirements of national law and requirements of the member body. They should not, however, list services provided or the firm's specialization.

Staff Recruitment--Staff vacancies may be communicated to the public through any medium where such items normally appear. The announcement may present details as to services provided to clients but it should not contain promotional elements. Moreover, the announcement should not contain any suggestion that the firm's services are superior to other firms as a consequence of size, associations, or other reasons. More latitude is available in a section of the medium devoted to vacancies than elsewhere in that medium.

Publicity on Behalf of Clients--Accountants/**auditors** may publicize staff vacancies on behalf of clients provided the announcement is for the client.

Inclusion of the Accountant's/Auditor's Name in a Document Issued by a Client--When clients publish documents that contain the accountant's/**auditor's** name, the accountant/**auditor** should advise the client that his or her permission must be obtained before the document is published. This requirement protects the public from being misled. The same consideration applies when the accountant/ **auditor** holds an office in a private capacity in an organization (for example, a charitable organization). That is, the accountant/**auditor** should ensure that the public is not misled to believe that his or her association is that of an independent **auditor**.

Part C: Applicable to Employed Professional Accountants[14] (applies, when applicable, to auditors)

Section 15

Conflict of Loyalties to Employers and the Profession	An employed professional accountant, **including an auditor**, cannot be required to

1. Break the law.
2. Breach the rules and standards of the profession.
3. Put their name on, or be associated with, a statement that materially misrepresents facts.

Furthermore, an employed professional accountant cannot lie to or mislead **auditors**, including misleading by keeping silent.

Differences in views between an employed professional accountant and the employer entity about accounting or ethical matters should be resolved within the entity according to the entity's policy. If following such policy does not resolve the matter, the employed professional accountant should discuss the matter with his or her immediate supervisor (unless the supervisor is involved in the matter), and if still not resolved, with higher levels of management or nonexecutive directors. If the matter cannot be resolved, the employed professional accountant may have no other course of action but to consider resigning. The employed professional accountant should communicate his or her reasons for resigning in an information memorandum to the entity but not to others unless legally or professionally required to do so.

Section 16

Support for Professional Colleagues	An employed professional accountant, **including an auditor**, having authority over others should deal with differences of opinion in a professional manner.

[14] *A professional accountant employed in industry, commerce, the public sector, or education.*

Section 17

Professional Competence (of Employed Professional Accountants)	An employed professional accountant should not mislead the employer as to his or her expertise or experience when undertaking significant tasks for which the employed professional accountant has not had sufficient training or experience. In addition, the employed professional accountant should seek appropriate expert advice and assistance.

Section 18

Presentation of Information	An employed professional accountant/**auditor** should present financial information fully, honestly, and professionally so that users can understand in its context.
	An employed professional accountant should maintain financial and nonfinancial information in a manner that describes clearly the true nature of transactions, assets or liabilities. A professional accountant should also record entries in a timely and proper manner.

37 WHERE TO GO FOR MORE INFORMATION

Introduction

A member may have additional questions about how to apply ethics guidance that are not addressed in this book. He or she will then need to do additional research or know where to go to ask questions.

Guidance Within a Member's Firm

A member's firm may have

- Ethics/independence policies tailored for the firm. Such policies may be more restrictive than AICPA, SEC, ISB, state society or state board requirements.
- An individual responsible for ethics matters in an office, region or line of service.
- Materials on ethics in the firm's library (electronic or paper-based).
- An independence system or database. This system or database usually contains information on the firm's clients (e.g., a restricted client list) so that members of the firm can monitor their compliance with independence requirements.

A member should always check his or her firm's policy first on how to deal with ethics questions. If additional research is needed, the following are sources of information.

AICPA

The AICPA's *Code of Professional Conduct* is reproduced at www.aicpa.org/about/code/index.htm.

For questions, call the AICPA's Professional Ethics Team at 1-888-777-7077 (or e-mail to ethics@aicpa.org).

Inquiries can also be submitted in writing to

> Professional Ethics Team
> American Institute of Certified Public Accountants
> Harborside Financial Center
> 201 Plaza Three
> Jersey City, NJ 07311

SECPS

For the AICPA's SEC Practice Section (SECPS) Independence Quality Controls, go to www.aicpa.org/members/div/secps/inmerefinal.htm.

For questions, call the AICPA's SECPS staff at 1-888-777-7077.

For the SECP's restrictions on consulting services, see item h. of the SECPs's *Requirements of Members* at www.aicpa.org/members/div/secps/require.htm (see Chapter 13 for additional information on these restrictions).

Independence Standards Board

The ISB materials are reproduced at www.cpaindependence.org.

The ISB staff answers questions about independence issues for **publicly-held entities** on a formal or informal basis.

- Formal inquiries must be submitted in writing. They result in written staff interpretations that are authoritative guidance for the requesting party when dealing with the SEC. If the staff interpretation is then ratified by the ISB Board, it becomes authoritative guidance for all registrants and auditors.

  - To submit a formal written inquiry online, go to www.cpaindependence.org and click on "Request Interpretation."
  - Formal written inquiries can also be sent to

    > The Independence Standards Board
    > 1211 Avenue of the Americas
    > New York, New York 10036

- Informal inquiries are made by calling 1-212-596-6133 or by going to www.cpaindependence.org and clicking on "Contact Us."

SEC	Guidance on independence can be found in Rule 2-01 of Regulation S-X. Contact publishers such as CCH at www.cch.com or RIA at www.riahome.com.

The SEC's no-action letters can be found in publications such as

> *SEC No-Action Letters*, published by CCH, Incorporated. For more information, go to www.cch.com
>
> *Analysis of Key SEC No-Action Letters* by Robert J. Haft, 1999-2000 edition, West Group, St. Paul, MN.

For questions about the SEC's independence rules, contact the ISB.

The SEC's website contains additional information on contacting the SEC staff. Go to www.sec.gov and click on "About SEC." Electronic mailboxes are found at www.sec.gov/asec/mailboxs.htm. Addresses are found at www.sec.gov/asec/secaddr.htm.

Department of Labor

DOL Regulation 2509.75-9, *Interpretive Bulletin Relating to Guidelines on Independence of Accountant Retained by Employee Benefit Plan*, is at (www.dol.gov/dol/allcfr/Title_29/Part_2509/29CFR2509.75-9.htm).

Questions should be addressed to the Office of Chief Accountant Help Desk at 202-219-8770.

GAO

The GAO's Yellow Book requirements are at www.gao.gov/govaud/ybhtml/index.html.

For questions on the independence requirements of the Yellow Book, contact the Project Manager for Government Auditing Standards at 202-512-9535 or e-mail to yellowbook@gao.gov.

FDIC

Information about the Federal Deposit Insurance Corporation's (FDIC) rules and regulations can be found at www.fdic.gov/regulations/laws/rules/2000-8500.html#2000part363.

APPENDIX A
GLOSSARY

Affiliates--Construed broadly, affiliates include persons associated with the client in a decision-making capacity such as officers, directors, and substantial stockholders, as well as entities that, directly or indirectly, control, are controlled by, or are under common control with the client. An example might be either a subsidiary or a parent company.

Alternative Practice Structures (APS)--A nontraditional structure for the practice of public accounting in which a traditional CPA firm engaged in auditing and other attestation services might be closely aligned with another organization, public or private, that performs other professional services (e.g., tax and consulting).

American Institute of Certified Public Accountants (AICPA)--The national professional organization for all certified public accountants (CPAs).

Audit sensitive position--A position is audit-sensitive (even though not of "significant influence"), if the person's activities are (1) an element of, or (2) subject to, significant controls over financial reporting.

Client's records--Any accounting or other records belonging to the client that were given to the member by, or on behalf of, the client.

Close relative--Close relatives are the member's nondependent children (including grandchildren and stepchildren), brothers and sisters, grandparents, parents, and parents-in-law. Spouses of any of the above are also close relatives. The SEC definition of close relatives expands the above to include a spouse's brothers and sisters and their spouses.

Code of Professional Conduct (the Code)--The Code was adopted by the membership of the AICPA to provide guidance and rules to all members on various ethics requirement. The Code consists of (1) Principles, (2) Rules, (3) Interpretations, and (4) Ethics Rulings.

Conflict of interest--A conflict of interest may occur if a member performs a professional service for a client or employer, and the member or his or her firm has a relationship with another person, entity, product, or service that could, in the member's professional judgment, be viewed by the client, employer, or other appropriate parties as impairing the member's objectivity.

Consulting process--The analytical approach applied in performing a consulting service. The process typically involved some combination of the following:

- Determining the client's objective
- Fact-finding
- Defining problems or opportunities
- Evaluating alternatives
- Formulating proposed actions
- Communicating results
- Implementing
- Following up

Consulting services--Professional services that use the practitioner's technical skills, education, observations, experiences, and knowledge of the consulting process.

Consulting services practitioner--Any AICPA member holding out as a CPA while performing consulting services for a client, or any other individual performing consulting services for a client for an AICPA member or member's firm holding out as a CPA.

Contingent fee--A fee for performing any service in which the amount of the fee (or whether a fee will be paid) depends on the results of the service.

Council--The Council of the American Institute of Certified Public Accountants.

Direct financial interest--A direct financial interest is created when a member invests in a client entity.

Disqualifying services--Term used to refer to the following services, which when performed for a client prohibit the member form accepting a contingent fee or commission:

- a. An audit or a review of a financial statement.
- b. An examination of prospective financial information.
- c. A compilation of a financial statement expected to be used by third parties except when the compilation report discloses a lack of independence.

See Chapter 29 on contingent fees and Chapter 32 on commissions.

Ethics Rulings--Part of the *Code of Professional Conduct*. Rulings summarize the application of rules and interpretations to a particular set of factual circumstances.

Firm--A form of organization permitted by state law or regulation whose characteristics conform to resolutions of Council that is engaged in the practice of public accounting, including the individual owners thereof.

Former practitioner--A proprietor, partner, shareholder or equivalent of a firm, who leaves by resignation, termination, retirement, or sale of all or part of the practice.

Holding out as a CPA--Includes any action initiated by a member, whether or not in public practice, that informs others of his or her status as a CPA.

Indemnification agreement--A contract between two parties whereby one party agrees to compensate or reimburse a second party for certain losses or expenses incurred.

Independence in fact--To be *independent in fact* (mental independence), the CPA must have integrity and objectivity. If there is evidence that independence is actually lacking, the auditor is not independent in fact.

Independence in appearance--If there are circumstances that a reasonable person might believe are likely to impair independence, the CPA is not independent in appearance. To be **recognized** as independent, the auditor must be free from any obligation to or interest in the client, its management, or its owners.

Independence Issues Committee (IIC)--A committee of the ISB that is charged with assisting the ISB in establishing standards by identifying and discussing emerging independence issues within the framework of existing authoritative literature. Its members are drawn from SECPS member firms.

Independence Standards Board (ISB)--A standard-setting body designated by the AICPA and SEC to establish independence requirements for auditors of public companies. The ISB operates as an independent body, but is funded by the AICPA's SEC Practice Section of its Division for CPA Firms (SECPS). The ISB, as well as all other SECPS activities, operate under the general oversight of the Public Oversight Board (POB). (The POB's **Panel on Audit Effectiveness** has recommended that the ISB operate under the direct oversight of the POB.)

Indirect financial interest--An indirect financial interested is created when a member invests in a nonclient entity that has a financial interest in a client.

Integrity--An element of character fundamental to professional recognition. It is the quality from which public trust derives and the benchmark against which a member must ultimately test all decisions.

Internal audit outsourcing--Internal audit outsourcing involves performing audit procedures that are generally of the type considered to be extensions of audit scope applied in the audit of financial statements. Examples of such procedures might include confirming receivables, analyzing fluctuations in account balances, and testing and evaluating the effectiveness of controls.

Interpretations of rules of conduct--Part of the *Code of Professional Conduct*. Interpretations are pronouncements issued by the AICPA's Division of Professional Ethics to provide guidelines concerning the scope and application of the rules of conduct.

Investment club--A group of individuals who pool their money, select investments, and invest the pooled funds in the selected investment.

ISB--see Independence Standards Board.

JEEP--see Joint Ethics Enforcement Program.

Joint closely held business investment--An investment that is subject to control by the member, or the member's firm, client or its officers, directors, or principal stockholders, or any combination of the above.

Joint Ethics Enforcement Program (JEEP)--The AICPA and most state societies cooperate in the Joint Ethics Enforcement Program (JEEP) in bringing enforcement actions against their members.

Joint Trial Board--The Joint Trial Board hears cases referred by the ethics committee and recommends appropriate disciplinary, remedial, or corrective action.

Member--In its broadest sense, "member" is a term used to describe a member, associate member, or international associate of the AICPA. All members must adhere to the AICPA's *Code of Professional Conduct*. For the purposes of applying the independence rules, the term "member" identifies the people in a CPA firm and their spouses, dependent, and cohabitants who are subject to the independence requirements. The definition of member is discussed in detail in Chapter 8.

Multidisciplinary practices (MDP)--Arrangements in which CPAs share fees with attorneys or other professionals.

National Association of State Boards of Accountancy (NASBA)--A voluntary organization composed of the state boards of accountancy. It promotes communication, coordination, and uniformity among state boards.

Objectivity--The principle of objectivity imposes the obligation to be impartial, intellectually honest, and free of conflicts of interest. Objectivity is a state of mind, a quality that lends value to a member's services.

Office participating in a significant portion of the engagement--Offices include the office having primary client responsibility (i.e., the engagement office) for a multi-office engagement and depends on the significance of work performed relative to the overall engagement effort. (Guidance on assessing this significance is provided in Chapter 8.)

PEEC--see Professional Ethics Executive Committee.

Period of professional engagement--The period of engagement starts when the member begins the service requiring independence and ends upon termination of the relationship (by the member or the client) or, if later, when the report is issued. The period does not stop when the report is issued and restart with the beginning of the next engagement. The period of engagement typically covers many periods.

Practice of public accounting--According to the *Code of Professional Conduct,* the practice of public accounting consists of the performance for a client, by a member or a member's firm, while holding out as CPA(s), of the professional services of accounting, tax, personal financial planning, litigation support services, and those professional services for which standards are promulgated by bodies designated by Council, such as Statements of Financial Accounting Standards, Statements on Auditing Standards, Statements on Standards for Accounting and

Review Services, Statement on Standards for Consulting Services, Statements on Standards for Tax Services, Statements of Governmental Accounting Standards, and Statements on Standards for Attestation Engagements. However, a member or member's firm, while holding out as CPAs, is not considered to be in the practice of public accounting if the member or the member's firm does not perform, for any client, any of the professional services described in the preceding paragraph.

Principles--Positive statements of responsibility in the *Code of Professional Conduct* that provide the framework for the rules, which govern performance.

Professional Ethics Executive Committee (PEEC)--The AICPA's senior technical committee that promulgates professional ethics requirements. The objectives of the PEEC are to develop standards of ethics, promote understanding and voluntary compliance with such standards, establish and present changes of violations of the standards and the AICPA's bylaws to the Joint Trial Board for disciplinary action in cooperation with the State Societies under the Joint Ethics Enforcement Program (JEEP), improve the profession's enforcement procedures, coordinate the subcommittees of the Professional Ethics Division, and promote the efficiency and effectiveness of JEEP Program.

Professional services--Includes **all services** performed by a member while **holding out** as a CPA.

Rules--Broad but specific descriptions of conduct that would violate the responsibilities stated in the principles in the *Code of Professional Conduct.*

Securities and Exchange Commission (SEC)--A federal government regulatory agency with responsibility for administering the federal securities laws.

Significant influence--According to Accounting Principles Board Opinion No. 18, *The Equity Method of Accounting for Investments in Common Stock*, significant influence exists when the investor owns from 20-50% of the investee's voting shares, although circumstances exist where such influence is present with under 20% ownership, or conversely is absent with holdings of 20% or greater.

State boards of accoutancy--State government regulatory organizations. Each state government issues a license to practice within the particular state under that state's accountancy statute.

State societies of CPAs--Voluntary organizations of CPAs within each individual state.

Statements on Standards for Tax Services (SSTS)--SSTS superseded and replaced the AICPA's Statements on Responsibilities in Tax Practice (SRTP). They are enforceable standards of conduct for tax practice under the *Code of Professional Conduct.*

Unpaid fees--Fees for (1) audit and (2) other professional services that relate to certain prior periods that are delinquent as of the date the current year's audit engagement begins, if the client is an SEC registrant, or the date the audit report is issued for non-SEC clients (i.e., AICPA rule).

Yellow Book--*Governmental Auditing Standards* issued by the General Accounting Office.

APPENDIX B

HOW TO CONTACT THE STATE BOARDS AND STATE SOCIETIES

State	*State Board*	*State Society*
Alabama	Alabama State Board of Public Accountancy P.O. Box 300375 Montgomery, AL 36130-0375 Phone: 334-242-5700 Fax: 334-242-2711 No website	Alabama Society of CPAs 1103 South Perry Street Montgomery, AL 36103 Phone: 334-834-7650 or 800-227-1711 www.accpa.org
Alaska	Alaska State Board of Public Accountancy Dept. of Community and Economic Development Division of Occupational Licensing, Box 110806 Juneau, AK 99811 Phone: 907-465-3811 Fax: 907-465-2974 www.dced.state.ak.us/occ/pcpa.htm	Alaska Society of CPAs 341 W. Tudor Road, #105 Anchorage, Alaska 99503 Phone: 907-562-4334 or 800-478-4334 Fax: 907-562-4025 www.akcpa.org
Arizona	Arizona State Board of Accountancy 3877 North Seventh Street-106 Phoenix, AZ 85014 Phone: 602-255-3648 Fax: 602-255-1283 www.accountancy.state.az.us	Arizona Society of Certified Public Accountants 2120 North Central Avenue, Suite 100 Phoenix, AZ 85004 Phone: 602-252-4144 or 888-237-0700 (in Arizona) Fax: 602-252-1511 www.ascpa.com
Arkansas	Arkansas State Board of Accountancy 101 East Capitol, Suite 430 Little Rock, AR 72201 Phone: 501-682-1520 Fax: 501-682-5538 www.state.ar.us/asbpa	Arkansas Society of Certified Public Accountants 11300 Executive Center Drive Little Rock, AR 72211-4352 Phone: 501-664-8739 or 800-482-8739 (in Arkansas) Fax: 501-664-8320 www.arcpa.org

California

California Board of Accountancy
2000 Evergreen Street, Suite 250
Sacramento, CA 95815-3832
Phone: 916-263-3680
Fax: 916-263-3674
www.dca.ca.gov/cba

California Society of CPAs
1235 Radio Road
Redwood City, CA 94065-1217
Phone: 800-9CALCPA
www.calcpa.org

Colorado

Colorado State Board of Accountancy
1560 Broadway
Suite 1340
Denver, CO 80202
Phone: 303-894-7800
Fax: 303-894-7802
www.dora.state.co.us/accountants

Colorado Society of CPAs
7979 East Tufts Avenue, Suite 500
Denver, CO. 80237-2845
Phone: 303-773-2877 or
800-523-9082 (in Colorado)
www.cocpa.org

Connecticut

Connecticut State Board of Accountancy
Secretary of the State
30 Trinity Street, P.O. Box 150470
Hartford, CT 06115
Phone: 860-509-6179
Fax: 860-509-6247
www.sots.state.ct.us/SBOA/SBOAindex.html

Connecticut Society of Certified Public
  Accountants
845 Brook Street, Building 2
Rocky Hill, CT 06067-3405
Phone: 860-280-1100
Fax: 860-280-1101
www.cs-cpa.org

District of Columbia

District of Columbia Board of Accountancy
941 North Capitol Street, N.E.
Room 7200
Washington, DC 20002
Phone: 202-442-4461
Fax: 202-442-4528
www.dcra.org/acct/dcbahome.shtm

Greater Washington Society of CPAs
1023 15th Street, N.W., 8th Floor
Washington, DC 20005-2602
Phone: 202-789-1844
Fax: 202-789-1847
www.gwscpa.org

Delaware

Delaware State Board of Accountancy
Cannon Building, Suite 203
861 Silver Lake Blvd.
Dover, DE 19904
Phone: 302-739-4522
Fax: 302-739-2711
No website

Delaware Society of CPAs
3512 Silverside Road
8 The Commons
Wilmington, Delaware 19810
Phone: 302-478-7442
Fax: 302-478-7412
www.dscpa.org

Florida

Florida Board of Accountancy
240 NW 76 Drive., Ste 1
Gainesville, FL 32607
Phone: 352-333-2500
Fax: 352-333-2508
www.state.fl.us/dbpr/cpa/index.shtml

Florida Institute of Certified Public
  Accountants
P.O. Box 5437
Tallahassee FL 32314
Phone: 850-224-2727
Fax: 850-222-8190
www.ficpa.org

Georgia

Georgia State Board of Accountancy
237 Coliseum Drive
Macon, GA 31217-3858
Phone: 478-207-1400
Fax: 478-207-1410
www.sos.state.ga.us/ebd-accountancy

Georgia Society of CPAs
3340 Peachtree Road N.E., Suite 2700
Atlanta, GA 30326-1026
Phone: 404-231-8676 or
800-330-8889
Fax: 404-237-1291
www.gscpa.org

Guam	Guam Territorial Board of Public Accountancy P.O. Box P Agana, GU 96910 Phone: 671-475-2672 Fax: 671-477-7770	Guam Society of CPAs 361 South Marine Drive Tamuning, GU 96911 Phone: 671-646-3884 Fax: 671-649-4265
Hawaii	Hawaii Board of Public Accountancy Department of Commerce & Consumer Affairs P.O. Box 3469 Honolulu, HI 96801-3469 Phone: 808-586-2696 Fax: 808-586-2689 No website	Hawaii Society of CPAs P.O. Box 1754 Honolulu, HI 96806 Phone: 808-537-9475 Fax: 808-537-3520 www.hscpa.org
Idaho	Idaho State Board of Accountancy P.O. Box 83720 Boise, ID 83720-0002 Phone: 208-334-2490 Fax: 208-334-2615 Email: isba@boa.state.id.us www.state.id.us/boa	The Idaho Society of Certified Public Accountants 250 Bobwhite Ct., Suite. 240 Boise, ID, 83706 Phone: 208-344-6261 www.idcpa.org
Illinois	Illinois Board of Examiners 505 E. Green, Room 216 Champaign, IL 61820-5723 Phone: 217-333-1565 Fax: 217-333-3126 www.illinois-cpa-exam.com/cpa.htm Illinois Public Accountants Registration Committee Public Accountancy Section 320 W. Washington Street, 3rd Floor Springfield, IL 62786 Phone: 217-785-0800 Fax: 217-782-7645 www.dpr.state.il.us	Illinois Society of CPAs Chicago Office 222 South Riverside Plaza, Suite 1600 Chicago, Illinois 60606 Phone: 312- 993-0407 Fax: 312-993-9954 www.icpas.org
Indiana	Indiana Board of Accountancy Indiana Prof. Licensing Agc., Indiana Gov. Ctr. S. 302 West Washington St., Room E034 Indianapolis, IN 46204-2246 Phone: 317-232-5987 Fax: 317-232-2312 www.ai.org/pla/accountancy/index.html	Indiana Society of CPAs 8250 Woodfield Crossing Blvd., #305 Indianapolis, IN 46240-2054 Phone: 317-726-5000 Fax: 317-726-5005 www.incpas.org
Iowa	Iowa Accountancy Examining Board 1918 S.E. Hulsizer Avenue Ankeny, IA 50021-3941 Phone: 515-281-4126 Fax: 515-281-7411 www.state.ia.us/iacc	Iowa Society of CPAs 950 Office Park Road, Suite 300 West Des Moines, IA 50265-2548, Phone: 515-223-8161 or 800-659-6375 (in Iowa) Fax: 515-223-7347 www.iacpa.org

Kansas

Kansas Board of Accountancy
Landon State Office Building
900 S.W. Jackson, Suite 556
Topeka, KS 66612-1239
Phone: 785-296-2162
Fax: 785-291-3501
www.ink.org/public/ksboa

Kansas Society of Certified Public
 Accountants
400 SW Croix
P.O. Box 5654
Topeka, KS 66605-0654
Phone: 785-267-6460
FAX: 785-267-9278
www.kscpa.org

Kentucky

Kentucky State Board of Accountancy
332 West Broadway, Suite 310
Louisville, KY 40202-2115
Phone: 502-595-3037
Fax: 502-595-4281
www.state.ky.us/agencies/boa

Kentucky Society of Certified Public
 Accountants
1735 Alliant Avenue
Louisville, Kentucky 40299-6326
Phone: 502-266-5272 or
800-292-1754 (in Kentucky)
Fax: 502-261-9512
www.kycpa.org

Louisiana

State Board of CPAs of Louisiana
601 Poydras Street, Suite 1770
New Orleans, LA 70139
Phone: 504-566-1244
Fax: 504-566-1252
No website

Society of Louisiana Certified Public
 Accountants
2400 Veterans Blvd., Suite 500
Kenner, LA 70062-4739
Phone: 504-464-1040 or
800-288-5272
Fax: 504-469-7930
www.lcpa.org

Maine

Maine Board of Accountancy
Department of Prof. & Fin. Regulation
Division of Lic. & Reg., 35 State House Station
Augusta, ME 04333
Phone: 207-624-8603
Fax: 207-624-8637
www.state.me.us/pfr/led/account/index.html

Maine Society of Certified Public
 Accountants
153 U.S. Route 1, Suite 8
Scarborough, ME 04074-9053
Phone: 207-883-6090 or
800-660-2721
Fax: 207-883-6211
www.mecpa.org

Maryland

Maryland State Board of Public Accountancy
500 N. Calvert Street, Room 308
Baltimore, MD 21202-3651
Phone: 410-333-6322
Fax: 410-333-6314
www.dllr.state.md.us/license/occprof/account.html

Maryland Association of Certified Public
 Accountants
1300 York Road, Building C
P.O. Box 4417
Lutherville, MD 21094
Phone: 410-296-6250
Fax: 410-296-8713
www.macpa.org

Massachusetts

Massachusetts Board of Public Accountancy
239 Causeway Street
Suite 450
Boston, MA 02114
Phone: 617-727-1806
Fax: 617-727-0139
www.state.ma.us/reg/boards/pa/default.html

Massachusetts Society of Certified Public
Accountants
105 Chauncy Street 10th floor
Boston, MA 02111
Phone: 617-556-4000 or
800-392-6145
Fax: 617-556-4126
www.mscpaonline.org

Michigan	Michigan Board of Accountancy Dept. of Consumer & Industry Services P.O. Box 30018 Lansing, MI 48909-7518 Phone: 517-241-9249 Fax: 517-241-9280 www.cis.state.mi.us/bcs/acct/	Michigan Association of Certified Public Accountants PO Box 5068 Troy, MI 48007-5068 Phone: 248-267-3700 Fax: 248-267-3737 www.michcpa.org
Minnesota	Minnesota State Board of Accountancy 85 East 7th Place, Suite 125 St. Paul, MN 55101 Phone: 651-296-7938 Fax: 651-282-2644 No website	Minnesota Society of Certified Public Accountants Wells Fargo Plaza 7900 Xerxes Avenue South, Suite 1230 Bloomington, MN 55431-1183 Phone: 952-831-2707 or 800-331-4288 Fax: 952-831-7875 www.mncpa.org
Mississippi	Mississippi State Board of Public Accountancy 653 North State Street Jackson, MS 39202-3304 Phone: 601-354-7320 Fax: 601-354-7290 Email: email@msbpa.state.ms.us www.msbpa.state.ms.us	Mississippi Society of CPAs Highland Village, Suite 246 Jackson, MS 39236 Phone: 601-366-3473 or 800-772-1099 Fax: 601-981-6079 www.ms-cpa.org/
Missouri	Missouri State Board of Accountancy P.O. Box 613 Jefferson City, MO 65102 Phone: 573-751-0012 Fax: 573-751-0890 www.ecodev.state.mo.us/pr/account	Missouri Society of CPAs 275 N. Lindbergh Blvd., Suite 10 St. Louis, MO 63141 Phone: 314-997-7966 or 800-264-7966 Fax: 314-997-2592 www.mocpa.org

Montana	Montana State Board of Public Accountants
	301 S Park
	P O Box 200513
	Helena, MT 59620-0513
	Phone: 406-841-2388
	Fax: 406-841-2309
	www.com.state.mt.us/license/pol/pol_boards/pac_
	  board/board_page.htm
		Montana Society of Certified Public
		  Accountants
		P.O. Box 138
		Helena, MT 59624-0138
		  Phone: 406-442-7301 or 800-272-0307
		Fax: 406-443-7278
		www.mscpa.org

Nebraska	Nebraska State Board of Public Accountancy P.O. Box 94725 Lincoln, NE 68509-4725 Phone: 402-471-3595 Fax: 402-471-4484 Email: nbpa01@nol.org www.nol.org/home/BPA	Nebraska Society of CPAs 635 South 14th Street, Suite 330 Lincoln, Nebraska 68508 Phone: 402-476-8482 or 800-642-6178 (in Nebraska) Fax: 402-476-8731 www.nescpa.com

Nevada	Nevada State Board of Accountancy 200 South Virginia Street Suite 670 Reno, NV 89501-2408 Phone: 775-786-0231 Fax: 775-786-0234 www.state.nv.us/accountancy	Nevada Society of CPAs 5250 Neil Rd. Suite 205 Reno, NV 89502-6567 Phone: 775-826-6800 or 800-554-8254 Fax: 775-826-7942 www.nevadacpa.org
New Hampshire	New Hampshire Board of Accountancy 57 Regional Drive Concord, NH 03301 Phone: 603-271-3286 Fax: 603-271-2856 www.state.nh.us/accountancy	New Hampshire Society of CPAs 1750 Elm Street, Suite 403 Manchester, NH 03104 Phone: 603-622-1999 Fax: 603-626-0204 www.nhscpa.org
New Jersey	New Jersey State Board of Accountancy 124 Halsey Street, 6th Floor P.O. Box 45000 Newark, NJ 07101 Phone: 973-504-6380 Fax: 973-648-2855 www.state.nj.us/lps/ca/nonmed.htm	New Jersey Society of CPAs 425 Eagle Rock Avenue Roseland, NJ 07068-1723 Phone: 973-226-4494 Fax: 973-226-7425 www.njscpa.org
New Mexico	New Mexico Public Accountancy Board 1650 University N.E. Suite 400-A Albuquerque, NM 87102 Phone: 505-841-9108 Fax: 505-841-9113 www.rld.state.nm.us/b&c/accountancy/index.htm	The New Mexico Society of Certified Public Accountants 1650 University NE, Suite 450 Albuquerque, NM 87102-1733 Phone: 505-246-1699 or 800-926-2522 Fax: 505-246-1686 www.nmcoa.org
New York	New York State Board for Public Accountancy State Education Department Cultural Education Center, Room 3013 Albany, NY 12230 Phone: 518-474-3836 Fax: 518-473-6282 www.op.nysed.gov/cpa.htm	New York State Society of Certified Public Accountants 530 Fifth Avenue New York, NY 10036 Phone: 800-537-3635 Fax: 212-719-3365 www.nysscpa.org
North Carolina	North Carolina State Board of CPA Examiners 1101 Oberlin Road, Suite 104 P.O. Box 12827 Raleigh, NC 27605-2827 Phone: 919-733-4222 Fax: 919-733-4209 www.state.nc.us/cpabd	North Carolina Association of Certified Public Accountants PO Box 80188 Raleigh, NC 27623-0188 Phone: 919-469-1040 Fax: 919-469-3959 www.ncacpa.org
North Dakota	North Dakota State Board of Accountancy 2701 S. Columbia Road Grand Forks, ND 58201-6029 Phone: 701-775-7100 Fax: 701-775-7430 Email: ndsba@pioneer.state.nd.us www.state.nd.us/ndsba	North Dakota CPA Society 2701 S. Columbia Rd. Grand Forks ND 58201 Phone: 701-775-7100 Fax: 701-775-7430 www.ndscpa.org

Ohio

Accountancy Board of Ohio
77 South High Street, 18th Floor
Columbus, OH 43266
Phone: 614-466-4135
Fax: 614-466-2628
www.state.oh.us/acc

The Ohio Society of CPAs
535 Metro Place South
Dublin, OH 43017-7810
Phone: 614-764-2727 or
800-686-2727
Fax: 614-764-5880
www.ohioscpa.org

Oklahoma

Oklahoma Accountancy Board
4545 Lincoln Blvd., Suite 165
Oklahoma City, OK 73105-3413
Phone: 405-521-2397
Fax: 405-521-3118
Email: okaccybd@oklaosf.state.ok.us
No website

Oklahoma Society of CPAs
50 Penn Place, Suite 910
Oklahoma City, OK 73118-1804.
Phone: 405-841-3800 or
800-522-8261 (in Oklahoma)
Fax: 405-841-3801
www.oscpa.com

Oregon

Oregon State Board of Accountancy
3218 Pringle Road, S.E. #110
Salem, OR 97302-6307
Phone: 503-378-4181
Fax: 503-378-3575
www.boa.state.or.us/boa.html

The Oregon Society of Certified Public
  Accountants
PO Box 4555
Beaverton, Oregon 97076-4555
Phone: 503-641-7200
Fax: 503-626-2942
www.orcpa.org

Pennsylvania

Pennsylvania State Board of Accountancy
124 Pine Street
1st Floor
Harrisburg, PA 17101-2649
Phone: 717-783-1404
Fax: 717-705-5540
www.dos.state.pa.us/bpoa/accbd/mainpage.htm

Pennsylvania Institute of CPAs
1650 Arch Street, 17th Floor
Philadelphia, PA 19103
Phone: 215-496-9272 or
888-CPA-2001 (in Pennsylvania)
Fax: 215-496-9212
www.picpa.org

Puerto Rico

Puerto Rico Board of Accountancy
P.O. Box 3271
Old San Juan Station
San Juan, PR 00904-3271
Phone: 809-722-2122
Fax: 809-721-8399

Colegio de Contadores Publicos
  Autorizados de Puerto Rico
Edif. Capital Center
Avenue Arterial Hostos #3
Buxon 1401, Hato Rey, PR 00918
Phone 787-754-1950
Fax: 787-753-0212
www.prscpa.org

Rhode Island

Rhode Island Board of Accountancy
233 Richmond Street, Suite 236
Providence, RI 02903-4236
Phone: 401-222-3185
Fax: 401-222-6654
No website

Rhode Island Society of CPAs
45 Royal Little Drive
Providence, RI 02904
Phone: 401-331-5720
Fax: 401-454-5780
www.riscpa.org

**South
 Carolina**

South Carolina Board of Accountancy
110 Centerview Drive-Kingstree Building
P.O. Box 11329
Columbia, SC 29211
Phone: 803-896-4492
Fax: 803-896-4554
www.llr.state.sc.us/bac.htm

South Carolina Association of CPAs
570 Chris Drive
West Columbia, SC 29169
Phone: 803-791-4181 or
888-557-4814 (in South Carolina)
Fax: 803-791-4196
www.scacpa.org

South Dakota

South Dakota Board of Accountancy
301 East 14th Street, Suite 200
Sioux Falls, SD 57104
Phone: 605-367-5770
Fax: 605-367-5773
www.state.sd.us/dcr/accountancy

South Dakota CPA Society
P.O. Box 1798
Sioux Falls, SD 57101-1798
Phone: 605-334-3848
Fax: 605-334-8595
www.sdcpa.org

Tennessee

Tennessee State Board of Accountancy
500 James Robertson Parkway
2nd Floor
Nashville, TN 37243-1141
Phone: 615-741-2550
Fax: 615-532-8800
www.state.tn.us/commerce/tnsba

Tennessee Society of CPAs
201 Powell Place
Brentwood, TN 37027
Phone: 615-377-3825 or
800-762-0272
Fax: 615-377-3904
www.tncpa.org

Texas

Texas State Board of Public Accountancy
333 Guadalupe
Tower III, Suite 900
Austin, TX 78701-3900
Phone: 512-305-7800
Fax: 512-305-7854
www.tsbpa.state.tx.us

Texas Society of Certified Public
Accountants
14860 Montfort Drive, Suite 150
Dallas, TX 75240-6705
Phone: 800-428-0272
Fax: 972-687-8500
www.tscpa.org

Utah

Utah Board of Accountancy
P.O. Box 146741
Salt Lake City, UT 84114-6741
Phone: 801-530-6720
Fax: 801-530-6511
www.commerce.state.ut.us

Utah Association of CPAs
220 East Morris Avenue, Suite 320
Salt Lake City, UT. 84115
Phone: 801-466-8022
Fax: 801-485-6206
www.uacpa.org

Vermont

Vermont Board of Public Accountancy
Office of Professional Regulation
26 Terrace Street, Drawer 09
Montpelier, VT 05609-1106
Phone: 802-828-2191
Fax: 802-828-2465
www.vtprofessionals.org/accountants

Vermont Society of CPAs
100 State Street, Suite 500
Montpelier, VT 05602
Phone: 802-229-4939
Fax: 802-223-0360
www.vtcpa.org

Virginia

Virginia Board of Accountancy
3600 West Broad Street
Richmond, VA 23230-4917
Phone: 804-367-8507
Fax: 804-367-2475
Email: accountancy@dpor.state.va.us
www.state.va.us/dpor

Virginia Society of CPAs
4309 Cox Road
Glen Allen, VA 23060
Phone: 804-270-5344
Fax: 804-273-1741
www.vscpa.com

Virgin Islands

Virgin Islands Board of Public Accountancy
P.O. Box 3016
No. 1A Gallows Bay Market Place
Christiansted, St. Croix, VI 00822
Phone: 809-773-4305
Fax: 809-773-9850

Virgin Islands Society of CPAs
P.O. Box 3016
Christiansted, St. Croix, VI 00822-3016
Phone: 809-773-4305
Fax: 809-773-9850

Washington	Washington State Board of Accountancy P.O. Box 9131 Olympia, WA 98507-9131 Phone: 360-753-2585 Fax: 360-664-9190 www.cpaboard.wa.gov	Washington Society of CPAs 902 140th Ave NE Bellevue, WA 98005-3480 Phone: 425-644-4800 Fax: 425-562-8853 www.wscpa.org
West Virginia	West Virginia Board of Accountancy 200 L & S Building 812 Quarrier Street Charleston, WV 25301-2695 Phone: 304-558-3557 Fax: 304-558-1325 www.state.wv.us/wvboa	West Virginia Society of CPAs P. O. Drawer 1673 Charleston, West Virginia 25326 Phone: 304-342-5461 Fax: 304-344-4636 www.wvscpa.org
Wisconsin	Wisconsin Accounting Examining Board 1400 East Washington Avenue P.O. Box 8935 Madison, WI 53708-8935 Phone: 608-266-5511 Fax: 608-267-3816 www.drl.state.wi.us	Wisconsin Institute of CPAs P.O. Box 1010 Brookfield, WI 53008-1010 Phone: 262-785-0445 or 800-772-6939 Fax: 262-785-0838 www.wicpa.org
Wyoming	Wyoming Board of Certified Public Accountants 2020 Carey Avenue Cheyenne, WY 82002-0610 Phone: 307-777-7551 Fax: 307-777-3796 www.cpaboard.state.wy.us	Wyoming Society of CPAs 1603 Capitol Avenue, Suite 413 Cheyenne, WY 82001 Phone: 307-634-7039 Fax: 307-634-5110 www.wyocpa.org

APPENDIX C
SEC PROPOSED RULES ON INDEPENDENCE[*]

On June 27, 2000, the SEC proposed the following new rule changes that would affect independence requirements:

We are proposing amendments to Rule 2-01 of Regulation S-X and Item 9 of Schedule 14A under the authority set forth in Schedule A and Sections 19 and 28 of the Securities Act; Sections 3, 10A, 12, 13, 14, 17, 23, and 36 of the Exchange Act; Sections 5, 10, 14, and 20 of the Public Utility Holding Company Act of 1935; Sections 8, 30, and 38 of the Investment Company Act of 1940; and Sections 203 and 211 of the Investment Advisers Act of 1940.

List of Subjects

17 CFR Part 210

Accountants, Accounting.

17 CFR Part 240

Reporting and recordkeeping requirements, Securities.

Text of Amendments

In accordance with the foregoing, Title 17, Chapter II of the Code of Federal Regulations is proposed to be amended as follows:

PART 210 - FORM AND CONTENT OF AND REQUIREMENTS FOR FINANCIAL STATEMENTS, SECURITIES ACT OF 1933, SECURITIES EXCHANGE ACT OF 1934, PUBLIC UTILITY HOLDING COMPANY ACT OF 1935, INVESTMENT COMPANY ACT OF 1940, AND ENERGY POLICY AND CONSERVATION ACT OF 1975

1. The authority citation for Part 210 continues to read as follows:

   Authority: 15 U.S.C. 77f, 77g, 77h, 77j, 77s, 77z-2, 77aa(25), 77aa(26), 78j-1, 78l, 78m, 78n, 78o(d), 78u-5, 78w(a), 78ll(d), 79e(b), 79j(a), 79n, 79t(a), 80a-8, 80a-20, 80a-29, 80a-30, 80a-37(a), unless otherwise noted.

[*] *This material appears on the SEC website at www.sec.gov.*

2. By amending § 210.2-01 by revising paragraphs (b) and (c) and adding paragraphs (d), (e) and (f) to read as follows:

    § 210.2-01 <u>Qualifications of accountants</u>.

    (a) * * *

    (b) The Commission will not recognize an accountant as independent, with respect to an audit client, if the accountant is not, or would not be perceived by reasonable investors to be, capable of exercising objective and impartial judgment on all issues encompassed within the accountant's engagement. Under this standard, an accountant is not independent whenever, during the audit and professional engagement period, the accountant:

    (1) Has a mutual or conflicting interest with the audit client;
    (2) Audits the accountant's own work;
    (3) Functions as management or an employee of the audit client; or
    (4) Acts as an advocate for the audit client.

    (c) An accountant is not independent under the standard of paragraph (b) of this section if, during the audit and professional engagement period, the accountant has any of the financial, employment or business relationships with, provides any of the non-audit services to, or receives a contingent fee from, the accountant's audit client or an affiliate of the audit client, as specified in paragraphs (c)(1) through (c)(5) of this section, or otherwise does not comply with the standard of paragraph (b) of this section.

    (1) <u>Financial relationships</u>. An accountant is not independent under the standard of paragraph (b) of this section if the accountant has a direct financial interest or a material indirect financial interest in the accountant's audit client, such as the financial relationships specified in this paragraph (c)(1).

    (i) <u>Investment in audit client</u>. An accountant is not independent when:

    (A) The accounting firm, any covered person in the firm, or any of his or her immediate family members, has any direct investment in an audit client or an affiliate of an audit client, such as stocks, bonds, notes, options, or other securities.

    (B) Any partner, principal, shareholder, or professional employee of the accounting firm, any of his or her immediate family members, any close family member of a covered person in the firm, or any group of the above persons has filed a Schedule 13D or 13G with the Commission indicating beneficial ownership of more than five percent of an audit client's equity securities, or otherwise controls an audit client.

    (C) The accounting firm, any covered person in the firm, or any of his or her immediate family members, serves as voting trustee of a trust or executor of an estate containing the securities of an audit client.

(D) The accounting firm, any covered person in the firm, any of his or her immediate family members, or any group of the above persons has any material indirect investment in an audit client, including:

(1) Ownership of more than five percent of an entity that has an ownership interest in the audit client; or

(2) Ownership of more than five percent of an entity of which the audit client has an ownership interest.

(ii) Other financial interests in audit client. An accountant is not independent when the accounting firm, any covered person in the firm, or any of his or her immediate family members has:

(A) Loans/debtor-creditor relationship. Any loan (including any margin loan) to or from an audit client, an affiliate of an audit client, or an audit client's or an affiliate of an audit client's officers, directors, or record or beneficial owners of more than five percent of the audit client's or affiliate's equity securities, except for the following loans obtained from a financial institution under its normal lending procedures, terms and requirements:

(1) Automobile loans and leases collateralized by the automobile;

(2) Loans fully collateralized by the cash surrender value of an insurance policy;

(3) Loans fully collateralized by cash deposits at the same financial institution; and

(4) A mortgage loan collateralized by the accountant's primary residence provided the loan was not obtained while the borrower was a covered person in the firm or an immediate family member of a covered person in the firm.

(B) Savings and checking accounts. Any savings, checking or similar account at a bank, savings and loan or similar institution that is an audit client or an affiliate of an audit client, if the account has a balance that exceeds the amount insured by the Federal Deposit Insurance Corporation or any similar insurer.

(C) Broker-dealer accounts. Any brokerage or similar accounts maintained with a broker-dealer that is an audit client or an affiliate of the audit client, if:

(1) Any such accounts include any asset other than cash or securities (within the meaning of "security" provided in the Securities Investor Protection Act); or

(2) The value of assets in the accounts exceeds the amount that is subject to a Securities Investor Protection Corporation advance, for those accounts, under Section 9 of the Securities Investor Protection Act.

    (D) <u>Futures commission merchant accounts</u>. Any futures, commodity, or similar account maintained with a futures commission merchant that is an audit client or an affiliate of the audit client.

    (E) <u>Credit cards</u>. Any credit card balance in excess of $10,000 owed to a lender that is an audit client or an affiliate of an audit client.

    (F) <u>Insurance products</u>. Any individual policy or professional liability policy originally issued by an insurer that is an audit client or an affiliate of an audit client.

    (G) <u>Investment companies</u>. Any investment in any entity in an investment company complex if the audit client is also an entity in the same investment company complex. When the audit client is an entity that is part of an investment company complex, the accountant must be independent of each entity in the investment company complex.

(iii) <u>Exceptions</u>. Notwithstanding paragraphs (c)(1)(i) and (c)(1)(ii) of this section, the accountant will not be deemed not independent if:

    (A) <u>Inheritance and gift</u>. Any person acquires a financial interest through an unsolicited gift or inheritance that would cause an accountant to be not independent under paragraphs (c)(1)(i) or (c)(1)(ii) of this section, and the financial interest is disposed of as soon as practicable, but no longer than 30 days after the person has the right to dispose of the financial interest.

    (B) <u>New audit engagement</u>. Any person has a financial interest that would cause an accountant to be not independent under paragraphs (c)(1)(i) or (c)(1)(ii) of this section, and:

        (<u>1</u>) The accountant did not audit the client's financial statements for the immediately preceding fiscal year; and

        (<u>2</u>) The accountant is independent under paragraphs (c)(1)(i) and (c)(1)(ii) of this section before the earlier of:

            (<u>i</u>)   Accepting the engagement to provide audit, review, or attest services to the audit client; or

            (<u>ii</u>) Commencing any audit, review or attest procedures (including planning the audit of the client's financial statements).

(iv) <u>Audit clients' financial relationships</u>. An accountant is not independent when:

    (A) <u>Investments by the audit client in the auditor</u>. An audit client or an affiliate of an audit client has, or has agreed to acquire, any direct investment in the accounting firm or its affiliate, such as stocks, bonds, notes, options, or other securities.

    (B) <u>Underwriting</u>. An audit client or an affiliate of an audit client, including a broker-dealer or other entity, performs any service for the accounting firm related to underwriting, offering, making a market in, marketing, promoting, or selling securities issued by the accounting firm, or issues an analyst report concerning the securities of the accounting firm.

(2) <u>Employment relationships</u>. An accountant is not independent under the standard of paragraph (b) of this section if the accountant has an employment relationship with an audit client or an affiliate of an audit client, such as the employment relationships specified in this paragraph (c)(2). An accountant is not independent when:

    (i) <u>Employment at audit client of accountant</u>. A current partner, principal, shareholder, or professional employee of the accounting firm is employed by the audit client or an affiliate of an audit client or serves as a member of the board of directors or similar management or governing body of the audit client or an affiliate of the audit client.

    (ii) <u>Employment at audit client of certain relatives of accountant</u>. A close family member of a covered person in the firm is in an accounting or financial reporting oversight role at an audit client or an affiliate of an audit client, or was in such a role during any period covered by an audit for which the covered person in the firm is a covered person.

    (iii) <u>Employment at audit client of former employee of accounting firm</u>. A former partner, shareholder, principal, or professional employee of an accounting firm is in an accounting or financial reporting oversight role at an audit client or an affiliate of an audit client, unless the individual:

        (A) Does not influence the accounting firm's operations or financial policies;

        (B) Has no capital balances in the accounting firm; and

        (C) Has no financial arrangement with the accounting firm other than one providing for regular payment of a fixed dollar amount (which is not dependent on the revenues, profits, or earnings of the firm) pursuant to a fully funded retirement plan or rabbi trust.

    (iv) <u>Employment at accounting firm of former employee of audit client</u>. A former officer, director, or employee of an audit client or an affiliate of an audit client becomes a partner, shareholder, or principal of the accounting firm, unless the individual does not participate in, and is not in a position to influence, the audit of the financial statements of the audit client or an affiliate of the audit client covering any period during which he or she was employed by or associated with that audit client or an affiliate of the audit client.

(3) <u>Business relationships</u>. An accountant is not independent under the standard of paragraph (b) of this section if the accounting firm or any covered person in the firm has any direct or material indirect business relationship with an audit client, an affiliate of an audit client, or with an audit client's or an affiliate of an audit client's officers, directors, or record or beneficial owners of more than five percent of the audit client's or affiliate's equity securities. The relationships described in this paragraph do not include a relationship in which the accounting firm or covered person in the firm provides professional services or is a consumer in the ordinary course of business,

(4) <u>Non-audit services</u>.

(i) Even if the audit client accepts ultimate responsibility for the work that is performed or decisions that are made, an accountant is not independent under the standard of paragraph (b) of this section when the accountant provides certain non-audit services to an audit client or an affiliate of an audit client, such as:

(A) <u>Bookkeeping or other services related to the audit client's accounting records or financial statements</u>. Any service involving:

(1) Maintaining or preparing the audit client's or an affiliate of the audit client's accounting records;

(2) Preparing the audit client's or an affiliate of the audit client's financial statements; or

(3) Generating financial information to be disclosed by the audit client or an affiliate of the audit client to the public.

(B) <u>Financial information systems design and implementation</u>. Designing or implementing a hardware or software system used to generate information that is significant to the audit client's financial statements taken as a whole, not including services an accountant performs in connection with the assessment, design, and implementation of internal accounting controls and risk management controls.

(C) <u>Appraisal or valuation services, fairness opinions, or contribution-in-kind reports</u>. Any appraisal or valuation service for an audit client or an affiliate of an audit client, or any service involving a fairness opinion or contribution-in-kind report where it is reasonably likely that, in performing an audit in accordance with generally accepted auditing standards, the results will be audited by the accountant.

(D) <u>Actuarial services</u>. Any advisory service involving the determination of policy reserves and related accounts for the audit client or an affiliate of an audit client, unless the audit client or its affiliate uses its own actuaries or third-party actuaries to provide management with the primary actuarial capabilities.

(E) <u>Internal audit outsourcing</u>. Internal audit services for an audit client or an affiliate of an audit client, not including nonrecurring evaluations of discrete items or programs and operational internal audits unrelated to the internal accounting controls, financial systems, or financial statements.

(F) <u>Management functions</u>. Acting, temporarily or permanently, as a director, officer, or employee of an audit client or an affiliate of an audit client, or performing any decision-making, supervisory, or ongoing monitoring function for the audit client or affiliate of the audit client.

(G) <u>Human resources</u>. Recruiting, hiring, or designing compensation packages for officers, directors, or managers of the audit client or an affiliate of the audit client; advising about the audit client's or affiliate of the audit client's management or organizational structure; developing employee evaluation programs; or conducting psychological or other formal testing of employees.

(H) <u>Broker-dealer, investment adviser, or investment banking services</u>. Acting as a securities professional, such as a broker-dealer, promoter, underwriter, analyst of the audit client's or an affiliate of the audit client's securities, investment adviser, or in any capacity recommending the purchase or sale of an audit client's or an affiliate of an audit client's securities, or designing the audit client or an affiliate of the audit client's system to comply with broker-dealer or investment adviser regulations.

(I) <u>Legal services</u>. Providing any service to an audit client or an affiliate of an audit client that, in the jurisdiction in which the service is provided, could be provided only by someone licensed to practice law.

(J) <u>Expert services</u>. Rendering or supporting expert opinions for an audit client or an affiliate of an audit client in legal, administrative, or regulatory filings or proceedings.

(ii) <u>Transition</u>. Until [insert date two years from the effective date of this section], providing to an audit client or an affiliate of an audit client the non-audit services set forth in paragraph (c)(4)(i) of this section will not impair an accountant's independence with respect to the audit client if:

(A) The non-audit services are performed pursuant to a written contract in effect on or before [insert the effective date of this section]; and

(B) Performing those services did not impair the auditor's independence under pre-existing requirements of the Commission, the Independence Standards Board, or the accounting profession in the United States.

(5) <u>Contingent fees</u>. An accountant is not independent under the standard of paragraph (b) of this section if the accountant provides any service to an audit client or an affiliate of an audit client for a contingent fee, or receives a contingent fee from an audit client or an affiliate of an audit client.

(d) <u>Quality controls</u>. An accounting firm's independence will not be impaired solely because a covered person in the firm is not independent of an audit client provided:

(1) The covered person did not know, and was reasonable in not knowing, of the circumstances giving rise to the lack of independence;

(2) The covered person's lack of independence was corrected promptly after the covered person or accounting firm became aware of it; and

(3) The accounting firm has a quality control system in place that provides reasonable assurance, taking into account the size and nature of the accounting firm's practice, that the accounting firm and its employees do not lack independence. For an accounting firm that annually provides audit, review, or attest services to more than 500 companies with a class of securities registered with the Commission under Section 12 of the Securities Exchange Act of 1934, a quality control system will not provide such reasonable assurance unless it has at least the following features:

(i) Written independence policies and procedures;

(ii) An automated system to identify financial relationships that might impair the accountant's independence;

(iii) An annual or on-going firm-wide training program about auditor independence;

(iv) An annual internal inspection and testing program to monitor adherence to independence requirements;

(v) Notification to all firm members, officers, directors, and employees of the name and title of the member of senior management responsible for compliance with auditor independence requirements;

(vi) Written policies and procedures requiring all firm professionals to report promptly to the firm when they are engaged in employment negotiations with an audit client, and requiring the firm to remove immediately any such professional from that audit client's engagement and to review promptly all work the professional performed related to that audit client's engagement; and

(vii) A disciplinary mechanism to ensure compliance with this section.

(e) In determining whether an accountant is independent, the Commission will consider all relevant circumstances, including all relationships between the accountant and the audit client or the affiliates of the audit client, and not just those relating to reports filed with the Commission.

(f) Definitions of terms. For purposes of this section:

(1) Accountant, as used in paragraphs (b) through (e) of this section, means a certified public accountant or public accountant performing services in connection with an engagement for which independence is required. References to the accountant include any accounting firm with which the certified public accountant or public accountant is affiliated.

(2) Accounting firm means the organization (whether it is a sole proprietorship, incorporated association, partnership, corporation, limited liability company, limited liability partnership, or other legal entity) that is engaged in the practice of public accounting or furnishing accountant's reports with respect to financial statements, reports, or other documents filed with the Commission, and all departments, divisions, parents, subsidiaries, and affiliates of the accounting firm, including its pension, retirement, investment or similar plans.

(3) Accounting or financial reporting oversight role means that the person is in a position to, or does influence the contents of the accounting records or financial statements or anyone who prepares them, such as when the person is a member of the board of directors or similar management or governing body, chief executive officer, president, chief financial officer, chief operating officer, general counsel, chief accounting officer, controller, director of internal audit, director of financial reporting, treasurer, vice president of marketing, or any equivalent position.

(4) Affiliate of the accounting firm.

(i) "Affiliate of the accounting firm" means:

(A) Any person directly or indirectly controlling, controlled by, or under common control with the accounting firm, including:

(1) Any person or entity directly or indirectly owning, controlling, or holding the power to vote five percent or more of the accounting firm's outstanding voting securities, partnership units, or other interest entitling a person to vote; and

(2) Any person or entity five percent or more of whose outstanding voting securities, partnership units, or other interest entitling a person to vote are directly or indirectly owned, controlled, or held by the accounting firm;

(B) Any officer, director, partner, copartner, or shareholder of more than five percent of the voting securities of a person described in paragraph (f)(4)(A) of this section;

(C) Any joint venture, partnership, or other undertaking in which the accounting firm participates and in which the parties agree to any form of shared benefits, including any form of shared revenue, income, or equity appreciation;

(D) Any entity that provides non-audit or other professional services to one or more of the accounting firm's audit clients, and in which the accounting firm has any equity interest in, has loaned funds to, or shares revenues with, or with which the accounting firm or any covered person in the firm has any direct business relationship;

(E) All persons and entities with which the accounting firm is publicly associated by co-branding; using the accounting firm's name, initials, or logo; cross-selling services; or using co-management; and

(F) If the accounting firm leases, or otherwise routinely acquires on a temporary or continuous basis, the services of personnel employed full- or part-time by another party (the "lessor") and the leased personnel perform a majority of the hours worked on the engagement or supporting the accountant's reports filed with the Commission, the lessor and the lessor's board of directors, executive officers, and all persons with management, supervisory, compensation, or other oversight responsibility for the leased personnel, and shareholders of five percent or more of the lessor's equity securities.

(ii) "Affiliate of the accounting firm" does not include parties that share with an accounting firm training facilities, technical knowledge, databases, or billing facilities but that have no other business or financial relationship with the accounting firm, provided that the accounting firm pays a reasonably proportionate and fair share of the costs and expenses associated with such items, and the party charges all participants no more than the costs and expenses incurred to operate or maintain the shared facility or database.

(5) <u>Affiliate of the audit client</u> means an entity that has significant influence over the audit client, or over which the audit client has significant influence, including the audit client's parent and subsidiary.

(6) <u>Audit and professional engagement period</u> includes both:

(i) The period covered by any financial statements being audited or reviewed (the "audit period"); and

(ii) The period of the engagement to audit or review the client's financial statements or to prepare a report filed with the Commission (the "professional engagement period").

(A) The professional engagement period begins when the accountant either signs an initial engagement letter (or other agreement to review or audit a client's financial statements), or begins review or audit procedures, whichever is earlier; and

(B) The professional engagement period ends when the client or the accountant notifies the Commission that the client is no longer that accountant's audit client.

(7) <u>Audit client</u> means the entity whose financial statements or other information is being audited, reviewed, or attested.

(8) <u>Audit engagement team</u> means all partners, principals, shareholders, and professional employees participating in an audit, review, or attestation engagement of an audit client, including those conducting concurring or second partner reviews and all persons who consult, formally or informally, with others on the audit engagement team during the audit, review, or attestation engagement regarding technical or industry-specific issues, transactions, or events.

(9) <u>Chain of command</u> means all persons having any supervisory, management, quality control, compensation, or other oversight responsibility over either any member of the audit engagement team or over the conduct of the audit. The "chain of command" includes all partners, principals, shareholders, and managers who may review, determine, or influence the performance appraisal or compensation of any member of the audit engagement team and any other person in a position to influence the audit engagement team's decisions during the conduct of the audit, review, or attestation engagement.

(10) <u>Close family members</u> means a person's spouse, spousal equivalent, parent, dependent, nondependent child, and sibling.

(11) <u>Consumer in the ordinary course of business</u> means a purchaser of routine products or services on the same terms and conditions that are available to the seller's other customers or clients, as long as the purchaser does not resell the product or service or receive a commission or other fee for selling the product or service.

(12) <u>Contingent fee</u> means any fee where payment, or the amount of the fee paid or due, is contingent, in whole or in part, on the result, including the value added, of any transaction or event, other than completion of the work or delivery of the product giving rise to the fee. A fee is not a "contingent fee" if it is fixed by a court or by any federal, state, or local governmental agency.

(13) <u>Covered persons in the firm</u> means the following partners, principals, shareholders, and employees of an accounting firm:

(i) The "audit engagement team;"

(ii) The "chain of command;"

(iii) Any other partner, principal, shareholder, or professional employee of the accounting firm who is, or during the audit client's most recent fiscal year was, involved in providing any professional service to the audit client or an affiliate of the audit client; and

(iv) Any other partner, principal, or shareholder from an "office" of the accounting firm that participates in a significant portion of the audit.

(14) <u>Group</u> means when two or more persons act together for the purposes of acquiring, holding, voting, or disposing of securities of a registrant.

(15) <u>Immediate family members</u> means a person's spouse, spousal equivalent, and dependent.

(16) <u>Investment company complex</u>.

(i) "Investment company complex" includes:

(A) An investment company and its investment adviser or sponsor;

(B) Any entity controlled by, under common control with or controlling the investment adviser or sponsor in paragraph (f)(16)(A) of this section; or

(C) Any investment company or entity that would be an investment company but for the exclusions provided by section 3(c) of the Investment Company Act of 1940 (15 U.S.C. § 80a-3(c)) that has an investment adviser or sponsor included in this definition by either paragraphs (f)(16)(A) or (f)(16)(B) of this section.

(ii) An investment adviser, for purposes of this definition, does not include a sub-adviser whose role is primarily portfolio management and is subcontracted with or overseen by another investment adviser.

(iii) Sponsor, for purposes of this definition, is an entity that establishes a unit investment trust.

(17) <u>Office</u> means a distinct sub-group within an accounting firm, whether distinguished along geographic or practice lines.

(18) <u>Rabbi trust</u> means an irrevocable trust whose assets are not accessible to the accounting firm until all benefit obligations have been met, but are subject to the claims of creditors in bankruptcy or insolvency.

PART 240 - GENERAL RULES AND REGULATIONS, SECURITIES EXCHANGE ACT OF 1934

3. The authority citation for Part 240 continues to read, in part, as follows:

Authority: 15 U.S.C. 77c, 77d, 77g, 77j, 77s, 77z-2, 77eee, 77ggg, 77nnn, 77sss, 77ttt, 78c, 78d, 78f, 78i, 78j, 78j-1, 78k, 78k-1, 78*l*, 78m, 78n, 78o, 78p, 78q, 78s, 78u-5, 78w, 78x, 78*ll*(d), 78mm, 79q, 79t, 80a-20, 80a-23, 80a-29, 80a-37, 80b-3, 80b-4 and 80b-11, unless otherwise noted.

* * * * *

4. By amending § 240.14a-101 to add paragraph (e) to Item 9 to read as follows:

     § 240.14a-101 <u>Schedule 14A Information required in proxy statement</u>.

* * * * *

Item 9. <u>Independent public accountants</u>.* * *

* * * * *

(e)(1) Describe each professional service provided during the most recent fiscal year by the independent public or certified public accountant (as defined in Article 2 of Regulation S-X, 17 CFR 210.2-01) that is the registrant's principal accountant. A service does not have to be disclosed if the fee for that service was, is, or will be less than the lesser of $50,000 or 10 percent of the fee for the audit of the registrant's annual financial statements.

<u>Instruction to paragraph (e)</u>

(1) Specifically describe each service. Broad general categories such as "tax matters" or "management advisory services" or "management consulting services" are not sufficient.

(2) Indicate whether, before each disclosed professional service was rendered, the audit committee of the board of directors, or if there is no such committee then the board of directors, approved the service and considered the possible effect of the service on the principal accountant's independence.

(3) Disclose the fee for each disclosed professional service.

(4) Disclose the aggregate fee for the audit of the registrant's financial statements for the fiscal year most recently completed and for the reviews of the financial statements included in the registrant's Forms 10-Q (17 CFR 249.308a) or 10-QSB (17 CFR 249.308b) for that fiscal year.

(5) If greater than 50 percent, disclose the percentage of the hours expended on the principal auditor's engagement to audit the registrant's financial statements for the most recent fiscal year that were attributed to work performed by persons other than the principal accountant's full-time, permanent employees.

THE CPA'S GUIDE TO PROFESSIONAL ETHICS

SELF-STUDY
CPE PROGRAM

JOHN WILEY & SONS, INC.

New York • Chichester • Weinheim • Brisbane • Toronto • Singapore

About This Course

We are pleased that you have selected our course. A course description that is based on the *CPA's Guide to Professional Ethics* follows:

Prerequisites:	**None**
Recommended CPE credits:	**8 hours**
Knowledge level:	**Basic**
Area of study:	**Accounting and Auditing**

The credit hours recommended are in accordance with the AICPA Standards for CPE Programs. Since CPE requirements are set by each state, you need to check with your State Board of Accountancy concerning required CPE hours and fields of study.

If you decide to take this course, follow the directions on the following page. Each course unit costs $59.00. Methods of payment are shown on the answer forms.

Each CPE exam is graded no later than two weeks after receipt. The passing score is at least 70%. John Wiley & Sons, Inc. will issue a certificate of completion to successful participants to recognize their achievement.

Photocopy one copy of the answer sheet for each additional participant who wishes to take the CPE course. Each participant should complete the answer form and return it with the $59 fee for each self-study course.

The enclosed self-study CPE program will expire on December 31, 2002. Completed exams must be postmarked by that date.

Directions for the CPE Course

The course includes reading assignments and objectives, discussion questions and answers, and a publisher-graded examination. To earn eight hours of CPE credit, follow these steps:

1. Read the learning objectives.
2. Study chapters 1 to 33 in *The CPA's Guide to Professional Ethics.*
3. Answer the discussion questions and refer to the answers to assess your understanding of the respective chapter.
4. Study material in any weak areas again.
5. Upon completion, take the publisher-graded examination. Record your answers by writing true, false, or a letter (a-e) on the line for that question on the answer form.
6. Upon completion of the examination, cut out the answer sheet, put it in a stamped envelope, and mail to the address below:

> The CPA's Guide to Professional Ethics
> CPE Program Director
> Wiley-ValuSource
> 7222 Commerce Center Drive
> Suite 210
> Colorado Springs, CO 80919

CONTINUING PROFESSIONAL EDUCATION: SELF-STUDY

OBJECTIVES

Studying Chapters 1 through 33 should enable you to:

- Apply the ethics guidance of
  - The AICPA Code of Professional Conduct
  - Independence Standards Board
  - SEC
  - DOL (audits of employee benefit plans)
  - GAO (audits of state and local governmental units)

- Apply this guidance in firms of all sizes having public company, private entity, governmental entity, and employee benefit plan clients.

- Describe the Joint Ethics Enforcement Program (JEEP) and the conduct of an investigation and trial board hearing.

- Describe the steps a member should take if involved in a disciplinary action under JEEP.

- Explain the importance of independence, integrity, and objectivity to public confidence in audit, examination (SSAE terminology), review and agreed-upon procedures engagements.

- Describe the rationale underlying independence rules and their interpretations and their general economic and social framework.

- Distinguish between the independence requirements of the various organizations and identify where the ISB, SEC, and DOL have more stringent requirements than the AICPA.

- Summarize the key elements of a firm's quality assurance policies and procedures relevant to independence.

- Distinguish between the general standards of professional competence, due professional care, planning and supervision, and sufficient relevant data.

- Explain the member's duty to comply with the standards promulgated by bodies designated by Council.

- Describe the representations by members in public practice when departures from generally accepted accounting principles exist.

- Describe a member's responsibility to keep client information confidential.

- Determine when a member is or is not permitted to receive commissions, referral fees, and contingent fees.
- Explain what constitutes a discreditable act.
- Distinguish between prohibited and permitted forms of advertising and solicitation.
- Explain the requirements for permitted forms of organization and firm names.

DISCUSSION QUESTIONS

1. If an auditor is technically proficient and applies extensive auditing procedures, but lacks independence, the financial statements are
   a. Unaudited.
   b. Semireliable.
   c. Reliable.
   d. None of the above.

2. Rule 102 on integrity and objectivity applies to all CPAs
   a. In public practice who provide professional services.
   b. Who provide professional services, no matter where employed.
   c. In public practice who provide auditing and attestation services.
   d. Who provide professional services imbued with the public interest.

3. The organization that is charged with establishing independence requirements for auditors of public companies is
   a. AICPA.
   b. ISB.
   c. SECPS.
   d. DOL.

4. A member or member's firm that is not independent can issue
   a. An audit report.
   b. An examination report under the SSAE.
   c. A review report.
   d. A compilation report for a private company.

5. Which of the following investments does **not** impair independence?
   a. A partner's spouse buys an immaterial number of common stock shares in an audit client.
   b. An audit manager in the firm's Santa Fe office invests in a company audited by that office.
   c. A staff accountant or associate in the firm's Boston office invests in a client of the firm's Denver office.
   d. None of the above.

6. Company A, an audit client, owns 50% of a joint venture. Company Z, a nonclient, owns the remaining 50% of the joint venture. CPA auditor has a material financial interest in Company Z. CPA is independent with respect to
   a. The joint venture.
   b. Company A.
   c. Company Z.
   d. None of the above.

7. An audit client has unpaid fees outstanding as of the date that fieldwork begins for the current audit. The client has paid those past due fees by the time the audit report is issued.
   a. Independence is impaired under the AICPA and SEC rules.
   b. Independence is not impaired under the AICPA rule and **may** not be impaired under the SEC rule.
   c. Independence is impaired under the AICPA rule, but not under the SEC rule.
   d. Independence is not impaired under either AICPA or SEC rules.

8. Which of the following bookkeeping services would the AICPA regard as not impairing independence?
   a. Authorizing or approving transactions.
   b. Determining the proper classification of transactions without obtaining client approval.
   c. Posting client-approved entries to the client's trial balance.
   d. None of the above.

9. A joint, closely held business investment with a **public** company audit client will impair independence if the investment
   a. Is material to the client.
   b. Is material to the member's net worth or his or her firm.
   c. Is material or immaterial to the member or the client.
   d. None of the above.

10. Which of the following services or occupations is not prohibited under SEC rules?
    a. Providing legal advice to a client's CEO.
    b. Serving as a director of a nonclient bank.
    c. Acting as legal counsel to a client.
    d. Being a broker-dealer.

11. Loans to and from clients that are not financial institutions
    a. Will impair independence without regard to materiality.
    b. If material, will cause an impairment of independence.
    c. Will not impair independence if the loan is "permitted."
    d. Will not impair independence if the loan is "grandfathered."

12. A member serves as treasurer of a campaign organization that is supporting a candidate for mayor. The member is not independent with respect to
    a. The candidate's political party.
    b. The municipality of which the candidate may become mayor.

   c.   The campaign organization.

   d.   All of the above.

13. An audit manager is performing an audit engagement. Which of the following employment relationships may impair independence?

   a.   Employment of the auditor's spouse by the client.

   b.   Employment of the auditor's dependent relative by the client.

   c.   Employment of the auditor's dependent child by the client.

   d.   All of the above.

14. A partner of a CPA firm retires and becomes the CFO of one of the firm's clients. Which of the following best describes the effect of this relationship on the firm's independence?

   a.   The firm's independence is impaired no matter what the arrangements are with the partner.

   b.   The firm will be considered independent based on the fact that the partner has permanently left the firm.

   c.   The firm may be considered independent if certain restrictions are met concerning retirement payments and concerning the partner's actual and appearance of participation in firm activities.

   d.   The firm will be considered independent as long as the partner no longer participates in firm activities.

15. Acceptance of a gift from a client will not impair independence if

   a.   The recipient discloses the gift to the CPA firm.

   b.   The gift is lavish, but not excessive considering the audit fee.

   c.   The gift is a wedding present.

   d.   The item received is a token gift.

16. A lawsuit is brought against a CPA firm by an audit client. Independence would be considered to be impaired in all of the following circumstances except

   a.   The present management alleges audit scope was inadequate.

   b.   The present management alleges an audit adjustment violated GAAP.

   c.   The present management alleges a state tax return prepared by the CPA firm incorrectly computed the tax liability for a minor amount.

   d.   The present management alleges failure to communicate a reportable condition in internal control.

17. If the client agrees to indemnify the member for knowing misrepresentations, the member

   a.   Is not independent under AICPA or SEC rules.

   b.   Is not independent under AICPA rules, but is independent under SEC rules.

   c.   Is not independent under SEC rules, but may be independent under AICPA rules.

   d.   Is independent under both AICPA and SEC rules.

18. To remain independent, a member performing a client's internal audit function may do all of the following except

    a. Be satisfied management and the board understand that the member cannot act or appear to act in a capacity equivalent to a member of management or an employee.

    b. Direct, review, and supervise day-to-day performance of internal audit procedures.

    c. Assist in performing preliminary risk assessments and preparing audit plans.

    d. Report to the audit committee on behalf of management the audit findings.

19. Which of the following situations would impair independence for a city government client?

    a. The auditor is elected to the city council.

    b. The auditor serves on a citizen's advisory committee to study a possible new structure in the form of government.

    c. The auditor owned city bonds but sold the bonds upon being engaged as the auditor.

    d. The auditor's spouse is running for mayor at the next election.

20. DOL independence rules differ from AICPA requirements in which of the following areas?

    a. Definition of materiality.

    b. Permitted employment of member by benefit plan.

    c. Definition of member.

    d. Acceptable financial interests in clients.

21. The definition of member for an agreed-upon procedures engagement includes

    a. All partners or owners in the firm.

    b. Only partners or owners in the firm.

    c. Only partners or owners who participate in the engagement and have a position of significant influence with the client.

    d. None of the above.

22. A CPA firm is in an alliance with a public company in an alternative practice structure. The partners of the firm are also employees of a professional services subsidiary of the public company. The chief executive of the professional services subsidiary has a direct financial interest in an audit client of the CPA firm. The partners report directly to the chief executive in their capacity as employees. Which of the following best describes the effect on independence of the CPA firm?

    a. Independence is not impaired because the chief executive is not an owner or employee of the CPA firm.

    b. Independence is impaired because the chief executive is subject to the same requirements as a member and any direct financial interest impairs independence.

    c. The chief executive is not a member, but independence would nevertheless be impaired if the financial interest is material to the chief executive's net worth.

    d. None of the above.

23. A firm's responsibilities for the adherence of its personnel to professional requirements on independence can be fully satisfied by

    a. Adoption of adequate quality control policies and procedures related to independence.

    b. Adherence by its personnel to professional requirements on independence.

    c. Both a. and b. together.

    d. Either a. or b. individually.

24. Which of the following bodies is **not** designated to issue standards by AICPA Council?
    a. Consulting Services Executive Committee.
    b. Independence Standards Board.
    c. Tax Executive Committee.
    d. Auditing Standards Board.

25. Which of the following is **true**?
    a. A member should never disclose the name of a client without the client's specific consent.
    b. A member may use a records retention agency to store client's records.
    c. A member may not accept an engagement to perform services that involve examining confidential information about competitors.
    d. A member may not be compelled by a subpoena to disclose confidential client information.

26. According to AICPA rules, a member in public practice may accept a contingent fee from a client
    a. Only when the contingent fee is disclosed.
    b. Only if the member does not perform an audit or review for the client.
    c. Only if the member does not perform an audit, review, or certain other attest or compilation services for the client.
    d. A member in public practice may never accept a contingent fee.

27. After an engagement is complete, a member is obligated to provide which of the following upon request of the client?
    a. Analyses and schedules prepared by the client at the request of the member.
    b. Member's workpapers.
    c. Consolidating journal entries found in the member's workpapers that are not in the client's books and records.
    d. All of the above.

28. Which is a prohibited form of advertising, even if it is not false, misleading, or deceptive?
    a. In-person solicitation of clients.
    b. Comparison of services provided to those of another firm.
    c. Celebrity endorsements.
    d. None of the above.

29. Which of the following organizations would allow a member to accept a commission for providing investment advisory services to the owner of an attest client?
    a. AICPA.
    b. SEC.
    c. DOL.
    d. ISB.

30. Which of the following is **not** one of the requirements of the Council Resolution concerning Rule 505--*Form of Organization and Name* ?

a. CPAs must own a majority of the financial interests and voting rights.
b. A CPA must have ultimate responsibility for all compilation services.
c. A non-CPA owner is not eligible for membership in the AICPA.
d. A non-CPA owner cannot use the title of "Principal."

ANSWERS TO DISCUSSION QUESTIONS

1. **The answer is a.** If an auditor is not independent, any procedures that the auditor might perform, no matter how extensive, would not be in accordance with GAAS. The auditor is precluded from expressing an opinion on the financial statements and the financial statements would be, for all practical purposes, unaudited.

2. **The answer is b.** Rule 102 applies to all CPAs who provide professional services, no matter where employed. This includes CPAs in industry, government, and education who provide tax, consulting, and a variety of other services.

3. **The answer is b.** The Independence Standards Board establishes independence requirements for auditors of public companies. The SEC enforces these requirements. SECPS has the Joint Task Force on Independence and Quality Controls that establishes membership requirements related to independence quality controls.

4. **The answer is d.** Independence is not required for compilation engagements. The auditor should disclose the lack of independence in the compilation report but not the reason for the lack of independence. All of the other engagements--audits, reviews, and examination reports under the SSAE--require independence.

5. **The answer is c.** The staff accountant is in an office that is not participating in the engagement. Therefore, independence is not impaired. Answer a. is not correct because any purchase of common shares, whether material or immaterial, is considered a direct financial interest and impairs independence. The spouse of a partner is considered to be a member for the purpose of applying the rules on financial interests. Answer b. is not correct because the audit manager owns a direct financial interest in an audit client of his or her office, which is prohibited.

6. **The answer is d.** CPA auditor has a material financial interest in the nonclient investee, Company Z. The member could be influenced by the nonclient investor, thereby impairing the member's independence with respect to Company Z. Independence is also impaired with respect to the nonclient and the joint venture. Therefore, the CPA would not be independent with respect to the joint venture, Company A, or Company Z.

7. **The answer is b.** Under the AIPCA rules, independence is impaired if the fees are delinquent for more than one year prior to the current audit report date. Therefore, since the fees were paid by the report date, independence is not impaired under the AICPA rule. Under SEC rules, fees that are material in relation to the current audit fee should be paid before the current audit begins, to avoid impairing independence. Such fees were **not** paid at the time that current audit work began in this example. However, since there are two exceptions to the SEC rule that (1) allow for a commitment to pay the fees prior to the audit report being issued

or (2) allow for an agreement to make periodic payments, the correct answer is that independence may not be impaired under SEC rules.

8. **The answer is c.** Posting client-approved entries to a client's trial balance would not impair independence. According to AICPA rules, answers a. and b., authorizing and approving transactions or determining the proper classification of transactions without client approval, would impair independence. Functions such as these are considered management functions.

9. **The answer is c.** The SEC prohibits any joint closely held investment without regard to materiality.

10. **The answer is b.** Serving as a director of a nonclient bank is not prohibited by the SEC. The AICPA does, however, discourage a member from serving as a director of a nonclient bank, if the member has clients that are customers of the bank.

11. **The answer is a.** Loans to and from clients that are not financial institutions will impair independence without regard to materiality. Answers c. and d. are not correct because exceptions for grandfathered loans and permitted loans apply only to loans from financial institutions.

12. **The answer is c.** A member who serves as treasurer of a campaign organization that supports a candidate for mayor would not be independent with respect to the campaign organization.

13. **The answer is d.** All of the relationships listed--spouse, dependent relative, or dependent child--are ascribed to the member. Thus, if the member's spouse, dependent relative, or dependent child has a position of significant influence over operating, financial, or accounting policies, the CPA firm is not independent.

14. **The answer is c.** In determining whether a former practitioner has an impact on a firm's compliance with independence requirements, the key is deciding whether a former practitioner is included in the definition of member or member's firm. The criteria for making this determination relate to payments to the former practitioner and participation in, or the appearance of participation in, the firm's business or professional activities. Answer a. is not correct because the firm's independence may **not** be impaired if arrangements with the partner meet the criteria described in this chapter. Answer b. is not correct because the key criteria are the firm's arrangements with the former practitioner concerning payments and participation in the firm's activities, not the fact that the partner has left the firm. Answer d. is not correct because the fact that the partner no longer participates in firm activities is only one element in determining whether the former practitioner is a member. The other element involves the payments made to the former practitioner.

15. **The answer is d.** A member should not accept more than a token gift from a client. Answer a. is not correct because an individual cannot mitigate the appearance of a lack of independence by disclosing the gift to the CPA firm. Answer b. is not correct because the gift cannot be accepted if it is lavish, no matter what its relationship to the audit fee. Answer c. is not correct because a wedding present is a gift that might give the appearance of impairing

independence. However, the prohibition against accepting gifts has to be interpreted sensibly and handled diplomatically.

16. **The answer is c.** Litigation impairs independence when present management of a client brings litigation alleging deficiencies in the member's audit work. Therefore, independence would be impaired for the situations described in answers a., b., and d. Independence would **not** be impaired if litigation relates to an engagement that does not require independence, such as tax work, and the alleged damages are not material to the member's firm or the client company.

17. **The answer is c.** The AICPA permits a member to include an indemnification clause in an engagement letter without impairing independence if the indemnification is restricted to knowing misrepresentations made by the client's management. However, the member who inserted such a clause in an engagement letter would not be independent under SEC rules because the SEC considers indemnification to be against public policy.

18. **The answer is d.** Reporting the audit findings to the audit committee on behalf of management is an example of an activity that would impair independence. The member is acting, or appearing to act, in a capacity equivalent to a member of client management or an employee.

19. **The answer is a.** If a member serves as an elected city legislator, such as on city council, independence is impaired with respect to the city even though the city manager is elected, rather than appointed, by the legislature. Answers b. and d. are both examples of situations that would not impair independence. Answer c. is also not correct because the city bonds were sold before independence was required. If, however, a member owned even an immaterial amount of the bonds at the beginning of the work on the engagement, independence would be impaired.

20. **The answer is c.** According to the DOL, "member" includes all owners, partners, or shareholders in the CPA firm, all professional employees participating in the audit, and all professional employees located in an office of the CPA firm participating in a significant portion of the audit. This is different from the AICPA definition of member described in Chapter 8.

21. **The answer is d.** The definition of members presented in Chapter 8 does not apply to agreed-upon procedures engagements. The key concept is engagement team independence. Answers a., b., and c. do not correctly define members of the engagement team.

22. **The answer is b.** The chief executive of the professional services subsidiary is a direct superior and is subject to the same independence requirements as a member with respect to New Firm's audit and attest services clients. A direct financial interest would impair independence for a member.

23. **The answer is c.** A firm's responsibilities for the adherence of its personnel to professional requirements on independence is fully satisfied only by both adopting adequate quality control policies and procedures related to independence and by the adherence of all professional personnel to all applicable professional requirements on independence.

24. **The answer is b.** The Independence Standards Board is not an AICPA body, but instead is a separate entity that provides guidance on independence issues.

25. **The answer is b.** A member may use a records retention agency. Answer a. is false because a member may disclose the name of a client as long as doing so does not reveal confidential information. Answer c. is incorrect because a member may accept such an engagement as long as the member does not violate confidentiality. Answer d. is false because Rule 301 does **not** relieve a member of an obligation to comply with a legally enforceable subpoena or summons.

26. **The answer is c.** A member in public practice may only receive a contingent fee if the member does not perform an audit, review, or certain other attest or compilation services for the client.

27. **The answer is c.** These entries should be provided to allow the client to complete the client's financial records. The other answers represent the member's workpapers, which do not need to be provided to the client.

28. **The answer is d.** All of the above are permitted forms of advertising, as long as they are not false, misleading, or deceptive.

29. **The answer is a.** The AICPA would allow a member to accept a commission for providing investment advisory services to the owner of an attest client. The SEC, DOL, and ISB disagree with the AICPA's position.

30. **The answer is d.** All of answers are requirements except for d. A non-CPA owner may use the title of Principal.

PUBLISHER-GRADED EXAMINATION

Multiple-
Choice

1. Which of the following is true of the Independence Standards Board?
   a. It is charged with establishing independence requirements that apply to auditors of private companies.
   b. It is charged with establishing independence requirements that apply to auditors of public companies.
   c. It can remove a CPA's license to practice for violation of independence requirements.
   d. All of the above.

Multiple-
Choice

2. Which of the following loans from a client would impair independence?
   a. A line of credit from a nonfinancial institution client for an amount that was immaterial to the member's net worth.
   b. A loan made from a financial institution client prior to its becoming an audit client.
   c. A credit card balance of $4500.
   d. All of the above.

Multiple-
Choice

3. Client owes Auditor fees for services performed for professional services provided from January 15 to January 30, 20X1. Auditor expects to begin work on the current year's engagement on February 1, 20X2, and issue the report on March 1, 20X2. Under the AICPA rules, the client must pay the fees by which date to avoid impairing independence?
   a. January 15, 20X1.
   b. January 30, 20X1.
   c. February 1, 20X2.
   d. March 1, 20X2.

Multiple-
Choice

4. Which of the following would **not** be included in the definition of member?
   a. A brother.
   b. A spouse.
   c. An unrelated dependent.
   d. All of the above would be included in the definition of member.

Multiple-
Choice

5. Which of the following **would** impair independence for a member who provides consulting or advisory services to an audit client on corporate finance matters?
   a. Assisting in identifying or introducing the client to possible sources of capital that meet the client's specifications or criteria.
   b. Maintaining custody of client securities.
   c. Assisting in drafting an offering document or memorandum.
   d. Being named as a financial advisor in a client's private placement memoranda.

Multiple-
Choice

6. Independence is required for all of the following **except**
   a. A comfort letter.
   b. A review report.
   c. A compilation report.
   d. An examination of a financial forecast.

Multiple-Choice

7. Which of the following statements is true?
   a. Independence is required under Statements on Auditing Standards (SAS), but not Statements on Standards for Attestation Engagements (SSAE) or Statements on Standards for Accounting and Review Services (SSARS).
   b. Independence is required under SAS and SSAE, but not SSARS.
   c. Independence is required under SAS and SSARS, but not SSAE.
   d. Independence is required under SAS, SSAE, and SSARS.

Multiple-Choice

8. Which of the following organizations cooperate in the Joint Ethics Enforcement Program (JEEP) in bringing enforcement actions against their members?
   a. AICPA and SEC.
   b. AICPA and state societies.
   c. AICPA, SEC and ISB.
   d. AICPA, SEC, ISB and state societies.

Multiple-Choice

9. An audit manager has XYZ Manufacturing as an audit client. The manager receives a substantial discount on products from XYZ. This discount is not available to members of the general public. What is the effect on independence?
   a. Independence is impaired.
   b. Independence is not impaired if the discount is disclosed to the firm.
   c. Independence is not impaired if the discount is disclosed to the firm and to the client.
   d. Independence is not impaired.

Multiple-Choice

10. The definition of member, according to **both** the AICPA **and** the SEC rules, includes all of the following **except**:
    a. The spouse of a staff accountant who participates in the audit engagement.
    b. A manager in consulting services who develops a new customer complaint system for the audit client.
    c. A staff accountant in the office conducting the engagement, but who personally does not participate in, or have association with, the engagement.
    d. A tax partner who provides only tax services to the audit client.

Multiple-Choice

11. Which of the following exceptions to indemnification agreements is allowed by the AICPA?
    a. A client indemnifies a member for damages from lawsuits and claims relating to client acts.
    b. A client indemnifies a member for knowing misrepresentations made by client's management.
    c. A member indemnifies the client for damages from lawsuits and claims relating to client acts.
    d. All of the above are permitted under AICPA rules, but not SEC rules.

Multiple-Choice

12. Ownership of which of the following would be considered a prohibited direct financial interest?
    a. Shares of a client's common stock.
    b. Shares of a client's preferred stock.
    c. Investment in a client's common stock through an investment club.
    d. All of the above.

Multiple-
Choice

13. Which of the following bookkeeping services would impair independence under **SEC** requirements?
   a. Posting coded transactions to a client's general ledger.
   b. Preparing source documents.
   c. Preparing financial statements based on information in the trial balance.
   d. All of the above.

Multiple-
Choice

14. All of the following organizations tend to have more stringent **independence** requirements than the AICPA except
   a. The Independence Standards Board (ISB).
   b. The SEC.
   c. State societies.
   d. Department of Labor (DOL).

Multiple-
Choice

15. Which of the following is **not** an example of a conflict of interest that impairs independence?
   a. A member has been approached to provide services in connection with the purchase of real estate from a client of the member's firm.
   b. A staff accountant in a firm's consulting department has been asked to develop a new customer complaint system for XYZ Company, an audit client.
   c. A member refers a client to ABC Service Bureau, in which a partner in the member's firm holds a material interest.
   d. A member has been asked to perform litigation services for the plaintiff in connection with a lawsuit filed against a client of the member's firm.

Multiple-
Choice

16. An audit manager invests in a client mutual fund that holds stock in one of the audit manager's clients. Which of the following is true concerning independence with respect to the client mutual fund?
   a. Independence is impaired only if the value of the stock is material to the member.
   b. Independence is impaired only if the value of the stock is material to the member's firm.
   c. Independence is impaired only if the value of the stock is material to the client.
   d. Independence is impaired without regard to materiality.

Multiple-
Choice

17. A CPA firm makes payments to a former practitioner who has accepted employment with a client after retirement from the firm. In order for the firm to be independent with respect to the client, all of the following provisions are required under AICPA rules **except**:
   a. The payments must be made subject to a written agreement.
   b. The payments must not be material to the CPA firm.
   c. The payments cannot be related to current firm revenues.
   d. The payments must be calculated based on an underlying formula that remains fixed during the payout period.

Multiple-
Choice

18. Auditors of public companies must follow the independence requirements of which of the following organizations?
    a.   The AICPA.
    b.   The ISB.
    c.   The SEC.
    d.   All of the above.

Multiple-
Choice

19. A member receives a wedding present from a client. The value of the gift exceeds the firm's policy on gifts. Which of the following is true?
    a.   Independence is not impaired because it is a wedding present.
    b.   Independence is not impaired if the gift is disclosed to the firm.
    c.   Independence is not impaired if the gift is disclosed to the firm and to the SEC.
    d.   Independence is impaired.

Multiple-
Choice

20. The concept of "engagement-team" independence applies to
    a.   Examinations of prospective financial statements.
    b.   Review engagements.
    c.   Agreed-upon procedures engagements.
    d.   Audit engagements.

Multiple-
Choice

21. All of the following would be examples of activities that would impair independence **except**:
    a.   Being responsible for a client's overall internal audit work plan.
    b.   Reporting to the audit committee on behalf of the member of management responsible for internal audit.
    c.   Being responsible for evaluating the effectiveness of internal controls.
    d.   Preparing source documents for transactions.

Multiple-
Choice

22. Which of the following is **not** true about a member in public practice who audits a state or local governmental unit?
    a.   The member who audits a state or local government's general-purpose financial statements fall into one of four categories for purposes of determining independence requirements.
    b.   If the member serves as an elected city legislator, independence is **not** impaired with respect to the city.
    c.   The member who audits a county and serves on a citizen's committee studying the financial status of the state does not impair independence with respect to that county.
    d.   If the member owns municipal bonds, he or she is not independent with respect to the municipality even if the amount of bonds is immaterial.

Multiple-
Choice

23. A CPA has begun an engagement to issue a review report for a client. Independence would be impaired if a member had which of the following?
    a.   A material indirect interest in a client.
    b.   A direct financial interest in a client.
    c.   Either a. or b.
    d.   Neither a. nor b.

Multiple-
Choice

24. A CPA firm is in an alliance with a public company in an alternative practice structure (APS). In addition to owners of the CPA firm, which category of people are subject to all of the same independence requirements as the owners/members?
    a. Direct superiors.
    b. Indirect superiors.
    c. Both direct and indirect superiors.
    d. Neither direct nor indirect superiors.

Multiple-
Choice

25. A firm should do which of the following with respect to quality control systems?
    a. Periodically obtain written representations from all professional personnel that affirm that the individual complied with independence policies.
    b. Designate a competent person or group as responsible for resolving questions on independence.
    c. Establish requirements for documentation of the resolution of independence questions.
    d. All of the above.

Multiple-
Choice

26. Which of the following is true concerning jointly held investments?
    a. Both the AICPA and SEC permit jointly held investments without regard to materiality.
    b. The SEC prohibits all jointly held investments without regard to materiality, but the AICPA only prohibits **material** jointly held investments.
    c. The AICPA prohibits all jointly held investments without regard to materiality, but the SEC only prohibits **material** jointly held investments.
    d. Both the AICPA and SEC prohibit jointly held investments without regard to materiality.

Multiple-
Choice

27. An auditor's independence with respect to an employee benefit plan is impaired whenever the auditor
    a. Has a material indirect financial interest in the plan.
    b. Serves as an investment advisor to the plan.
    c. Serves as the director of a plan sponsor.
    d. All of the above.

Multiple-
Choice

28. An audit partner in the Boston office of CPA Firm has a spouse who is the chief financial officer of ABC Company. ABC Company has just become a client of CPA Firm's Boston office. The partner will not participate in the engagement. Which of the following is correct concerning the relationship between CPA Firm and ABC Company?
    a. Independence is impaired under AICPA and SEC requirements.
    b. Independence is impaired under AICPA, but not SEC, requirements.
    c. Independence is impaired under SEC requirements, but not AICPA requirements.
    d. Independence is not impaired under AICPA or SEC requirements.

Multiple-Choice

29. Which of the following would impair independence without regard to materiality?
    a. A direct financial interest.
    b. An indirect financial interest.
    c. Both a. and b.
    d. Neither a. nor b.

Multiple-Choice

30. An audit manager invests in a nonclient mutual fund that holds stock in one of the audit manager's clients. Which of the following is true?
    a. Independence is impaired if the value of the stock is material to the manager.
    b. Independence is impaired if the value of the stock is material to the manager's firm.
    c. Independence is impaired if the value of the stock is material to the client.
    d. All of the above.

Multiple-Choice

31. Material cooperative arrangements are
    a. Permitted by the AICPA, but not by the SEC.
    b. Permitted by the SEC, but not the AICPA.
    c. Permitted by both the AICPA and SEC.
    d. Prohibited by both the AICPA and SEC.

Multiple-Choice

32. Under AICPA requirements, independence would be impaired in which of the following situations?
    a. A third-party litigant, such as an insurance company, brings litigation against a member in the name of the client under subrogation rights.
    b. The client and the member agree to binding arbitration to avoid litigation.
    c. A client sues member but settles out of court.
    d. All of the above.

Multiple-Choice

33. Which of the following CPAs would need to maintain integrity and objectivity?
    a. An audit manager who works only on audits of small companies.
    b. A corporate controller.
    c. A sole practitioner who does only tax returns.
    d. All of the above.

Multiple-Choice

34. Rule 201, *General Standards*, states that a member should comply with all of the following **except**:
    a. Planning and supervision.
    b. Sufficient relevant data.
    c. Monitoring.
    d. Due professional care.

Multiple-Choice

35. Which activity would violate client confidentiality?
    a. A member uses an outside service to process clients' tax returns.
    b. A member provides client information in response to an ethics inquiry from the AICPA's Professional Ethics Division.
    c. A predecessor auditor provides client information to a successor auditor without receiving permission from the client to speak freely.
    d. A member provides client information to a professional liability insurance carrier solely to help defend the member against actual or potential claims.

Multiple-
Choice

36. According to AICPA rules, a member in public practice should not accept a contingent fee for
   a. Preparing an original tax return.
   b. Preparing an amended tax return.
   c. Preparing a claim for a tax refund.
   d. All of the above.

Multiple-
Choice

37. Which of the following is **not** a violation of Rule 501, *Acts Discreditable?*
   a. A member fails to pay a tax liability in a timely manner.
   b. A member defaults on a business loan.
   c. A member is convicted of sexual harassment.
   d. A member retains client records after the client requests them.

Multiple-
Choice

38. The AICPA *Code of Professional Conduct*
   a. Prohibits advertising by all members.
   b. Allows advertising if member does not perform attest services.
   c. Allows advertising for all members as long as it is not false or misleading.
   d. Allows all forms of advertising.

Multiple-
Choice

39. A member's spouse refers products and services for a commission to a member's attest client. Rule 503 is not violated if
   a. The activities of the member's spouse are separate from the member's practice.
   b. The member is not significantly involved in those activities.
   c. No conflict of interest exists.
   d. All of the above.

Multiple-
Choice

40. Which of the following is **false** under Rule 505?
   a. A firm may designate itself as "Members of the American Institute of Certified Public Accountants" as long as a majority of its CPA owners are AICPA members.
   b. A successor firm **may** include the names of one or more past owners in the firm name.
   c. An association of members who are not partners may not use a letterhead showing the names of the members even if they share an office, employees, and work on each other's engagements.
   d. A firm may not use a designation such as "nonproprietary partner" to describe a high-ranking staff person who was a former partner of merged firms but is not a partner in the merging firm.

The CPA's Guide to Professional Ethics CPE Course

Record your CPE answers on the answer form provided below and return this page for grading.

Mail to:

The CPA's Guide to Professional Ethics CPE Director

Wiley-ValuSource, 7222 Commerce Center Drive, Suite 210, Colorado Springs, CO 80919

PAYMENT OPTIONS

☐ **Payment enclosed ($59.00).**
(Make checks payable to John Wiley & Sons, Inc.)
Please add appropriate sales tax.
Be sure to sign your order below.

Charge my:

☐ American Express   ☐ MasterCard   ☐ Visa

Account number _____

Expiration date _____
Please sign below for all credit card orders.

Signature _____

NAME _____

FIRM NAME _____

ADDRESS _____

PHONE (___) _____

CPA STATE LICENSE # _____

ISBN 0-471-43443-4

SEE THE OTHER SIDE OF THIS PAGE FOR THE CPE FEEDBACK FORM.

CPE ANSWERS

1. ___	2. ___	3. ___	4. ___	5. ___	6. ___	7. ___	8. ___	9. ___	10. ___
11. ___	12. ___	13. ___	14. ___	15. ___	16. ___	17. ___	18. ___	19. ___	20. ___
21. ___	22. ___	23. ___	24. ___	25. ___	26. ___	27. ___	28. ___	29. ___	30. ___
31. ___	32. ___	33. ___	34. ___	35. ___	36. ___	37. ___	38. ___	39. ___	40. ___

The CPA's Guide to Professional Ethics CPE Feedback

1. Were you informed in advance of the

   a. Course objectives? Y N
   b. Requisite experience level? Y N
   c. Course content? Y N
   d. Type and degree of preparation necessary? Y N
   e. Instruction method? Y N
   f. CPE credit hours? Y N

   c. Course content? Y N
   d. Type and degree of preparation necessary? Y N
   e. Instruction method? Y N
   f. CPE credit hours? Y N

2. Do you agree with the publisher's determination of

   a. Course objectives? Y N
   b. Requisite experience level? Y N

3. Was the content relevant? Y N

4. Was the content displayed clearly? Y N

5. Did the course enhance your professional competence? Y N

6. Was the course content timely and effective? Y N

How can we make the course better? If you have any suggestions please summarize them in the space below. We will consider them in developing future courses.

_____

_____

_____

_____